Speak STRONG

Say what you *Mean*.
Mean what you say.

Don't be Mean
when you say it.

MERYL RUNION

*Speak*STRONG

© 2009 PowerPotentials Publishing
www.powerpotentials.com
Power Potentials Publishing
4265 Outpost Road, Cascade, CO 80809

719–684–2633

PowerPhrases® is a registered trademark
of Meryl Runion and SpeakStrong, Inc.

Runion, Meryl.
Title: SpeakStrong: Say what you mean, mean what you say, don't be mean when you say it.
Meryl Runion; Editor Kristin Porotsky.

Publisher's Cataloging-in-Publication
(Provided by Quality Books, Inc.)

Runion, Meryl.
 SpeakStrong : say what you mean, mean what you say, don't be mean when you say it / Meryl Runion ; editor, Kristin Porotsky.
p. cm.
 ISBN-13: 978-0-9714437-8-5
 ISBN-10: 0-9714437-8-5

 1. Interpersonal communication. 2. Business communication. I. Title. II. Title: Speak strong.

BF637.C45R856 2009 153.6
 QBI08-600339

Copyrights and reuse policy

I wrote this book in a form that is easy to excerpt — and I want you to — if you follow the following guidelines.

Reprint/Reuse Policy

You have permission to use content from this book in your newsletter, publications, or on your web site up to one skill per publication, if you follow the following guidelines.

1. Let us know when and how you are using the excerpt via email.
   MerylRunion@speakstrong.com.

2. If it is a web posting, please link back to *www.speakstrong.com.*

3. Place my tag line at the end of the article with all my contact information. If on-line, please make certain that her web address links to her site.

4. If you alter the content, please submit for approval at Meryl's
   email address.

   Thanks!

Tag line

Meryl Runion and Speak Strong (SpeakStrong) provide Power Phrases (PowerPhrases) and other tools to help you improve communication skills at work and at home.

She is the author of the books **PowerPhrases!**, **How to Use PowerPhrases**, **Perfect Phrases for Managers and Supervisors** and **How to Say It: Performance Reviews.**

You can reach me at 719–684–2633 or by email:
MerylRunion@speakstrong.com.

www.speakstrong.com

Speak STRONG

Mean What You Say Skill Set #3: Be Resolute

Mean What You Say Skill Set #4: Retrain to Respond

■ SPEAKSTRONG STEP 4: Don't Be Mean When You Say It

Don't Be Mean When You Say It Skill Set #1: Check Your Attitude

Don't Be Mean When You Say It Skill Set #2: Assert, Don't Aggress

Speak softly enough for them to hear you

Nice girls (and boys) don't...

If I smile while I stick the knife in, will you still like me?

Don't Be Mean When You Say It Skill Set #3: Give up the Games

You're with me or you're against me

Pay no attention to the man behind the curtain

Like putty in my hands

Don't Be Mean When You Say It Skill Set #4: Purge the Poison

After all I've done for you ...

You have a great face for radio

You're an *$!#% *#

Nothing is the way it seems

■ SPEAKSTRONG STEP 5: Speak Your Simple Truth

■ APPENDIX

Disclaimer

I wrote this book to provide communication information and guidance. As publisher and author, I am not offering legal or other professional services.

I made every possible effort to provide you with accurate, sound and useful advice. Results vary in different situations.

As author and publisher I am not liable or responsible for any damages caused or allegedly caused directly or indirectly by the information in this book.

If that doesn't work for you, please return your book and I'll refund your money.

If that does work for you, have a great time reading and a greater time Speaking Strong.

Introduction: A Speak Strong Revolution

Your Speak Strong call to action

"Speak Strong!" It's a leadership skill, a success strategy and a moral imperative.

Speak Strong is a hero's journey, an awakening and an adventure.

It's a call to action and an invitation to remake yourself, your life and career on a higher level.

Speak Strong means to communicate powerfully & effectively. It means to speak the simple truth and to rise to the communication needs of every situation. It means when someone needs to take charge of the conversation and tell the simple truth, you say, "I'll go first."

This book paves your spoken path to success with a three-part appeal:

Say what you mean. Mean what you say. Don't be mean when you say it.

It's simple. That's what makes it so powerful.

Some boats need to be rocked

Has anyone ever told you not to rock the boat? Play it safe, go along to get along, don't stir up trouble—you've heard all the reasons—or lame excuses—why you should ignore reality and stay silent when something needs to be said. Here's a news flash for you…some boats NEED to be rocked—at the right time, for the right reasons and in the right way. *SpeakStrong* tells you why, when and how to initiate "boat-rocking conversations" that will elevate your relationships to their highest level of honesty, clarity and effectiveness.

Master the *skills* behind powerful communication scripts, words and phrases

I'm a big fan of scripts and phrases to guide communication. They help you hear and understand what powerful communication sounds like and looks like and feels like. They give you the quick edge you need to make a conversation turn out right—especially in a pinch. When people find the words to discuss an issue, they find the courage to SpeakStrong. When they don't have the words, they usually say nothing.

However, scripts and phrases are developed on the basis of powerful principles and communication skills. That's why this book reveals the over 50 communication skills that make PowerPhrases so effective. I clarify each *SpeakStrong* skill with practical tips and examples, dos and don'ts, and new PowerPhrases and Poison Phrases—to help you victoriously navigate the rocky waters of high-risk, high-reward conversations.

Read it cover to cover or pick out the skill you want to develop.

Audio bonus

Be sure to listen to my audio CD that details essential conversations to lay the foundation for productive working relationships—whether you're an executive, manager, supervisor, team leader and/or an ambitious employee. It outlines the conversations you will want to initiate with your newly developed SpeakStrong skills.

A welcome SpeakStrong surprise

Get ready. Life as you knew it is over. You are about to get more of what you want. You are about to become a bigger player in your own life. You are about to command more attention than ever before.

Here's what might surprise you. The stronger you become, the more others will enjoy being around you, working with you, being a part of your team and of your life. If you think that people won't like you when you speak up, think again. People who speak out are more successful at work and at home. *SpeakStrong* helps you become one of those people. I wish you a thrilling and satisfying communication journey.

Let me know how I can help you along the way. I answer communication questions, so ask them freely. You can email me at: *merylrunion@speakstrong.com.*

Keep on Speaking Strong—

Meryl Runion
www.speakstrong.com

Speak
STRONG

STEP 1:
COMMIT TO CODE WHITE

Commit to Code White Skill Set #1:
Awaken Your Inner Ostrich

Commit to Code White Skill Set #2:
Open Your Eyes

Introduction to Step One:
Commit to Code White

The power of attention

Health care organizations and hospitals all over the country have different codes for different kinds of events. Code blue is cardiac arrest. Code pink is infant abduction. Code BM is…well, you can imagine.

In Colorado Springs and some other places, there's a Code White. Here's what Code White is: if a physician verbally abuses a nurse within earshot, the nurses in the unit stand around and silently witness the conversation. That makes the physician aware of his or her inappropriate behavior. Usually all it takes to get the physician to stop the verbal abuse is for the staff to keep their eyes open to what's going on.

Power in numbers

This reminds me of the movie *Witness*. In the end of the movie, a group of dastardly criminals prepare to kill an Amish family who know of their crimes. The young son is able to ring the bell, and suddenly the entire Amish community shows up. These harmless people are able to stop a murder, simply by being witnesses. There is power in awareness. The ringing of the bell was a kind of Code White.

Code White starts with awakening your inner ostrich, even though it would prefer to keep its head in the sand.

There are two skill categories for your SpeakStrong first step to commit to Code White.

Commit to Code White Skill Category #1:
Awaken Your Inner Ostrich

Code White says—wake up! Take your head out of the sand and see things as they are. Admit what's in front of you. Code White doesn't even ask you to speak—it simply asks that you be willing to face truth with your eyes open. It asks that you stop saying things you don't mean and look for what needs to be said. It means you forget those lame excuses that you hide behind and get honest with yourself. It means you awaken your inner ostrich and pull your head out of the sand. Once there, you open your eyes wide.

Commit to Code White **Skill Category #2:**
Open Your Eyes

If you've been burying your head in the sand, when you pull your head out, your eyes will need to refocus to see what's right in front of you. You might be tempted to stick your head back into the ground. Don't do it. Learn to see.

Learn to let go of the excuses and cut to the core of truth. Establish standards of honesty that are realistic and integrous.

Life is full of Code Whites: situations that require your willingness to bear witness to the truth. Committing to Code White is the first step of Speaking Strong.

Read on to learn how.

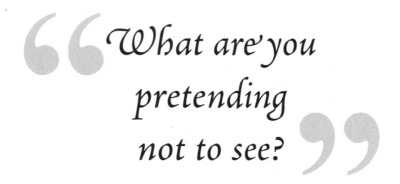

" *What are you pretending not to see?* "

MERYL RUNION

> " *Change comes from
> the willingness
> to see things
> as they are*. "

MERYL RUNION

Is that My Best Foot Forward — or a False Front?

Skill #1: Stop Saying Things You Don't Mean

A family of "Great Pretenders"

Jill's family has a day-long gathering every Christmas. While no one really wants to go, they make believe they do. They attend, pretend and extend themselves in false merriment. They have one eye on the clock as it creeps ahead to their secretly predetermined exit moments. They exchange hugs, say their goodbyes and feign regret about how they couldn't stay longer.

If you heard their private follow-up conversations, you'd never guess how tedious the whole family finds the gatherings. Jill gushes with the best of them. When she hangs up the phone, she wonders if she's the only one who would like to end this family tradition.

Jill has a picture perfect family with no real people in it.

It's a family addicted to saying things no one means.

It's a family that doesn't admit what everyone knows. No one wants to spend every Christmas together, and everyone lies when they say they do.

The charade continues

The pretense doesn't stop there. Jill goes to work and assures her client she'll meet a deadline that she doubts she can make. Her husband goes to work and tells his boss that the last-minute changes are no problem when in fact they are. Jill's brother Rod doesn't go to work — he calls in sick. Rod wants to attend his daughter's soccer game in the afternoon. He can't say that, so he uses his most pathetic-sounding voice to phone in and take the entire day off.

Can you imagine what it would be like if Jill's family faced reality and spoke nothing but truth for an entire day?

Just imagine...

Imagine what your day would be like if the people in your life stopped saying things they didn't mean. Your spouse might stay silent when you ask if your dress makes you look fat. Your kid might not have an answer for you when you ask where he's been since school let out. Your boss might not want to answer when you ask whether your job was secure.

It would be a very different world if we all stopped saying things we don't mean.

Envision a day in your world where you and everyone else only speak words they mean. If it looks a lot different than your normal day, ask yourself where and how you can stop saying things you don't mean.

There is another way

While Jill's family continues to plan for their next year's Christmas gathering, Cindy's family admitted they'd rather celebrate at home and schedule a family reunion in the summer when the weather is good and the kids can play outside. Cindy's family stopped saying things they didn't mean. Each had their best individual Christmases ever.

Cindy likes the new arrangement so much; she's considering making a few more changes. In fact, she just might tell her manager that she needs more lead time on a reoccurring project.

What a concept!

> *"A lie for a lie'*
> *makes the whole*
> *world a mirage."*

MERYL RUNION

Dos, Don'ts and Tips, Skill #1:
Stop Saying Things You Don't Mean

Some call it manners, others call it savvy. I call it dishonesty. If you pretend you think things you don't think, feel things you don't feel, and want things you don't want, you're being deceitful.

Some deceptions are relatively harmless or even helpful. But even your little lies come at the price of your integrity.

When you say something you don't mean like: "That's okay," "No problem," and "I agree."…you discount yourself.

When you say something you don't mean, like: "I hate you," "I'm perfect, so if something I do offends you, it's your problem," and "You'll never amount to anything." …you hurt others.

An occasional white lie doesn't turn you into a liar, but a *habit* of saying things you don't mean is a habit that undermines your relationships, your success and your personal integrity. Create a personal communication policy of not saying things you don't mean. Here's how.

1. Ask why you say things you don't mean

We all shade the truth at times. Sometimes it's habitual and unconscious. Other times it's deliberate. Notice when you speak inauthentically and ask yourself why.

Don't: be hard on yourself, but don't excuse yourself either.
> **Why not?** You do what you do for a reason. Uncover what you do and understand why. If you beat yourself up, you are less likely to be honest. If you make excuses, you're less likely to recognize the impact of your tales.

Do: examine what you avoid or experience when you say things you don't mean.
> **Why?** When you understand the reason behind a behavior, you can change it.

Example: Adam told his boss he was late due to traffic. In fact, he stayed late at a gathering to talk with prospective clients. Why did he lie? He didn't want to answer his boss' inevitable questions about the prospects. He was afraid his boss would try to micromanage his contacts.

2. Steer clear of set-ups
Avoid situations that invite dishonesty and/or punish truthfulness.

Don't: make promises you can't keep or put yourself in situations where you expect truth won't fly.
    Why not? It's like an alcoholic visiting a bar—it's harder to quit a habit in an environment that encourages it.
Do: make promises you can realistically keep and surround yourself with people who CAN handle the truth.
    Why? Even the most honest among us will find it difficult to stay honest in environments that don't support honesty. You will be more inclined to stop saying things you don't mean in environments that support truth.
Example: Katie worked for a CEO who liked yes-people. When she shared an honest opinion with him, he was annoyed. She tried being the yes-person her boss wanted, but she realized she needed to find a job where lying was not a part of her job description.

3. Examine the consequences of saying things you don't mean
What price do you pay for saying things you don't mean? Take the time to assess the price of your deceptions.

Don't: just think short-term.
    Why not? Most dishonesty is for short-term gratification or short-term avoidance at a long-term price.
Do: examine the long-range impact saying things you don't mean has on relationships, self-esteem, health and productivity.
    Why? You probably don't realize the price you pay for pretending. If you base your communication on long-term objectives, you'll reap great rewards.
Example: Ruby's administrator, Jules, was sensitive, so Ruby hesitated to say anything to her about errors. Ruby didn't want to offend Jules, but when she considered the long-range impact Jules' errors had on the team, Ruby realized by staying silent, she hurt the team.

4. Know that a well-intended lie is still a lie
Sometimes circumstances give you good reason to lie, but those circumstances don't whitewash your lie. Even when your higher angels guide you to distort the truth, you're still lying.

Don't: pretend that a good reason to lie erases it.
    Why not? Sir Walter Scott said: "Oh what a tangled web we weave when first we practice to deceive." It's true. The web you weave isn't just

external — it's internal too. The more you fake, the more fake you become. The more fake you become, the farther you stray from authentic power and communication.

Do: examine your motive to spin the truth and only do it when a higher principle dictates that you do.

Why? The first step to authentic, powerful communication is to fess up to yourself. That includes admitting your "little white lies."

Example: I used to gauge what to say by what I thought people wanted to hear. That left me feeling fragmented. Now I have developed such a habit of truthfulness that even the slightest excuse or pretense creates a great deal of discomfort in me. I wasn't comfortable with my pretense before, but it was such a familiar feeling that I didn't recognize my discomfort.

5. Start small

If this book inspires you to embrace new levels of honesty, (as I hope it does) start small. Set yourself up for success.

Don't: burn bridges — not immediately anyway. For example, don't go into your boss' office tomorrow and tell him you lied on your resume.

Why not? It's better to develop your skills more gradually on low risk conversations.

Do: start with less earth-shattering admissions…like small confessions to your kids — who can't leave because they don't have any money.

Why? This is a major new skill. It's best you establish it one step at a time.

Example: Tony started his new communication by telling the truth to telemarketers. (I'm serious. That was a stretch for him.) Eventually Tony stopped lying to the neighbors when they asked if he minded when their dog barked. He hasn't gotten himself to stop excusing his manager's gum smacking in the cubical next to his, but he's getting there.

6. Give people a heads-up

Don't: become a truth machine in a relationship that has a foundation of pretense without warning.

Why not? It rocks the boat too much too fast, and creates defensiveness. Give people a chance to buy into a new foundation for your relationship before you tear into the old one.

Do: let people know what you're doing, why and how it's healthy for the relationship.

Why? If people understand your reasons for new behavior, they are more likely to support your efforts.

PowerPhrase/What to Say: I'm trying to give and get more useful feedback by not sugar-coating my words anymore. Are you open to us gracefully telling it like it is to each other?

Poison Phrase/What NOT to say: I've been lying when I said I like the way you structured this form. It's trash.

7. Be willing not to know what to say at times

Don't: resort to old habits when you find yourself at a loss about how to communicate.

    Why not? That will reinforce old behavior.

Do: let yourself experience a void.

    Why? It will force you to develop new habits and behaviors.

Example: When Victoria stopped her "yes" habit, she didn't know how to respond to requests. She stopped pretending she wanted to do things when she didn't, but it took a while to figure out how to say what she wanted.

8. Develop your communication skills

Don't: make it up on your own as you go along.

    Why not? You can learn much more quickly and painlessly by learning from others.

Do: read the rest of this book (and other resources) and practice.

    Why? When you have the skills to say what you mean, you are more likely to stop saying what you don't mean.

Resources: My website has great articles, online tools and a variety of resources. Visit it at: *www.speakstrong.com*

Don't let your best foot become a false front

Some call it manners, others call it savvy. I call it dishonesty. Everyone wants to look good, and there's nothing wrong with that. Go ahead and put your best foot forward. But watch out for when your best foot becomes a false front.

Choose words that put a nice frame on your message. A great picture frame enhances a picture and draws out its beauty. Let your words frame your message in the same way. But don't enhance to the point of distortion and untruth. Stop saying things you don't mean. It's part of your commitment to Code White, and it's the first skill you need to Speak Strong.

I'm Not Saying and You Can't Make Me

Skill #2: Start noticing what you don't say

Forbidden topics

Jayne and several coworkers regularly met in secret to discuss the shocking, forbidden topic of the boss' poor management skills. The group of coworkers felt connected by their concealed conversations.

They should have done more than talk around the break room. They should have raised the issue with someone who could do something about it. Six months later, half the members of the "inner circle" — including Jayne — were laid off due to mismanagement.

But Jayne could have lost more than her job. She had covered up more than her boss' incompetence.

Dangerous complicity

A year before she was laid off, Jayne's boss instructed her to transfer investor funds to his private venture. Jayne tentatively voiced unease at the time, but backed off when her boss reprimanded her for questioning him. Jayne indirectly mentioned the transfer to her "inner circle," but never fully addressed her concerns.

She should have. That transfer led to criminal charges against her boss. Jayne narrowly missed being named as a codefendant.

Speak the unspeakable

What do you find difficult to discuss? Sex, religion and politics are the stereotypical hot-button topics that we've been counseled to avoid. But there are other "unspeakable" topics. Research shows most employees are aware of dishonesty, incompetence and rule avoidance and most say nothing.

Jayne used to avoid those risky conversations. She doesn't anymore.

While Jayne initially laid all the responsibility for her problems at her former boss' feet, she eventually came to accept her own contribution. It was a tough lesson and she learned it well. She committed to speak up effectively to the people who need to know.

That's a commitment she will never break.

Dos, Don'ts and Tips, Skill #2:
Start noticing what you don't say

You don't miss what you don't see — or say

Out of sight, out of mind. If you habitually avoid an issue, you just might forget you have one. Verbalization clarifies and validates reality. Silence negates it.

Start noticing what you don't say. Here are some tips to do that.

1. Observe when you feel shut down

Have you heard of the book title: *Been Down So Long it Looks Like Up to Me?* Here's another title for you. *Been Shut Down So Long it Feels Like Open to Me.* (I don't believe anyone has written it yet — you're welcome to if you want.) Pay attention — notice that shut down feeling.

Don't: ignore the feelings that being silenced creates.

Why not? Those feelings give powerful clues that you need to speak.

Do: take your attention to your body to notice how you feel when you have a thought that you don't express.

> **Why?** Change starts with observation. If you don't even know you shut down, you won't be able to open back up. Once you learn to recognize that shut down feeling, you'll be better able to respond differently.

Example: This example is mine. A vendor indicated that my issues with his work were my own fault. He was defensive, offensive and dismissive when I tried to clarify my issues with him. I felt five years old all over again. However, when I was five years old, if someone dismissed me this way, I'd shut down. Now I see that five-year old feeling as a signal that I need to talk.

2. Examine how silence affects you

Do you know what it does to you to have something you need to talk about and stay silent? Explore the price you pay for silence.

Don't: limit your examination to catastrophic and short-term impact.

> **Why not?** Even when the short-term impact doesn't seem so bad, the long-term implications can be extreme.

Do: Notice how it feels to stay silent when something needs to be said. Observe how you feel in the moment as well as any lingering feeling and behaviors. Include the impact of silence on health, relationships, your self-esteem and productivity.

> **Why?** Each time you censor yourself, you lose a bit of your personal integrity and power.

Example: Kyle consistently discounts Midge's ideas. When Midge considered the impact Kyle's dismissals have on her, she realized they cause her to second-guess herself and stop offering her ideas.

3. Journal

I write in part to clarify my thoughts. I often discover something I didn't know I knew. Journal freely and find out what you don't know you know. Then compare your writing to what you say.

Don't: block, edit or evaluate as you write.
>   **Why not?** This exercise is to get past your standard censors. You can evaluate your words later. If you write unedited, surprising things can emerge.

Do: write three pages without stopping. Then review to see what you wrote. Finally, compare what you write to what you say.
>   **Why?** It will help you be aware of what you don't say.

Example: Joe does the writing exercise. He noticed a continual theme of discouragement about lack of support for his new ideas. After a few weeks, he realized he needed to talk about it.

4. Get a confidant / mentor

Find someone you can talk to about anything. In that safe environment, you might find yourself talking about things that you suppress elsewhere. Let that illuminate what you're not saying.

Don't: practice openness in an unsafe environment.
>   **Why not?** It could reinforce silence.

Do: use a safe friend as a sounding board.
>   **Why?** It will help you open up.

Example: Julie had grown accustomed to the cursing in her workplace, but it wasn't until she had a long open conversation with her mentor that she realized how it affected her. She also realized she never addressed the issue because she was afraid they'd curse her if she did.

Who knew?

There's a whole world of thought, feelings, opinions and desires inside of you. Notice what they are, and then notice how closely what you think, feel and want matches up with what you say.

> *"You can't play it safe by playing it silent."*

MERYL RUNION

I can't talk about that because they...

Skill #3: Uncover eight lame excuses (and one shameful one)

Can you believe they bought it?

In 1999, *Candid Camera* filmed an actor playing a doctor inoculating employees for the Y2K bug in a corporate break room. The employees rolled up their sleeves one by one for the vaccination. No one questioned the authority of a "doctor" vaccinating them against a computer virus.

I watched incredulous. Don't they get it? You don't get vaccinated for a computer virus! How could they be so blinded by a white coat and stethoscope?

It's easy to laugh at their folly. Yet you and I have stayed silent against our better judgment for reasons that couldn't pass the smell test either.

Endless tales of unspoken truths

The stories abound. There's the shipping agent who followed his boss' instructions to dispatch a crate to Portland, Oregon even though he knew the client was in Portland, Maine. There's the manager who tolerated a worker's offensive body odor for five years because they didn't want to offend the offender. (Catch the irony?) There's the employee who quit because he was unwilling to risk angering her boss by asking for a raise.

Then there's the business owner who ignored his favorite employee's incompetence. (Never mind that the other overworked employees had to pick up the slack.) There's the gentle soul who never confronted an issue in her life and wasn't about to start now, even though her coworker had stolen her idea. She wouldn't know what to say or how to say it anyway.

Oh, yes, there's the employee who figured if the new marketing campaign was as bad as it sounded to her, someone else at the meeting surely would have said so. And there's the wife who assumed every time her opinion differed from her husband's, he must know something she didn't. And there's an employee who never pointed out the accounting error because that error meant extra money in his own pocket.

So many excuses — so little time

We've all made excuses for not speaking up about errors, incompetence and issues. I've done it, I've seen it and so have you. That's why the 1999 *Candid Camera* episode shouldn't have surprised me.

That's also why I am surprised and delighted when someone drops the excuses and speaks up.

> *A misleading silence*
> *is as dishonest as*
> *a misleading word.*

MERYL RUNION

Dos, Don'ts and Tips, Skill #3:
Uncover eight lame excuses (and one shameful one)

How do you excuse your silence? Let us count the ways.
There are eight lame excuses and one shameful excuse for staying silent when something needs to be said. We'll look more closely at how to overcome these excuses in later chapters. Now I'll help you uncover the ones you hide behind.

1. The *misplaced respect for authority* lame excuse
Do you hesitate to question a perceived authority even when your own knowledge contradicts what they say?

Don't: under or overvalue experience and/or position.
> **Why not?** People have authority for a reason, and experience adds to accuracy — but authorities are not infallible and experience does not mean all knowing.

Do: examine your interaction with anyone you respect, admire and emulate. Notice if you ever dismiss your own knowing for theirs.
> **Why?** You are responsible for your own choices. If you make a poor choice because you listened to an "expert," you're the one who suffers.

Example: Angela didn't think peeking into a coworker's files was such a good idea — but her friend and colleague Carla egged her on until she did it. Angela let Carla's values take authority over her own.

2. The *fear of negative consequences* lame excuse
Do you stay silent because you fear retaliation?

Don't: underestimate how fear of retaliation affects you.
> **Why not?** You might shut down so quickly you don't know it.

Do: conduct a cost-benefit analysis. Focus on long-term costs and benefits of speaking AND not speaking. Complete the Risky Conversation Assessment Form in the appendix and on my website at: *www.speakstrong.com/articles/ speak-strong/risky_conversation.html*
> **Why?** You'll never Speak Strong if you let retaliation control you.

Example: Roy resented how his wife spent money, but never said a word when she came home with shopping bags full of things they didn't need. He tried talking about it a few years back, and regretted it because his wife responded with the silent treatment.

On reflection, Roy realized it was not acceptable for him to be unable to discuss a subject that mattered so much to him.

3. The *fear of offending* lame excuse

Do you avoid issues because the truth might offend someone?

Don't: assume your desire not to offend is altruistic.
   Why not? You may tiptoe around feelings to avoid your own discomfort with a sensitive topic. But if they need to know about something and you're not telling, what's so altruistic about that?
Do: ask—who really bears the burden from the unaddressed issue?
   Why? Your "kindness" may be misplaced.
Example: Theresa didn't want to hurt Jay's feelings when he asked for feedback on his presentation, so she didn't point out the flaws. When Jay's presentation bombed, Theresa realized she should have spoken more honestly.

4. The *avoidance* lame excuse

Do you wait to speak up until a tomorrow that never comes?

Don't: kid yourself that the relief that comes from ignoring something is a form of resolution. Don't pretend you're waiting for better timing when you're really making an excuse to avoid the issue.
   Why not? There's never a perfect time to talk. Waiting for one is a common lame excuse.
Do: require yourself to identify the reason why you're waiting. If the reason is a good one, commit to when you will speak.
   Why? Sure, you may not want to break bad news to someone on their wedding day, but you can commit to when you will.
Example: Terry's wife was grumpy so he decided to wait to tell her he didn't want to go to her mother's for Christmas. The next day, her mood had improved. Terry was enjoying her company and didn't want to ruin her good mood. Eventually he realized there never was a good time, and he needed to go ahead and say it.

5. The *habit* lame excuse

Do you have a habit of not speaking up?

Don't: think you know what your habits are.
   Why not? Habits are usually invisible.
Do: observe your trends.
   Why? To find out what habits you need to change.
Example: It didn't even occur to Jessica to discuss finances with her fiancé before they married because she was not accustomed to addressing issues. After a rocky start to her marriage, she realized she and her husband could have avoided some of the conflict had she sought agreements instead of made assumptions.

6. The *no-one-else-is saying-anything* lame excuse

Do you assume if there was anything to say, someone else would say it?

Don't: count on other people to be more committed to truth than you are.
> **Why not?** 1) History is full of examples of mass deception. Consensus doesn't make it right. 2) Others might be waiting for you to say something.

Do: ask why you trust others' ideas about what needs to be said over your own.
> **Why?** You'll uncover a very passive pattern.

Example: Could she really be the only one that hated the new logo? No one else objected so Jolene stayed silent. She figured since no one else objected, everyone else must like it.

7. The *self-doubt* lame excuse

Do you let your own self-doubt silence you?

Don't: pretend you need certainty to speak.
> **Why not?** If certainty was a prerequisite, no one would ever say anything.

Do: notice when you let doubt silence you.
> **Why?** Doubt is a legitimate reason to educate yourself before you speak, but not a legitimate reason to silence yourself.

Example: Cybil didn't trust the applicant. Everyone else seemed charmed by what she saw as slickness. She didn't express her concerns to the hiring committee because she questioned her own perceptions.

8. The *don't know what to say* lame excuse

Do you stay silent because you don't have the words?

Don't: accept poor communication skills as a legitimate excuse for silence.
> **Why not?** You can learn.

Do: assess your lack of skills, develop skills, and practice, practice, practice.
> **Why?** It will enhance your life.

Example: Seven years into her marriage, Amy still hasn't told her mother-in-law that her put-downs are hurtful. Her mother-in-law has a way of twisting Amy's words that Amy doesn't know how to respond to. Amy stayed silent because she didn't know what to say. That might have been understandable for a few months, but seven years later, it's a lame excuse. She should have learned long ago, and it's time for her to start now.

Shameful excuse

9. Ask if you stay silent out of self-interest

Do you stay silent when something needs to be said because ignoring the issue works for you?

Don't: ignore your own deceitfulness.
   Why not? Your complicity implicates you.
Do: be honest with yourself about your motivation.
   Why? Your integrity is worth more than anything you gain from hiding the truth.
Example: Jeremy's partner Margot told their boss the report was late because the consultant didn't get back to them on time. It wasn't true, but Jeremy didn't correct her. After all, her lie vindicated him as well as her.

So many excuses — so much to gain by naming them.

Do you have an excuse-based life? You can't Speak Strong and make excuses at the same time. Name your lame excuses so you'll know where to start when you're ready to lose them. That's coming up in skill #7. We have groundwork to lay first.

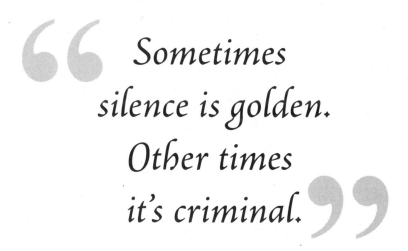

Sometimes silence is golden. Other times it's criminal.

MERYL RUNION

We get along great ... as long as...

Skill #4: Get honest

An insufferable boss

My seminar participants tell fascinating and amusing stories — and they often tell them with great passion. That's what Julie did.

Her eyes were wide, her voice lively and her whole body animated as Julie told me about her boss.

Years of insensitivity came to a head the week Julie's father died. She worked overtime and left clear instructions so no one would miss her when she took the day of the funeral off. That didn't stop her boss from suggesting that she come in that morning. After all, the funeral wasn't until the afternoon. Julie politely declined.

Julie was surprised when her boss called the morning of the funeral. She assumed it was important, so she answered. Her boss asked if she could pick up a print order and drop it by the office on her way to the funeral home.

All's I can take, I can't take no more

Julie did as requested, but when she delivered the goods to her boss, she not-so-politely shared her pent-up rage. She called him names I won't repeat and unloaded a laundry list of complaints. She concluded by informing her boss that she quit.

Julie couldn't believe what happened next. Her boss said, "Julie, I think you could use some time off. Why don't you take a week of paid vacation and come back in a week from tomorrow?"

Stunned, Julie agreed. Her boss didn't call her once during her sabbatical, and she still had her job months later when she told me her tale.

A new beginning

Julie's relationship with her boss became much healthier after that. She learned that she could express her needs as they arose, and she stopped waiting until she was ready to explode to set a firm boundary.

Julie discovered an unexpected benefit to her new approach. She started actually liking her job. And, resentment, which once was her dominant emotion toward her boss, all but disappeared.

It could have turned out differently. Her boss might have accepted her resignation and found someone else who was willing to take whatever he dished out. Had that happened, Julie thinks (and I agree) it would not have been much of a loss.

You're as healthy as the things you can talk about

I often hear people say they don't address important issues because they want to protect a good relationship. That doesn't give the relationship much credit. If you can't politely address an important issue, the relationship isn't all that good.

Be who you are and honor yourself. Your good friends, best associates and true family will love you for it. Those who don't are probably not the ones you want in your life anyway. Use truth to keep your relationships healthy.

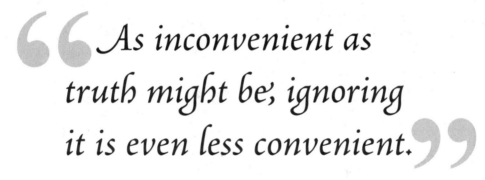

As inconvenient as truth might be, ignoring it is even less convenient.

MERYL RUNION

Dos, Don'ts and Tips, Skill #4:
Get honest

Why is it so hard to be honest with the people you're closest to?

Do you think the people who care the most about you should be able to handle your honesty better than anyone else? After all, they know you, understand you and love you. But that doesn't mean they can handle your honesty. The more personal and entwined your relationship, the greater their stake in your thoughts, feelings and actions. That can make them want to block free expression that threatens the status quo. For example, if you express dissatisfaction with your high-paying job, someone who benefits from the money you bring in might not want to hear it.

Truth can seem like a threat to relationships. Off-limit topics are a greater threat. Forbidden subjects cause gradual relationship numbing. If you want your business and personal relationships to remain healthy, use these tips to get honest in your relationships.

1. Review what topics you've learned not to raise (or taught others to avoid) in your relationships

Don't: explain anything away.

> **Why not?** While it may be appropriate and even wise to agree to avoid certain topics, if you begin by listing them all, you'll get a more accurate list to work from and a more comprehensive picture of the overall situation.

Do: list every topic you avoid.

> **Why?** You need a complete picture to work with.

Examples: Cindy can't talk to her brother about how to divide their parent's estate. Joe's business is off-limits to his wife. Katherine gets defensive when her business partner brings up the topic of money.

2. Assess the impact of being unable to discuss things

Don't: leave any forbidden topic out.

> **Why not?** Any topic you're tempted to leave out is likely to be one you need to evaluate.

Do: document the impact each off-limit topic has on you, the relationship and events.

> **Why?** Even if you accept being unable to discuss some things, the prohibition affects you. This step assesses how.

Example: Gloria is angry that she brings in more clients than her partner Joe, but they share the revenue equally. She attempted to discuss it once, but Joe acted so affronted that she was afraid to bring it up again. She notices she feels cooler toward Joe, but doesn't want to risk addressing the issue again.

3. Consider talking to someone else instead

Don't: replace a necessary conversation with a principal with a conversation with a surrogate. Don't get intimacy needs met at the expense of a primary relationship. However, don't expect one person to meet you at every level.

> **Why not?** People often discuss issues with everyone except the person they have the issue with. That can create emotional barriers. However, sometimes other people are better able to listen, and talking to others can take undue pressure off the relationship.

Do: ask, is this a conversation I need to have with this person? Can I get satisfaction by talking to someone else? If I talk to someone else, will it enhance the relationship, or undermine it?

> **Why?** To be sure you Speak Strong to the right people at the right time.

Example: Gloria noticed she'd been complaining about Joe to other people and decided she needed to have a conversation with Joe about compensation structure. She initiated that conversation and stayed steady despite his resistance.

They found an arrangement she could live with, but after that, she decided to do her bragging about the great deals she landed to someone other than Joe, because now that they divided profits based more on results, he wasn't interested in hearing the details of her successes.

4. Determine which conversations are necessary for a healthy relationship and pursue them

Don't: expect to break down a long-standing wall in a single conversation.

> **Why not?** You'll trigger a reaction that is likely to fortify the walls.

Do: consistently and persistently let others know how essential these conversations are to you.

> **Why?** While it may be uncomfortable and create disruption, it's ultimately the best for the relationship. If you can't discuss critical issues, the relationship won't thrive.

Example: Keith's boss blamed him for not understanding his instructions, even though his instructions weren't clear. When Keith brought it up, his boss resisted. Keith persisted, because he didn't want to work for someone who treated him with that kind of disrespect.

5. Develop your communication skills to help you approach sensitive topics adeptly

Don't: assume the topic itself is the whole reason someone reacts to your words.

Why not? They might be able to hear what you have to say if you voice your message differently.

Do: Examine your words for possible triggers.

Why? Even a small change in wording can open a previously closed conversation.

Example: Keith discovered that the way he expressed his confusion to his boss sounded critical. When he removed the criticism, his boss was more able to respond to Keith's confusion without blame.

6. Be willing to risk the relationship for the relationship

Don't: resign yourself to an unhealthy dynamic to "preserve" a relationship.

Why not? It doesn't work. And, if your relationship falls apart because you were honest, you haven't lost much.

Do: Let people know when a conversation is a deal maker or breaker.

Why? The more you're willing to risk, the more you stand to gain.

Example: Mary was a supportive friend to Sandy, but Sandy didn't readily return her support. Mary was reluctant to address the issue until it came to a head one day. Mary asked Sandy for a small favor which Sandy declined for a petty reason. Mary let Sandy know how disappointed she was. Sandy responded by not asking Mary for support anymore so she wouldn't have to reciprocate. Mary was sad, but decided it was the best outcome.

To your own self be true, and encourage the same in others

You are as healthy as the things you can talk about. It's that simple. Few if any relationships are completely open and healthy, but the more open you can be with the people in your life, the more likely it is that your relationships will be vital and strong. If you go along to get along—if you get along great as long as you lie, pretend, or hide your true nature—it's time to get honest. You just might like it—and so might they.

> " *What would you
> say if you could
> say anything?* "

MERYL RUNION

Just What DO I Mean?

Skill #5: Cut to the core

An undercover employer

He came to my administrative assistant's conference, not to learn about being an assistant, but to hire an assistant. He figured his odds were good in a room with 250 of them. Did he succeed? I didn't find out. But he did teach me something important.

He asked me to tell the assistants in my classes that employers aren't looking for order-takers these days…they want creative thinkers. He complained that schools don't teach kids how to think. Schools, he told me, teach kids to look for the established right answer. They teach kids to guess what the instructor wants to hear. Business requires people to assess situations for themselves and make good judgment calls. Few of us have learned to do that.

A dearth of critical thinking

I knew what he was talking about. I've had assistants post things that were clearly wrong, and explain their actions by saying, "That's how you gave it to me." As if that's a reason. Yes, I sometimes pass things on with errors. Does anyone really think I want it posted that way?

We don't know how to think! My friend Sandy can cook a great meal with a recipe but is helpless without one. If she's missing an ingredient, she can't make the dish. She also can sew an elaborate outfit with a pattern, but she can't sew a hem without one. She thinks there's one right way to do everything, and either she has learned the "right way" and resents those who don't follow it, or she hasn't learned the "right way" and she looks outside herself for how it's "supposed" to be done.

Then there's Anthony, who swallows a political ideology whole and parrots the talking points of the day. I don't enjoy discussing politics with him because I don't believe he has found his own meaning. He borrows his meaning from talk-show hosts. If I want to hear the host's message, I'll listen to the show.

We learned a lot in school but few of us learned to be our own authorities. It's time to inquire deeply or to cut to the core of our OWN message.

A glimmer of hope

But there's hope. Last week my assistant pointed out a flaw in my strategy and suggested I rethink my instructions. After looking for the "right way" to grieve her father's passing, Sandy found her own way. And Anthony stopped listening to his political shows because he found they left him enraged. Good choice. He's been more pleasant to speak with ever since.

It's nice to be around self-directed people and it's nicer still to be one.

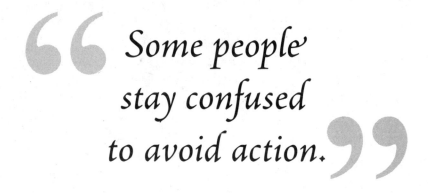

Some people stay confused to avoid action.

MERYL RUNION

Dos, Don'ts and Tips, Skill # 5:
Cut to the core

If you don't know what you mean, you can't say what you mean

Just what *do* you mean? If you don't know, how do you expect anyone else to get it? If you're confused, they're sure to be confused too.

Before you speak, cut to the core of your message.

The core of my message here is simple. You have to know what you mean to say what you mean. That's my bottom line, my main point and my key concept for this chapter. What's your bottom line? Here are some things you can do to find out.

Right Brain Techniques

Use right brain and left brain techniques to figure out what you really have to say. Here are a few of the right brain approaches.

1. Quickly summarize your point in fifteen words or less

Quick — pick a topic and, in fifteen seconds and fifteen words or less, tell me what you mean. What's your bottom line?

Don't: think.
    Why not? Your thoughts will filter your inner knowing
Do: practice speaking or writing as if your life, happiness and/or success depend on having an answer in the next fifteen seconds.
    Why? The sense of urgency will help you bypass your mental filters, and allow you to come up with some surprising answers.

2. Brainstorm twenty ideas

Don't: edit as you go.
    Why not? Evaluation blocks your creativity.
Do: come up with at least twenty messages without worrying about them being either good or accurate.
    Why? In order to think of twenty ideas, you'll relax your filters. You'll come up with some "wild ideas" that contain truth.
Example: At a seminar I led for the Department of Defense, we brainstormed until we had 20 ideas about how to make morning meetings more productive and civil. Some of the ideas were far-fetched. One person suggested that they not allow any ideas. That morphed into the concept that all ideas should be submitted to the supervisor first. The whole group liked that suggestion. They implemented that recommendation along with five others we established.

3. Allow your core message to be contradictory

Don't: expect your message to be 100% rational or consistent.

>**Why not?** Life is full of contradictions so your experience of it will be too.

Do: acknowledge contradictions without editing them.

>**Why?** Conflicting ideas are part of what you mean. You can simplify your thoughts and look for unifying principles later.

Example: Karla advocates a management style that empowers workers to make their own decisions. She also advocates extensive mentoring, training and support. Her positions seemed contradictory to her at first. She later concluded they weren't. Her philosophy was to give employees the tools to do their jobs independently and to provide them the room to do it.

4. Take a "core message hike"

Don't: sit at your desk as you track down your deepest meaning.

>**Why not?** Sitting at your desk is associated with left-brain, linear thinking. You'll get better results if you use your whole brain.

Do: take a walk, move around, be in nature and participate in other activities that elicit right-brain, non-linear thinking.

>**Why?** Your right brain is more closely associated with your unconscious than your left brain is.

Example: When I am stuck in my writing, I'll often take a walk. I walk with a concrete idea of what I want to deliberate about, but I'll let my mind go where it will. I usually have clarity by the time my walk is complete.

5. Use sentence stems to jumpstart your expression

Don't: worry about getting it right.

>**Why not?** If you're willing to get it "wrong" on the way to getting it "right," you'll explore more ideas and reach a better conclusion.

Do: allow yourself to guess at the best way to complete your sentence stems.

>**Why?** An idea that you want to reject on first impulse might later prove accurate.

PowerPhrases/What to Say/Sentence Stems
- If I could say anything without guilt, shame or criticism, I would say…
- If I did know the answer, it would be…
- In summary I say…

Example: I suspected Jean wanted to accept her new job offer but was reluctant to admit it to me, since it would mean ending her work with me. When I asked if she wanted to take the job she said she didn't know. When I asked, "If you did know, what would you say?" She told me she wanted to take the job.

6. Imagine exploring/explaining your point to a trusted friend (Or instead of imagining — actually do it)

Don't: imagine explaining it to someone you want to impress.

Why not? You'll feel pressure to have the "right" answers.

Do: Picture a trusted person listening and wanting to help you reach your core message.

Why? It humanizes your words and allows you to perceive what you say through someone else's eyes.

Example: My friend Barbara was having trouble writing her school papers. I suggested she pretend she was writing to explain things to me. She did — and her writing flowed more freely.

Left Brain Techniques

Let's balance our right brain techniques with left brain ones. Here are a few techniques for you.

1. Research and make a list of facts

Don't: evaluate your facts as you go.

Why not? That will limit your fact gathering.

Do: include anything that may be even remotely relevant.

Why? It will give you more to work with.

2. Organize your facts

Don't: judge the facts yet.

Why not? You're looking for themes.

Do: put the facts into categories.

Why? To help you see the big picture.

3. Evaluate your facts

Don't: include subjective impressions.

Why not? That's for the right-brain process.

Do: evaluate each fact according to importance, relevance and credibility.

Why? To weigh their merit.

4. Extract the underlying theme

Don't: pay too much attention to the specific details.

Why not? The details can keep you from recognizing the bigger picture.

Do: create a summary of each list.

Why? That is the bigger picture that contains your meaning.

Now What?

1. Alternate between your left and right-brained approach

Don't: use one to the exclusion of the other.

> **Why not?** The approaches complement each other.

Do: alternate between the two.

> **Why?** You'll get a broader picture.

Example: After I organized the facts for a recent article, I took a hike. The information fell into place.

2. Continue the process until you've nailed your core message

Don't: stop too soon.

> **Why not?** If your message doesn't sound and feel exactly right, you can do better.

Do: continue until you've hit the target.

> **Why?** Your message will be far more powerful.

Example: I've literally taught the same seminar hundreds of times—but in fact it's never exactly the same seminar. It took me hundreds of seminars to get the concept of PowerPhrases.

3. Update your message on an ongoing basis

Don't: rest on your laurels.

> **Why not?** Your message will change as you do.

Do: Constantly reevaluate.

> **Why?** In order to be perpetually true to yourself and thereby strengthen your message.

Example: I write a weekly newsletter. It helps my readers master the principles, but it also helps me continually rethink my message to make it fresh and new.

4. Ask if you already know but don't want to admit what you know

Don't: abandon ideas you initially reject.

> **Why not?** You might miss a truth that threatens you.

Do: look more closely at ideas that intimidate you.

> **Why?** They could be your orphaned message.

Example: Ruth believes that the younger workers have a sense of entitlement and resents how often they are promoted past her. She believes her experience should get her promoted before the younger workers. She planned to address the issue at her performance review. In preparing to make her case, she considered all the objections her boss would be likely to offer her. One such objection was the idea that these workers had better technical skills than she did.

As Ruth prepared her response to that objection, she began to consider the idea that some of her skills were obsolete. She decided to enroll in computer classes to update her skills so she would have a stronger argument about why she deserved a promotion. It was difficult for her to admit to herself that her skills were antiquated, but once she did, she was able to realistically compete — and leverage her experience on top of her newly updated computer skills.

Welcome to the core of your message

Do you know what you mean now? You may, you may not. And even if you do, your conclusions are subject to change. It can take a lifetime to get to know yourself; and as soon as you do, you'll evolve and change. Keep using these techniques to dig deeper. Your core message is closer…and more powerful than you think. You need to be as clear as you can in order to Speak Strong.

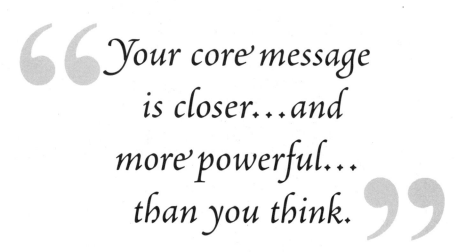

Your core message is closer…and more powerful… than you think.

MERYL RUNION

66 *There's more' to telling the truth than not lying.* 99

MERYL RUNION

What's the Truth About the Truth?

Skill #6: Establish Your Standard

A very mixed message

"Tell Grandma how much you love the socks she gave you for Christmas."

Ruth might as well have said, "Now, lie to Grandma."

So what did Ruth mean when she told her kids that honesty is the best policy? What were her kids supposed to think when Ruth said, "Don't ever let me catch you lying"?

Ruth's life is full of little lies she doesn't know she tells. Her kids know. Her kids know she rewrites events when she recounts them, embellishes her accomplishments when she relays them, and makes things up to get her way. When confronted, Ruth dismisses accusations, so her kids have given up correcting her.

Ruth's anti-mom

Ruth's daughter Kayla was so determined to not be like her mother that she embraced full disclosure. She provided a list of her hang-ups on her first dates. She over-explained herself because she didn't want to create a false impression by summarizing. She advised interviewers of the reasons why they might not want to hire her. Kayla didn't stop with her own limitations. She pointed out her friend's minor errors — particularly their inaccuracies. Kayla was self-righteously judgmental of anyone less truthful than she.

Balance

While Kayla didn't want to be like her mother, being the anti-mother didn't work well either. Eventually Kayla embraced a reasonable honesty policy. She decided that sometimes politeness is more important than truth and sometimes it isn't. (Her main criterion became: does it matter?) She evaluated what she thought people were open to hearing and picked her battles. (She started giving people — including her mother — a pass where she wouldn't have before.) She created a standard for putting her best foot forward that worked for her. (As long as no one would be likely to decide she had misled them, she felt okay about her self-promotion.)

There's a balance you must strike somewhere between saying whatever serves you and absolute truth-telling. Kayla is happy to have found her balance. Frankly, her family, coworkers and friends are glad she did too.

Dos, Don'ts and Tips, Skill # 6:
Establish your standard

We all know honesty is the best policy…or do we?
"The truth will set you free." "Beauty is truth, truth is beauty." "No legacy is so rich as honesty."

Kind of brings a tear to your eye, doesn't it? Truth gets great press in the quotation books. It gets great press other places too. Our parents, our pastors and our teachers taught us to tell the truth as children.

Or did they really? Think about it. Did anyone ever punish you for telling the truth? Did anyone ever reward you for telling a lie they wanted to hear? Did you discover the ground reality is that most people can't or don't always want to handle the truth?

The truth gets great lip service, but when it comes to real life, truth's welcome can depend on how convenient it is.

Truthfully, truth doesn't care if you welcome it or not. Truth doesn't care if you believe it or not. Truth doesn't care if you tell it or not. Truth is like gravity — it is what it is and it does what it does no matter who champions it and who maligns it.

Truth holds all the cards — remember that when you play yours.

Let's look at your truth about truth.

1. Examine what you learned about truth at a young age and what messages you get about it now
Don't: just consider what people said or say.
 Why not? When people's words conflict with their actions, actions make the deepest impressions.
Do: create a summary of your "truth lessons."
 Why? It will help you discover and understand your attitude toward truth now.
Example: I tell a formative tale about how my mother taught me to lie in my article: *Some Boats Need to Be Rocked. www.speakstrong.com/articles/boats. html*

2. Examine what your own behavior says about your attitude toward honesty.

Don't: change your behavior during this review.

> **Why not?** The purpose of this review is to examine your habits. If you change anything, it will skew the results.

Do: tell the truth to yourself about how consistently you tell the truth.

> **Why?** You might as well practice being more truthful now.

Example: Nora received an item she wasn't charged for in an order. She initially considered it a gift. On reflection, she realized calling it a gift was a lie — even if no one asked her about it. She reported the error.

On the other hand, Roy realized he wasn't charged for a 30 cent item when he checked out at the store. (Yes, 30 cent items still exist.) He decided it wasn't worth his trouble or the checker's to correct the error.

3. When you choose to temper the truth, examine what values your choices display

Don't: assume honesty always will be — or should be — your policy.

> **Why not?** Sometimes other worthy values trump truth.

Do: ask yourself what values your words reflect — whether noble, such as politeness, compassion or harmony — or not so noble — such as greed and meanness.

> **Why?** If you understand the underlying values behind your existing honesty policy, you can better create a relevant new one.

Example: Laura knew the product had defects, but didn't report it. She asked herself why — and realized she was motivated by: loyalty to the workers who made the mistake and her own desire to avoid confrontation. She realized by making that value choice, she overruled honesty and customer safety.

4. Decide if and when honesty is and isn't your best policy

Don't: create an unrealistic ideal.

> **Why not?** You want your policy to guide your decisions effectively. Your policy won't be effective if you're unrealistic.

Do: Decide what role you want truth to play in your life.

> **Why?** While honesty may not always be your best policy, you need a clear honesty policy to guide you in difficult situations.

Example: I have an 80 year old renter in Florida who asked me how I liked the carpeting she replaced the old carpeting with. I saw no reason to tell her I didn't like it, because I didn't *need* to like it. I didn't think quickly enough to say something non-committal, so I told her it was nice. That fits my honesty policy because I saw no value in telling her I thought it was hideous.

5. If you have a secret you deem too disruptive to confess to anyone, get help

Don't: go through life with a deep dark secret that no one knows.

    Why not? It alienates you from yourself and others.

Do: Find someone you can speak truthfully to, and make peace with your secret—and/or change.

    Why? It will set you free from the clutches of your secret.

Example: Criminals are known to bond with investigators who convince them to admit their secrets—because it can feel good to unburden themselves, even if it results in conviction.

6. Create a formal policy toward truth

Don't: skip this step.

    Why not? Your formal policy will reduce the "fudge factor" when truth becomes inconvenient.

Do: create a personal policy like a business would create a policy manual.

    Why? It will solidify what you really believe and remind you when you're tempted to act otherwise.

Resource: See when silence is golden at: *www.speakstrong.com/about/solutions.html*

Example: Roger created a beautiful design for Marge's website, but there were many technical and functional errors. Marge was tempted to forget the debacle, never use Roger again and not refer any of her business contacts to him. But her honesty policy wouldn't let her do that. Roger resisted Marge's feedback but Marge persisted to help Roger understand what the issues were.

7. Let your honesty policy create integrity in your life

Don't: make excuses in situations where honesty is uncomfortable.

    Why not? When you're committed to tell the truth about your behavior, you're more likely to behave in a way you're proud of.

Do: evaluate things you plan to do while knowing that if challenged, you will not lie.

    Why? It will encourage behaviors you're proud of.

Example: Sandra considered staying home instead of attending the seminar she had registered for. When she thought of how she would explain her absence to her boss, she realized she didn't have a strong enough reason. Since she was committed to truth and refused to lie, she attended the seminar.

A code you can live by

The song *Teach Your Children Well* opens with the following lyrics: "You, who are on the road, must have a code that you can live by." Those words suggest that while you don't need to adopt anyone else's rules, it's important to have some kind of meaningful code to guide your own behavior. It's like the US Constitution, which the framers wrote to guide day-to-day governmental decisions. Create your honesty policy and let it direct your decisions. It's your foundation for Speaking Strong.

> " *You, who are*
> *on the road,*
> *must have a code*
> *that you can live by.* "

CROSBY, STILLS, NASH AND YOUNG

> ## *Speak as if every word matters. It does.*
>
> MERYL RUNION

I Wasn't Going to Say Anything, But…

Skill #7: Lose Your Lame Excuses

Pollyanna got a bad rap

If I call someone a Pollyanna, they'll probably consider it an insult. They'd be wrong. Pollyanna knew how to Speak Strong. She challenged pretense and negativity, and her outspoken nature transformed an entire town. If you call me a Pollyanna, I'll thank you for the compliment.

Endless tales of spoken truths

You don't have to turn to children's books for inspiring stories about people who Speak Strong. You'll find abundant stories in the history books (Patrick Henry did a great job), business books (my books are full of them), and in homes and offices around the world. Scriptures speak of prophets who offered alternatives to the prevailing wisdom. Quotation books don't quote those who say what everyone says—they quote those who say things most people recognize as truth but few people speak.

A consulting company called Vital Smarts conducted compelling research of healthcare workers who speak up about incompetence and dishonesty. The research showed that 10% of healthcare workers habitually speak up about issues, and those 10% are more satisfied with their work, have better patient outcomes, feel better about themselves, stay longer, and give more discretionary effort.

So if you think that speaking up doesn't work, note that the research contradicts you.

And so do Patrick Henry, the prophets, thousands of my readers, and the ultimate (albeit fictional) authority, Pollyanna.

How can you argue with that?

How can you argue with the arguments above? Well, you might say they were born with it and you weren't. You might say you were like that once and you aren't any more. You might give a false argument that you're not about to become a truth zealot as if that's what I advocate.

You might use a lame excuse and settle back into your comfortable silence… until it stops being comfortable any more.

Or you might take inspiration from those who have spoken up before you and lose your lame excuses. Good riddance.

Dos, Don'ts and Tips, Skill # 7:
Lose Your Lame Excuses

An excuse-free life
Letting go of excuses is like moving out of a hut you know to move into a castle you don't know. It's tempting to delay and to cling to and hold on to the familiar. The transition time can be uncomfortable. Yet the end result is magnificent once you settle into it. Here are some things you can do to let go of your lame excuses.

1. Respect your own authority
Don't: consider what anyone says to be complete truth that trumps what you know.

Why not? Even if they're "right", their suggestions may not be best for you.
Do: compare what they say to what you know. Update your thinking accordingly.

Why? No authority is absolute. While they may know the subject, you know your own situation and experience.

Example: My physical therapist is exceptional. I've gone to her a few times with injuries and muscle strains. I am an active participant in the process. If something she suggests doesn't sound right or her diagnosis doesn't match my symptoms, I let her know. We work as a team to track down the source of stress and work out a plan to deal with it.

After all, while she knows physical therapy, I know my body.

And while tech support knows computers, you know what the error message says on your screen.

2. Risk short-term discomfort for long-term gain
Don't: let resistance to change drive your choices.

Why not? Resistance to positive change values short-term comfort over long-term benefits.
Do: complete the Risky Conversation Assessment Form in the appendix and on my website: *www.speakstrong.com/articles/speak-strong/risky_conversation. html*. Let the assessment help you differentiate between fears that create resistance and legitimate considerations that have merit.

Why? Reasonable assessment puts fears that create resistance in perspective and reminds you of what you have to gain.

Example: People often suggest to me that they can't talk to certain people even though they haven't tried. More often than not (by far) they are pleasantly surprised when they risk telling the truth.

3. Allow people to react to the truth you tell

Don't: try to control what others feel in response to your words.

>**Why not?** Your desire to control how they feel is your problem. Their reaction to something you need to say is their problem. You won't overcome either problem by pandering.

Do: speak as gently as you can and still be clear. Trust them to deal with their reaction.

>**Why?** Truth can hurt. It's natural to recoil from it. As long as you are non-attacking, you're not responsible for how they react.

Example: Joel gets angry when his secretary corrects his errors. For years, she tried to avoid his anger. Eventually she realized he needed to hear what she had to say. She spoke her peace and let him deal with his anger on his own.

4. Start with small issues and work up

Don't: wait to address issues until you're ready to handle the "big one."

>**Why not?** You'll either never start or you'll start in a way that is counterproductive due to your lack of experience.

Do: notice smaller issues you previously ignored and address at least one per week.

>**Why?** You'll build your communication muscle gradually. Eventually the "big one" won't seem so daunting.

Example: Robertah started by addressing the fact that her husband selected the movies they watched. After a few months she worked her way up to talking about how they managed their money.

At work, she started by addressing the assistant who left work in the conference room. She worked up to addressing her objections to the fact that her boss showed up to meetings late.

5. Pick one habit to change at a time

Don't: try to change everything at once.

>**Why not?** You'll end up not changing anything.

Do: commit to changing a single habit.

>**Why?** It's manageable.

Example: I started by replacing sarcasm with direct communication about the issues that motivated it. I had other areas of focus, but eliminating sarcasm was the one I worked to master before moving on to other habits.

Clarissa started by not expressing impatience when her colleagues didn't understand her point as quickly as she thought they should. By learning not to be so over-bearing, she became freer to address issues in ways that worked.

6. Speak from the level of knowledge you have

Don't: pretend you know things you don't, but don't wait for certainty to speak.

Why not? Neither approach honors truth and neither is productive.

Do: express how you see things and invite feedback.

Why? If your information is inaccurate or just plain wrong, you'll find out. If you're right, you'll find out. Otherwise you're guessing.

PowerPhrase/What to say: I believe the vendor was responsible for maintenance.

Poison Phrase/What NOT to say: The vendor should have maintained it. (When you're not certain.)

7. Ask people you trust to help you say what you mean to them

Don't: overlook friends and coworkers as powerful resources to develop your skills.

Why not? They can give you the best possible feedback.

Do: ask them if they'll work with you when you have issues to help you learn how to say what you mean in a way they can hear.

Why? It's concrete, real world training that will change how you communicate.

PowerPhrase/What to say: I have a habit of agreeing to do things I don't want to do or that take me away from my first priorities. I'd like to break that habit. Will you help me?

8. Read stories about people who speak nobly

Don't: take your cues from media or the culture at large.

Why not? The media often panders to the lowest common denominator.

Do: read success stories and inspiring tales of people who speak up and out.

Why? It shows you what it looks like and sounds like to Speak Strong. It proves that this is practical, real-world knowledge.

Resource: My *A PowerPhrase a Week* newsletter includes success stories. *www. speakstrong.com/newsletter/newsletbene.html*

An excuse-free life

I can summarize every lame excuse to justify silence in one excuse: the habit of making excuses. You'll find it inconvenient at times to lose that habit — but ultimately it will simplify your choices.

Eventually, you'll appreciate the rewards that come with an excuse-free life. You'll also appreciate the foundation it gives you to Speak Strong.

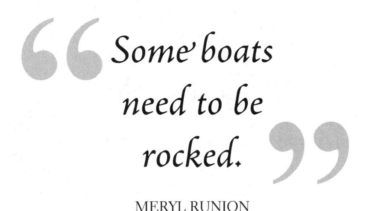

Some boats need to be rocked.

MERYL RUNION

" *Truth holds
all the cards—
remember that
when you play yours.* "

MERYL RUNION

Where Do I Begin?

Skill #8: Talk about how you talk

What could be scarier?

Women have the power to strike terror into men's souls with five simple words — "Honey, we need to talk." Suddenly the tough guy who can slay metaphorical dragons is reduced to a quivering broken shell of his former self.

Of course, it isn't just the men who find difficult conversations so threatening. Most all of us do. I suggest we're afraid we'll discover we're not who we think we are, that someone will run verbal circles around us, or that we will be exposed as frauds.

There's no complete cure for conversation phobia, but if you talk about how you talk, it can help.

A conversation worth having

Al Gore initiated a conversation about conversations in his book *Assault on Reason*. His book claims the national conversation is "broken" and Americans need to fix it. Gore charges that slogans and propaganda have replaced logic and reason. He encourages politicians and voters to talk about how they talk — and decide what standards they want to observe. That's an important conversation — one we all need to have. And not just about politics.

Conversations about conversations

Conversations about conversations provide timeouts to decide the rules of the communication game. They set the objectives and boundaries. They allow participants to play without fear of being fouled, sacked or tackled.

It's a manager telling her employee how she likes to be updated. It's a sister telling her brother she will not accept sarcasm. It's a moderator telling a political commentator to drop the personal attacks and stick to the issues.

It's life partners learning how they can best hear what the other has to say and helping each other through the difficult conversations.

Where do you begin?

Talk about how you talk. Speak Strong by having a conversation about conversations. Establish the rules of the game so the players can safely play. Then the words, "Honey, we need to talk" — or even the words "I'd like you to step into my office for a few minutes" — will be welcome ones.

Dos, Don'ts and Tips, Skill # 8:
Talk about how you talk

Make it safe to talk

Why should you talk about how you talk? To create the safety that effective communication depends on. Here's where you start.

1. Initiate a conversation about becoming more truthful

Don't: emphasize existing dishonesty — particularly not theirs.

Why not? It will create defensiveness.

Do: mention your own desire to be more truthful in your life and ask to negotiate a mutual standard of honesty.

Why? It removes the blame and therefore the defensiveness.

Power Phrases/What to say: I want to be able to tell you when something doesn't work for me and I'd like you to do the same. Sometimes we try too hard to protect each other's feeling and we skirt the truth. Can we agree to be more honest?

Poison Phrase/What NOT to say: You lie to me about how you feel all the time and I want that to stop.

2. Initiate a conversation about mutual civility

Don't: limit the discussion to a conversation about what you want them to change.

Why not? You may need to change too. This conversation is to establish standards for both of you to follow.

Do: let them know you want mutual respect.

Why? There's incentive for them, and it focuses on working together.

Power Phrases/What to say:
• Let's talk about how we can speak so we both feel respected.
• Let's discuss ways we come across as rude or harsh to each other, and how we can change that. Do I ever say things in a way that hits you wrong? What do I say? How could I say it better?

Poison Phrase/What NOT to say: I'm always polite to you, and you're rude to me.

3. Invite a collaborative approach

Don't: let them polarize you into opposing them.

Why not? If they maintain a polarized stance, it's easy to take the opposite stance. If you do that, you won't get anywhere.

Do: identify adversarial tones and suggest you work together.

Why? You'll get better results with less strain.

Power Phrases/What to say: We're getting adversarial. I'd like us to get back on the same team. How can we do that?

Poison Phrase/What NOT to say: You're antagonistic. Stop it.

4. Invite them to tell you how you can communicate better with them

Don't: use this as a ploy to tell them what you want.

> **Why not?** They'll feel manipulated when you reveal your hidden agenda. If you're raising the issue of how you communicate just to get them to change and aren't open to feedback, don't use this tip.

Do: ask them how they like to receive info, how detailed they like their information and what else they can tell you about how you can better communicate with them.

> **Why?** You might discover your communication style actually creates problems — and another style would work better.

Power Phrases/What to say:
- How do you like to be updated?
- Do you prefer I get to the point more quickly?
- Is there anything about how I communicate that doesn't work for you and you'd like for me to change?

Poison Phrase/What NOT to say: Now that I've listened to you, you have to listen to me.

5. Establish communication standards together

Don't: continue with conversational dynamics that don't work.

> **Why not?** You won't get anywhere.

Do: take a step back and address how you communicate.

> **Why?** You will be far more likely to have a satisfying result.

Power Phrases/What to say: When we have sensitive discussions, I notice we tend to get defensive. I'd like to set guidelines for our conversations that make it safe for us to talk to each other.

Poison Phrase/What NOT to say: Let's follow my rules to keep you from attacking me.

Example: For some people, civility standards mean they won't yell at each other. Others have no problem with yelling. Some will set clarity standards and ask for people to convey what they think, feel and want when things get contentious. Others will find that tedious. People have told me that they've set listening standards that require people to briefly reference the last thing the person before them said to make sure they listened instead of focused on their own words.

6. Use a facilitator to set standards

Don't: give up when you hit an impasse.

Why not? You might be caught up in your usual communication traps.

Do: invite a friend or a professional to help you set standards of communication.

Why? A professional can guide you past your usual pitfalls.

Resources: Recommended standards of communication: *www.speakstrong.com/commstds.html*; Meryl Runion, CSP coaching: *www.speakstrong.com/hire_meryl/*

You're as healthy as the things you can talk about

If you take a step back and talk about how you talk, you can ferret out unhealthy communication practices. You just might have some genuine interaction — where everyone Speaks Strong.

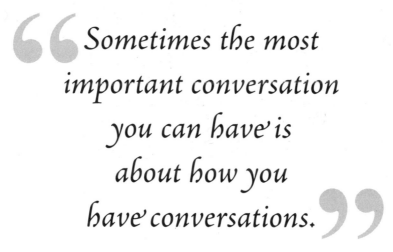

" *Sometimes the most important conversation you can have is about how you have conversations.* "

MERYL RUNION

Speak
STRONG

STEP 2:
SAY WHAT YOU MEAN

Say What You Mean Skill Set #1:
Say What You Think

Say What You Mean Skill Set #2:
Say What You Feel

Say What You Mean Skill Set #3:
Say What You Want

Say What You Mean Skill Set #4:
Add Persuasion

Introduction to Step Two:
Say What You Mean

Wouldn't it be great if Code White was all you needed? If pulling your head out of the sand and keeping your eyes wide open solved every problem? Code White is a great start—but it's just a start. Your second step is to say what you mean. That sounds simple—doesn't it?

Saying what you mean is a bit more involved than most of us think. There are four aspects to it. It takes awareness and skill to separate each aspect and put them into practice.

Say What You Mean Skill Category #1:
Say What You Think

Saying what you think is disclosing your objective look at a situation. What do you think? What's going on in your mind? What are your observations? Opinions? Concepts? Ideas? If you wrote a report on the situation, what would you write?

Say What You Mean Skill Category #2:
Say What You Feel

People are far more likely to express their thoughts about an issue than their feelings. Yet feelings are a driving force in every conversation. Not only is there is a secret power in communicating what you feel, but there is a secret peril in ignoring feelings. Include what you feel to add power to your message when you say what you mean.

Say What You Mean Skill Category #3:
Say What You Want

Saying what you want is your call to action. It gives your message a direction and tells people what to do and where to go with your words. It channels your thoughts and the feelings into your desired outcome.

Say What You Mean Skill Category #4:
Add Persuasion

Once you know what you think, feel and want, you can "sex up" your language for a more effective result. This section explores how to be persuasive without going into the realm of deception and propaganda.

Just the facts ma'am

Skill # 9: Separate fact from opinion

Courtroom conflation

Judge Judy has one thing in common with Dragnet's legendary Sergeant Joe Friday. She has little patience for people who can't separate fact from opinion. Like the Sergeant, Judy interrupts abruptly with dismissive insistence on "just the facts." At the first sign of opinion masquerading as fact, Judy waves her finger, stares disapprovingly at the speaker and sharply says something like:

"I didn't ask you if he worked slowly, I asked if he got the job done."

"Don't tell me you've been busy, tell me if you finished the project."

"I don't care if you think she's a loser. I want to know what happened."

Judge Judy beams her finely tuned radar to distinguish between fact and opinion.

Most of Judge Judy's plaintiffs and defendants don't have a clue. If they did, surely they wouldn't risk her wrath as they do. In Judge Judy's courtroom, you weaken your case and lose credibility when you conflate fact and opinion.

And even if your listeners don't have Judge Judy's cultured ear, you too will lose credibility when you conflate fact and opinion.

Like Senator Ted Kennedy did once in a Judiciary Committee meeting.

Decisive distinctions

Senator Ted Kennedy told Senator Arlen Specter that he knew Specter had received a report because he, Kennedy, had sent it. Kennedy's words failed the Judge Judy test.

Judge Judy would have accepted Kennedy's claim that he sent the info but she would have scolded him severely for insisting Specter had received it. Kennedy had no way to know that Specter had received it. That was Kennedy's opinion. It wouldn't have worked in Judge Judy's court and it didn't play well on the evening news either.

Specter looked irritated by Kennedy's remark.

Do you ever not get the respect you deserve? Perhaps it's because you conflate fact and opinion. When you know you can pass the Judge Judy test, you know you can say what you mean with confidence.

Dos, Don'ts and Tips, Skill # 9:
Separate fact from opinion

A vital distinction

You know what you said, but do you know what they heard? You know what you saw someone do, but do you know why they did it? You know how someone behaved in the past, but do you know what they will do in the future?

If you draw strong conclusions and informed opinions based on what you know, you are likely to be correct. But unless you can differentiate between the facts and the opinions you formed based on the facts, you will lose credibility with the Judge Judys in the world. That will provide ammunition to anyone who wants to discredit what you say when you say what you mean.

So make the differentiation and speak accordingly. Here's how.

1. Imagine an omnipresent video camera filming events

Picture a video camera recording the situations and events that you talk about.

Don't: interpret.
   Why not? This exercise is not about interpretation. It's about pure facts.
Do: observe events in a way a camera could confirm.
   Why? This step helps you neutrally observe.

2. Describe what you see on your imaginary camera

Don't: add commentary to your description…yet.
   Why not? That comes later. This step is to determine what is.
Do: describe events in a way that a camera could confirm.
   Why? Those are your facts.
Example: If you say, "Joe called me a %()# and slammed his fist on the table," you're describing fact. If you say, "Joe was hateful toward me," you're adding interpretation.

3. Make commentary on your imaginary video

Okay, now you can interpret. Now you can project and infer and construe.

Don't: limit yourself to what anyone watching the video would observe.
   Why not? This step is to uncover your opinion.
Do: explain the background, context and meaning of the events you described in earlier steps.
   Why? That's your opinion.

Example: This example starts with fact and moves to interpretation. "Joe called me a %()# and slammed his fist on the table. He's angry that I got his promotion."

4. Practice your "imaginary camera test" with your important conversations

Don't: edit.

Why not? You might edit out something significant.

Do: watch your imaginary video with the questions: who, when, how, what, why and where? Then ask which answers your imaginary omnipresent video camera can and can't confirm.

Why? The answers your imaginary camera confirms are your facts. The answers it doesn't confirm are your opinions.

Example: Fact: I received the promotion Joe applied for on June 20th. Since that date, Joe has not called me once to update me on production. Yesterday Joe called me a %()# and slammed his fist on the table.

Opinion: Joe wanted the promotion and is angry I got it. He is attempting to sabotage my performance.

5. Differentiate between judgment and opinion when you speak

Don't: state your judgments and opinions as if they were factual, but don't discount them either.

Why not? With proper attribution, your opinions matter.

Do: communicate both opinions and the facts you base them on.

Why? Opinions carry more weight when you support them with facts without conflating them with facts.

PowerPhrase/What to say: I believe you have the report because I sent it directly to your office.

Poison Phrase/What NOT to say: I know you have the report because I sent it.

Say exactly what you mean

The power to Speak Strong comes from the power of authenticity. That's why you need to speak accurately. If you're not accurate, you're not really saying what you mean. Use these techniques to stop conflating your facts and your opinions, to add power to your points and to Speak Strong.

> " *Clarity begins at home.* "

MERYL RUNION

Why should they listen to me?

Skill #10: Establish credibility

Simply incredible

"Why don't they listen to me?" Gina asked. "I've been here a long time, I know what I'm talking about, and yet I present an idea and they ignore me. Then someone else says the same thing and everyone acts like that person invented the iPhone. What's that about?"

Gina's colleague Sandy replied, "I know why they don't take you seriously. You point out possible limitations in your ideas. You say, 'This might not work because of this, that and the other reason, but it's worth a try.' Someone else will say, 'I know exactly what we should do. We should do A. If that doesn't work we should do B.' They sound committed to their ideas and you don't."

Gina is "incredible" because she doesn't sound like she believes in her own ideas.

Then there's Frank. Frank is Gina's credibility opposite. Frank is "incredible" because he doesn't allow himself to be "confused by facts." He ignores evidence that doesn't support what he promotes. He hedges numbers. He uses information out of context. He dazzled at the interview that got him the job, but his colleagues quickly learned that his words were empty.

Credible is something you are — not something you do

You can't do credible. You have to be credible. You have to know what you're talking about and know how to package what you know.

Gina was right, but it's not enough to be right. She was not convincing in her presentation. Frank was convincing, but it's not enough to be convincing. When his claims failed the test of time, his colleagues learned to discount his words. If you want to establish credibility, you need to know what you're talking about and be convincing when you talk.

Dos, Don'ts and Tips, Skill # 10:
 Establish credibility

Thoughts worth listening to
The world is full of opinions, so how do you get people to care about yours? How do you get your voice heard above the noise? How can you speak in a way that causes people to suspend their skepticism and hear what you say?

You develop the following credibility skills:

1. Be principle-based
Don't: forget to reference the principles that guide you, but don't speak about principles you don't live by.
   Why not? Credible people base their words AND actions on consistent principles.
Do: explain your point of view in terms of universally held principles that you evenly apply.
   Why? It associates your ideas with broader concepts that elevate the discussion.
PowerPhrase/What to say: This course of action supports our mission statement.
Poison Phrase/What NOT to say: This course of action will make us look good at the meeting on Friday,

2. Reference how your credentials inform your opinions
Don't: exaggerate.
   Why not? You might get busted, you'll know you're faking it and on some level they'll know too.
Do: support your points with your credentials and your experience.
   Why? It naturally provides a background for your remarks that boosts credibility.
Example: To get his colleagues to give his words more weight, Larry reminded the group that he had implemented an employee reward system in a previous job.
PowerPhrase/What to say: We found that when the rewards were non-competitive, cooperation was higher and output increased by 13%.

3. Be specific and thorough

Don't: neglect details.

Why not? People need specifics to relate to abstractions.

Do: include and/or reference precise examples and details that support your assertions.

Why? It anchors your broad principles to concrete ideas.

PowerPhrase/What to say: Eight out of nine witnesses recanted their testimony. That's unprecedented.

Poison Phrase/What NOT to say: The evidence is weak.

4. Communicate opinions as opinion and tie them to the facts you base them on

Don't: exclude fact or opinion.

Why not? They both are part of making a strong point.

Do: say what you think and why. Include facts that inform your opinions.

Why? You need both for a persuasive assertion.

PowerPhrase/What to say: Based on this month's figures I recommend we increase our projections by 40%.

Poison Phrase/What NOT to say: We're doing great. We should double our projections.

5. Share personal experience and expertise

Don't: explain when you can demonstrate.

Why not? Your experiences exhibit your topic knowledge in a tangible way.

Do: describe what you've seen, experienced and implemented.

Why? It sets you up as an authority.

PowerPhrase/What to say: When we increased warehouse capacity in 2003, it reduced our turnaround time by 23%.

Poison Phrase/What NOT to say: We need to expand the warehouse.

6. Listen to opposing views

Don't: quickly dismiss opposing ideas, even if you've already considered and rejected them.

Why not? You will appear closed-minded.

Do: respectfully consider and clarify opposing ideas.

Why? If you appear closed to any idea, it indicates that you form opinions based on selective input.

PowerPhrase/What to say: I asked that question myself the first time I faced this situation, and what I learned was…

Poison Phrase/What NOT to say: That's ridiculous.

7. Admit your mistakes

Don't: hide your errors.

    Why not? You will lose credibility.

Do: admit it when you discover you made a mistake—preferably before they bring it up.

    Why? You can discuss the issues on your own terms and enhance your credibility.

PowerPhrase/What to say: I know what can happen when you don't transfer a site properly. I neglected to transfer some important files on the first site I designed. It was a mess. That's a mistake I won't make again.

Poison Phrase/What NOT to say: You heard about that? Yeah. My clients didn't show me all the files so they weren't transferred. They should have been more thorough.

You can't do credible unless you are credible

Credibility comes from knowing what you're doing, and confidently communicating that knowing. You can't fake credibility for long.

A commitment to honesty is a commitment to become more credible. If you refuse to fake it, you increase your incentive to make it. If you're committed to putting your best foot forward but not a false front, you're likely to make sure your best foot looks pretty good. When you stop trying to do credible, you're more likely to be credible. It's important to be credible when you say what you think as part of Speaking Strong.

> " *If you have a*
> *horn worth blowing,*
> *take a deep breath*
> *and let it fly.* "
>
> MERYL RUNION

Judge and Jury

Skill #11: Express your opinion (without sounding opinionated)

What do you think?

Opinions: we all have them. Do you know how to offer yours? Most people don't. I know this from my many years as a trainer.

Seminar participants evaluate my presentation at the end of the day. Most of the evaluations are ego-gratifying but not useful. A few leave me feeling judged, misrepresented and beat up. Out of every fifty I read, I'll receive one that really provides me with useful information.

No trainer really minds when an audience member sings his or her praises on evaluations. But the greatest gift is when a participant expresses a unique observation, offers a concrete suggestion and provides tangible examples of what worked, didn't work or what might work better in the future. After all, who can I better learn from than someone who just spent an entire day listening to me? A well-expressed opinion can be a fabulous gift.

I have spoken

Well-expressed doesn't mean pronounced from on high. How many of us heard, "Because I said so!" as a child? Too many of us were told not to question, and as adults, we still encounter people who seem to think their opinions are law. Often, the more they insist on their perspective, the more others want to prove them wrong.

I think of the image consultant who replied to my email about how much I love my new red hair highlights by telling me that red coloring doesn't work for brunettes going grey. I think of the chiropractor who replied to my comment about how helpful my physical therapy was by telling me physical therapy has no value. And in an example that doesn't reference my age, I think of the colleague who had me pegged politically based on a single policy objection I referenced. These people didn't stop at having opinions—they were opinionated. Opinions are a gift. Opinionated is an imposition. Because of those impositions, I don't seek these people's opinions as I might.

Thinking doesn't make it so — but it does make it relevant

Opinionated people have too much confidence in their opinions. Compliant people have too little. The excessively humble know their thinking doesn't make something so, but they discount the legitimate value of their opinions. Your thoughts don't need absolute truth to have value. It's enough that you think them, so don't hoard your thoughts when someone could benefit.

Opinions as gifts

"I'm glad I know that." "Thanks for telling me." "Wow, that was useful." We've all have had our lives improved when someone told us something we needed to know.

Give your opinions as gifts.

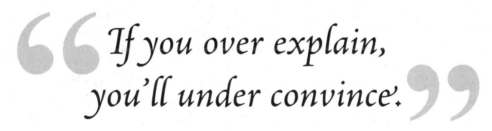

*If you over explain,
you'll under convince.*

MERYL RUNION

Dos, Don'ts and Tips, Skill # 11:
Express your opinion (without sounding opinionated)

Thoughts worth listening to

A hundred people will think a hundred different things. Every opinion has value, but the well-expressed opinions are the ones that make a difference. Here are some tips to get your opinion heard.

1. Express your opinion as how you see it, not how it is

Don't: claim omniscience.

Why not? It discredits your entire argument.

Do: express your opinion as an opinion.

Why? It's believable.

PowerPhrase/What to say: I find chiropractic to be more effective than physical therapy. Here are some of the limits I see in using Physical Therapy...

Poison Phrase/What NOT to say: Physical therapy is a waste of time.

2. Share the perspective that is uniquely yours

Don't: censor or minimize your opinions as "just your idea."

Why not? People can get consensus opinion anywhere. Your own thinking is something only you can provide.

Do: ask yourself how you personally perceive things and express that.

Why? It's your unique gift.

PowerPhrase/What to say: Here's how I see it.

Poison Phrase/What NOT to say: My opinion doesn't matter. Here's what others say.

3. Translate opinions into concrete suggestions

Don't: offer critical judgments about what's wrong without concrete suggestions of what would work.

Why not? It's negative and demoralizing.

Do: provide clear recommendations when you communicate critical opinions.

Why? It's constructive.

PowerPhrase/What to say: Let's rewrite the copy to emphasize benefits.

Poison Phrase/What NOT to say: This copy is too focused on features. No one cares about that.

4. Offer tangible examples that support your conclusions

Don't: assert your conclusions without explaining what you base them on.

Why not? It leaves people guessing.

Do: explain your reasoning with concrete with examples.

Why? It helps your listener understand your opinions and makes your ideas concrete.

PowerPhrase/What to say: I recommend you rework your presentation to eliminate slang that some people consider to be unprofessional such as "like" and "whatever."

Poison Phrase/What NOT to say: Your language is unprofessional.

5. Use "I" language or behavior language

Don't: make your opinion about the other person.

Why not? It triggers defensiveness.

Do: use "I" language to take ownership of your opinion or behavior language to focus your opinion on actions and events rather than your listener.

Why? It makes your opinion easier to listen to.

PowerPhrases/What to say:
- I recommend putting the footnotes at the end.
- The footnotes would work better at the end.

Poison Phrase/What NOT to say: You put the footnotes in the wrong place. You should have put them at the end.

6. Be open to opposing views

Don't: discount ideas without consideration—even if you've already evaluated them.

Why not? That's what opinionated people do.

Do: respectfully discuss and weigh opposing ideas.

Why? If you appear closed to any idea, it indicates that you form opinions based on selective input.

PowerPhrase/What to say: I usually find red hair coloring doesn't work well with skin tones for brunettes. I'm glad you found something that works.

Poison Phrase/What NOT to say: Brunettes who are going grey should never use red coloring.

Opinions don't make you opinionated. Rigid opinions do.

We all have opinions, but not all of us are opinionated. The distinction is in how rigidly we hold onto our opinions and how skillfully we share them. Offer your opinions as useful gifts. That's what your opinions are when you Speak Strong.

If it's not personal, why am I so triggered?

Skill #12: Get over rationality myths

Who cares what you feel?

I once heard a tale of a couple in counseling over the husband's infidelity. The wife snapped, "You just like her (the other woman) because she makes you feel special." The husband thought for a moment and said, "Yes, I think that might have something to do with it."

This story could trigger a thousand conversations (like how the husband's behavior makes his wife feel…), but for now, let's focus on this—how we make each other feel matters very much.

Patients sue the doctor who makes them feel discounted. Terminated employees attack the firing managers who took their job in ways that also took their dignity. Clients leave the vendors who blame them for their own delivery problems. Sure, the medical error, the firing and the lateness matter, but it's a myth to think that people make decisions rationally. It's the feelings that put us over the edge.

A manager's tale

An HR Director named Mike helped me bust the myth of rationality at a management seminar I led. One participant insisted feelings have no place in business conversations because no one at work cares how anyone feels. The HR Director disagreed. He shared the following tale of how he once turned a tense conversation around with Laura, a difficult employee, by disclosing his own feelings.

Three managers had tried to reason with Laura and failed. They referred her to Mike because they couldn't get past her defenses.

Mike reviewed the documentation and asked Laura what she saw as the problem. Laura immediately accused Mike of being selective in his review. Mike said, "Let me ask—your managers tell me you respond to input by going on the offensive and putting them on the defensive. What do you think about that?" Laura snapped, "I don't put anyone on the defensive."

Mike replied:

"Here's how I feel right now. I am here to help you succeed, but I feel under attack. I feel very much on the defensive."

By telling Laura how he felt in real time, Mike helped her understand what other managers had been unable to convey.

Mike helped me make my point at the seminar — we're not as rational as we like to think. By doing that, he helped me explain the importance of a key issue we often ignore — feelings.

Your conversations aren't about what you think they're about

Here are some common communication myths that will limit your ability to Speak Strong if you believe them.

1) We are rational beings who operate exclusively on reasoned review of facts
2) Feelings don't matter, especially not at work
3) If you ignore emotional issues, they'll go away
4) If no one brings up feelings, there's no reason for you to
5) You come across as weak when you say what you feel
6) If feelings drove you, you'd know it, and,
7) As long as your points are valid you don't need to consider emotion.

Business may not be personal, but it sure feels like it is. If you never say what you feel, you're telling just one part of the story. If you haven't gotten beyond the rationality myth, you're not Speaking Strong. So get over it and have your say.

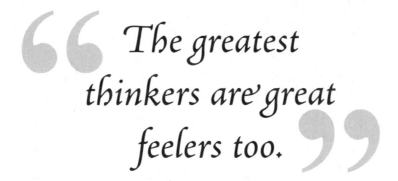

The greatest thinkers are great feelers too.

MERYL RUNION

Dos, Don'ts and Tips, Skill # 12:
Get over rationality myths

The inside of the story

The facts are part of every story. Your interpretations of the facts are another part of the story. But you don't just interpret facts intellectually. You interpret them emotionally too. Before you can Speak Strong, you need to get beyond your rationality myths. Here's how.

1. Explore the feeling behind your opinions

Don't: stop until you uncover feelings that strike you as a complete match.
  Why not? Like most of us, you are probably somewhat emotionally illiterate and need to develop your ability to recognize feelings.
Do: identify and name a feeling associated with each opinion you consider.
  Why? Every opinion has some kind of feeling associated with it. This step will make your feelings conscious.
Example: Carla felt angry that her mentor hadn't told her about the job opening in her department. But when she looked more deeply, she realized she felt hurt and betrayed. She finally felt an "emotional match" when she considered her deeper feeling might be fear — fear that perhaps her mentor didn't have confidence in her. That scared Carla because it led her to think that she might not be as good as she had thought.

2. Examine deceptive thinking patterns that masquerade as feelings

Don't: mistake thoughts for feelings.
  Why not? You need to be aware of both.
Do: flag blame, judgment and statements such as "I feel that" as thoughts that indicate some buried feelings you need to identify and probably communicate.
  Why? Blame and judgment are thoughts that cover feelings. The statement "I feel that" is often followed with an opinion, not a genuine feeling.
PowerPhrase/What to say: I'm hurt that you didn't recommend me.
Poison Phrase/What NOT to say: I feel it's your fault that I didn't get the job.

3. Consider major decisions you've made and ask what emotions might have guided them

Don't: assume rationality.
  Why not? You are a thinking and feeling being. Your emotions weighed in on your decision as well as your thinking — probably more than you knew.

Do: examine what emotions influenced your choices.

Why? It will help you recognize the role emotions play in your decisions.
Example: Carmen said she didn't promote Joy because she was unqualified, but when she looked deeper, she realized she was jealous that Joy had moved through the company so much more quickly than she had. She didn't think Joy realized how much harder those who went before her had it, and felt unappreciated.

4. Study brain structure, emotional IQ, and persuasion
Don't: limit your communication study to facts and logic.

Why not? Facts and logic are the tip of the communication iceberg.
Do: learn how your brain operates and how reason and emotion interrelate.

Why? It will help you understand how to include emotional references in your conversations.
Resource: Article: *www.speakstrong.com/articles/persuasion/anticipation.html*

5. When you hit a substantive impasse in a discussion, consider potential underlying emotional barriers
Don't: assume you or the other person would know if you had a "hidden emotional agenda."

Why not? Like you (and me), others often are unaware of motives.
Do: explore and ask about emotional motivators.

Why? Underlying unaddressed emotion can hinder substantive conversations.
PowerPhrase/What to say: Is there something else we need to talk about that is affecting this conversation? Did I offend you?
Poison Phrase/What NOT to say: You're not being rational here.

People are people are people
Try as we might to be professional work machines, in the end, we're all people with emotions, egos and self-images we protect. It's a myth to think otherwise. When you communicate based on myths, you're ineffective. The most effective and persuasive communicators know that feelings and emotions are important topics for communication. Develop your communication skills based on fact, not myth, as a foundation to Speak Strong. Say what you feel.

He hurt my feelings

Skill #13: Express emotion
(without sounding like a five-year old)

A simple expression of hurt

It happened on a 2004 episode of *The Apprentice* and I remember it like I saw it yesterday. When Troy selected Heidi to go to the boardroom with him to face being "fired," she reacted with such hostility that her words were censored. Troy's response was as straightforward as possible. He said:

- Ouch!

Heidi was silent. She and Troy entered the boardroom where Heidi was "fired."

Troy's simple reaction was a non-defensive and non-attacking acknowledgement of how Heidi's words left him feeling. Troy made his point without sounding weak, without appearing childish and without creating defensiveness. His lack of hostility turned Heidi's words back on to her. Heidi hugged Troy goodbye before she left.

Leave the violins behind

Do you think that emotional communication means extended, excruciating and gut-wrenching confessionals better left to church or therapy? It can. There are times and places for protracted emotional expression and processing. But as Troy reflexively demonstrated on *The Apprentice*, you can communicate your feelings with a single word that makes your point and leaves everyone's guts un-wrenched.

You get to be human

You're human. That means you're a thinking and feeling being. And that means when you're attacked or treated unfairly, it affects you. You don't need to pretend that it doesn't.

But that does not suggest you should have an emotional display, a dramatic confrontation or lay responsibility for your feelings at someone else's feet. Instead, decide what part of your feelings they need to know about and simply communicate it.

When you appropriately say what you feel, it adds to your power
There's a time and a place for all things. It's ironic that the strong dare to be more vulnerable than the weak would ever dare to be. There's a secret power in feelings, and knowing how to use that power is an important part of Speaking Strong.

> " *Pick words strong enough to pierce the barriers around the heart but gentle enough to protect the heart itself.* "
>
> MERYL RUNION

Dos, Don'ts and Tips, Skill # 13:
Express emotion (without sounding like a five-year old)

Feelings matter
A child having a tantrum at a store can wield a lot of power through emotional expression. I don't recommend tantrums as a strategy for either children or adults, but that doesn't mean you should abandon all emotional expression. If you do, you'll suppress your power. Feelings matter and these steps will help you express them without sounding like a five-year old.

1. Describe your feelings instead of dramatically displaying them
Don't: turn your emotional disclosure into a venting session or an exhibition.
> **Why not?** That's what children do. It's unbecoming in an adult and can backfire.

Do: describe what you feel. Keep your display of emotion moderate — not computer-like — without being theatrical.
> **Why?** It communicates a mature balance of heart and mind.

PowerPhrase/What to say: I am angry about the delay.
Poison Phrase/What NOT to say: <SNIFF> You never make my work a priority <GASP>. I hate you!

2. Do your emotional homework before you communicate
Don't: share every passing emotion.
> **Why not?** Fleeting emotions are often irrelevant — and you can muddy the waters by expressing them.

Do: distill raw emotions into more sophisticated, well-defined ones.
> **Why?** These emotions will be easier to hear, respect and respond to.

PowerPhrase/What to say: I'm disheartened by this omission.
Poison Phrase/What NOT to say: You hurt my feelings.

3. Respond, don't react
Don't: dump emotion without purpose.
> **Why not?** Your reaction can trigger a reaction in them which can trigger a reaction in you which can trigger a reaction...

Do: disclose with a selected purpose (such as clarity, honesty, inviting them to open up emotionally, etc.)
> **Why?** Your disclosure will have more power and be more effective.

PowerPhrase/What to say: I want to tell you how the team feels so you'll understand why they react the way they do.
Poison Phrase/What NOT to say: We're mad about your hypocrisy and we're not going to take it any more.

4. Be genuine

Don't: pretend you're not reacting emotionally when you are.

 Why not? It's confusing and mixes the message.

Do: acknowledge genuine emotion.

 Why? Emotion is a vital part of any communication.

Example: Julie pretended not to mind being bypassed for the promotion. She thought if she expressed her disappointment, she would appear immature. She later realized her apparent indifference led people to believe she didn't want the promotion. She recognized that could inhibit her chances for future promotions.

5. Develop a sophisticated vocabulary of feelings

Don't: rely on an inadequate emotional vocabulary.

 Why not? You can sound childish, and that will limit your willingness to express what you feel.

Do: develop an emotional vocabulary that enables you to communicate any feeling in any situation.

 Why? You will use the tools once you have them.

Resource: Emotional words: you'll find them in the appendix and at: www. speakstrong.com/articles/speak-strong/emotions.html

6. Differentiate between expressing emotions and being emotional

Don't: assume an emotional display is saying what you feel.

 Why not? You can behave highly emotionally without giving a clear indication of what you feel.

Do: before you say what you feel, be sure you know the difference between being emotional and expressing emotion.

 Why? If you don't, you'll confuse instead of clarify.

Example: Ted shouted at Katie, blaming her for undermining his project. He thought he had shared his feelings, but he hadn't. He told her what he thought at loud volumes, but he never conveyed sincere emotion.

An emotional adult

Not only is there nothing wrong with being emotional, emotions are the foundation of passion. Would you want to live without passion? I hope not.

If you want to free your passion, say what you feel in a way that adds to your communication effectiveness. Use these tips to communicate like an emotional adult. It will help you Speak Strong.

Mad, sad, glad, scared

Skill #14: Expand your emotional vocabulary

That ain't the way to have fun

When people don't know what to say, they often say nothing. That's what Patty did when her boss Bob's two daughters were the only ones who dressed in "costume" for the office "pajama party." The young women's "pajamas" were better described as lingerie. They seemed quite delighted to flaunt their voluptuousness. While some of Patty's male coworkers snickered and seemed to enjoy the display, Patty was certain she wasn't the only employee who found the scene inappropriate and distasteful.

Patty considered telling Bob that the carousing was an immoral affront to the professionalism of the women who worked for him. She wanted to call him a depraved father to allow it to continue. She was tempted to lecture him on how hard women have worked to overcome objectification, and how this exhibit was a step back for the evolution of women. She said none of those things. Instead, she took her coat and went home.

Patty thought she had two choices — either critically condemn her boss or silently condone him. She actually had more options. She could have simply told him she felt embarrassed by how his daughters were dressed and told him she was going home and would see him on Monday.

You need a vocabulary of emotions

Patty wanted to speak up, but she didn't know what to say. Her disclosure vocabulary consisted of opinions and judgments that said as much about her history as they did about the party. Had she had a vocabulary of feelings and known to reference it, she probably would have spoken and her boss would have understood the effect of the party. Had she had a vocabulary of feelings, Patty wouldn't have had an emotionally charged story to tell me four years after the event.

Opinions, judgments and feelings

Patty strongly condemned her boss. Underneath the judgment was a sensitive woman with a valid emotional reaction. A wider emotional vocabulary would have helped her Speak Strong about what was really going on.

Dos, Don'ts and Tips, Skill # 14:
Expand your emotional vocabulary

Get the words and you get the concept
I used to sort my emotions out by writing country songs. I'd work and rework my lyrics until I had the perfect words to communicate the essence of feelings I was trying to describe. It was remarkably therapeutic. When I found the perfect word, I felt released from the bondage of the emotion itself.

Develop your emotional vocabulary to help set you free — and to help you say what you feel when you need to. Here's how.

1. Make a list of everything you might be feeling about a difficult conversation
Don't (#1): limit yourself to your usual feeling agenda.
　　Why not? You probably have a standard repertoire of feelings that you allow yourself and a whole host of others you disown.
Don't (#2): try to be fair.
　　Why not? Feelings aren't fair.
Do: keep expanding your list until it matches your emotional state and/or you have a minimum of twenty emotions.
　　Why? You'll uncover the depth of your feeling.
Example: Clara was angry about accusations her brother made. She also was hurt. However, she was having a difficult time communicating why she was unwilling to talk to her brother about it—until she hit upon the word that captured the essence of her experience. She was feeling shell-shocked. Once she had the word that matched her feelings, she was able to communicate.

2. Jumpstart your feeling inquiry with the sentence stem: "I feel"
Don't: use the phrase "I feel *that*."
　　Why not? "I feel *that*" is usually followed by a thought, not a feeling.
Do: make sure your words reflect true emotions, not opinions or judgments.
　　Why? That's where the power is.
PowerPhrase/What to say: I feel disrespected.
Poison Phrase/What NOT to say: I feel that you don't respect me.

3. Trace emotions from the most aggressive to the most vulnerable, following the map in the appendix

Don't: resist if your experience takes you through the emotions in a different order.

Why not? Emotions follow patterns but can still be unpredictable.

Do: start your emotional review in order, using sentence stems to jumpstart you. When strong impulses take you through your emotions in a different order, go with them. Be sure to return to any emotions you skipped before you finish.

Why? You'll work your way to the core of your feeling.

Resource: appendix and *www.speakstrong.com/articles/speak-strong/emotional_map.html*

4. Highlight the most "vulnerable" feelings on your list

Don't: stop with victim emotions that make others look bad.

Why not? When you're triggered, you are likely to react with emotions that attack. That can backfire.

Do: communicate at the most vulnerable level appropriate to the relationship.

Why? Unless the other person is "shameless" (denies all accountability and exploits your willingness to take responsibility), that willingness to express vulnerability is likely to soften the dynamic.

PowerPhrase/What to say: This is a topic I feel sensitive about.

Poison Phrase/What NOT to say: You violated my trust.

5. Eliminate victim / villain language from your vocabulary

Don't: favor words that maximize your innocence and their culpability.

Why not? It makes you sound like a helpless victim—and that's rarely true.

Do: describe your emotion as YOUR reaction, not their insensitivity.

Why? It prevents polarizing the conversation—a dynamic that will get you nowhere.

PowerPhrase/What to say: I feel discounted.

Poison Phrase/What NOT to say: You never make me a priority.

6. Start with the feelings list in the appendix and build

Don't: start without a guide.

Why not? It is common to confuse judgments and feelings.

Do: use a list to jumpstart you.

Why? It will keep you on track.

Resource: *www.speakstrong.com/articles/speak-strong/emotions.html* and appendix.

Learn the language of feeling

In my perfect world, no one would need emotional lessons. We would all become fluent in the language of feelings as children. In that world, parents help their children explore, identify and name their emotions as they arise.

Let's get real. Chances are, if you want to Speak Strong you need remedial emotional work. It's humbling, but well worth the effort.

> " *Finding the perfect words is like finding your perfect prince. You might have to kiss a few frogs before you get there.* "
>
> MERYL RUNION

Good people don't want; strong people don't ask

Skill #15: Dare to desire

The price of never wanting

I lost my first husband to cancer in 1986. The experience was a devastating wake-up call. I learned a hundred lessons, and my books were born from those lessons. Here's one lesson I learned that previously seemed radical to me. Ready? Here it is. I learned that what I want is important. Not just for me personally, but for also those I care about.

What you want is important too — for you and for those you care about. But I'll focus on myself a little more before I get back to talking about you.

My grief and personal devastation were mixed with anger because I had put myself on hold while I supported my husband in his ambitions. I thought that once he realized his dreams, it would be my turn. He died before my turn came.

It became my turn by default. That uncovered a new challenge. I didn't know what I wanted. I was in the habit of asking what other people wanted. I was in the habit of putting other people's needs ahead of my own. I had mastered the art of anticipating and meeting others' needs and ignoring my own, as if not having needs made me noble. It didn't.

In fact, if I had been more willing to stand up for my own desires, I would have insisted my late husband get to the doctor when he showed early cancer symptoms. And if I had, he might still be with me today and our son might have grown up with a father.

See what I mean about how our not wanting can cost those we care about?

What YOU want is important

Where do people learn not to want or need anything? It's not like teachers hold mandatory "how not to need anything" classes. It's not like pastors deliver sermons titled "thou shall not need." We did receive training, but nothing as formal or overt as that.

"Don't want — don't need — don't ask" training is more subtle. It comes in forms like my father wincing when I asked for things. He loved (loves) me and overall he was (is) generous with me. However, he hated to say "no" to me so much that when I asked for something he couldn't give or didn't want to give, he was visibly uncomfortable. I felt guilty to have "pained him" (he really did look pained) and often I didn't ask for things to avoid the risk of triggering him.

My "don't ask" lessons were uncomfortable for me, but they were far gentler than Sandy's. When Sandy asked for things, she was treated to a lecture about what a burden she was. No wonder she learned not to desire.

You have needs too

I once participated in a seminar exercise where my partner and I looked in each other's eyes and took turns saying, "I have needs too." It hit me on a deep level. The tears rolled down my cheeks as I expressed what I hadn't felt permission to say before. It was a liberating feeling—and ultimately a healthy one. It was a powerful barrier buster that got me asking for what I want.

Try it sometime. Look in a partner's eyes and acknowledge that you have needs. Some of you will have no idea what the fuss is all about—but others will find the exercise stirs you emotionally on a very profound level.

Let's look at more ways to bust your request barriers.

> *When you dare to desire,*
> *you risk disappointment.*
> *When you don't dare to*
> *desire, you risk apathy.*
>
> MERYL RUNION

Dos, Don'ts and Tips, Skill #15:
Dare to desire

Do you ask for what you want? Let's examine and break the barriers that keep you from asking. Here are some tips that will help you admit and let the world know what you want.

1. Observe how often you don't ask for what you want

We're back to a code white exercise — daring to see things as they are. Start the process of asking for what you want by observing the times and ways you avoid wanting.

Don't: dismiss any desire.

> **Why not?** This is an inventory of what you don't ask for; not an inventory of what you should ask for.

Do: review your day to see how many times you wanted something you didn't ask for.

> **Why?** This makes your desires conscious. While some desires are best left unspoken, you won't know which ones you need to express if they're buried with desires you can't express.

Example: If you want your boss' job and don't ask, put that on the list, even though there are probably very good reasons not to ask. If you want your co-worker to shut off the radio and don't ask, that goes on the list too.

2. Understand why you don't ask

Review all the desires on your list and figure out why you don't express them.

Don't: assume you know why.

> **Why not?** You might be surprised.

Do: consider the following reasons for not asking: fear of rejection, habitual patterns, presumed futility, pride, low self-esteem and expecting them to guess.

> **Why?** To find out if your reason for not asking is really a lame excuse.

Example: The reason you don't ask for your boss' job may be because it would be career limiting. That sounds legitimate. The reason you don't ask you co-worker to shut the radio off could be that you think their preferences matter more than yours. That sounds self-defeating.

3. Conduct a cost-benefit assessment of the risks of speaking up

Don't: just consider short-term costs.

> **Why not?** Short term considerations can come with a long-term cost.

Do: apply the Risky Conversation Assessment Form in the appendix and on my website at:
www.speakstrong.com/articles/speak-strong/risky_conversation.html
>   **Why?** You'll get an objective assessment of whether or not you should ask for what you want.

Resource: Risky Conversation Assessment Form: Appendix, *www.speakstrong. com/articles/speak-strong/risky_conversation.html*

Example: If I ask my Dad for something and he can't or doesn't want to give it, I might have to deal with a wince. If I don't ask: 1) I won't get it, even if he would gladly give it, and 2) My Dad won't ever know what I want and, 3) I perpetuate the myth that I have to take care of my Dad's emotions.

4. Conduct a moratorium on complaining

Don't: complain for a predetermined amount of time.
>   **Why not?** Complaining is a lame and ineffective substitute for asking for what you want.

Do: either ask for what you want or resolve yourself to stay silent.
>   **Why?** Without the outlet of complaining, you will be more aware of your discomfort and more motivated to ask for what you want.

Example: George complained daily about how bad his boss' instructions were. When he decided to stop complaining, he was motivated to figure out how to get his boss to provide better instructions.

5. Start small and work up

Don't: begin with long shot requests.
>   **Why not?** The stakes are too high. Get some success under your belt before you up the ante.

Do: start by asking for things others are likely to be willing to give.
>   **Why?** Your success will motivate you and increase your inclination to say what you want.

Example: Rindy wanted bigger and more interesting assignments. She laid out a series of projects to ask for, starting small and increasing the scale of her requests.

Dare to desire

If you don't know what you want, you probably won't get it. Daring to desire is an important first step in Speaking Strong. It's important for your own well being — and for those you care about.

I don't know what I want, but I should have it...whatever it is

Skill #16: Prepare to ask

Julie

Julie has a reputation for whining. It's not that Julie is highly demanding. In fact, she rarely makes requests, let alone demands. Instead, she complains. She talks about how bad things are, how they shouldn't be the way they are, and how put-upon she is. But she rarely asks for anything.

Julie complains about how little she is paid even though she never asked for a raise. She complains that her husband doesn't spend time with her, but she doesn't know what she would want to do with him if he did. She complains that her coworker doesn't pull her weight but she never asks her coworker for anything specific.

Julie knows what she doesn't want, but she doesn't know what she wants. The irony is that Julie wouldn't ask for what she wanted even if she knew, because she's afraid to come across as demanding. Even though she never asks for anything, all her complaining has given Julie a reputation of being a nag.

Lisa

Lisa is the anti-Julie. Lisa knows what she wants and generally regards others as the means to get it. She asks people to do things for her that she would never do for them. She asks for things she really doesn't need. She pressures people when they refuse. She doesn't show appreciation because she appears to think she's entitled to get what she wants.

Lisa likes Julie because Julie won't ask for anything in return for all her favors. Julie complains about Lisa, but she always says "yes" to her requests anyway.

Kim

Then there's Kim. Kim knows how to get what she wants — she asks for it. She asked a famous author if she could have a job organizing his workshops. He thought it sounded like a great arrangement and agreed. She asked a local journalist to write a feature article about her. He liked the angle she offered and obliged. When she wasn't happy with her airline customer service, she asked to speak to manager after manager until she convinced the airline VP to send her two free tickets to South America. (Yes, they were round-trip.)

Kim likes to receive. But she also likes to give. She knows that giving is a two-way process. She enjoys being around people like herself who are clear about what they want and are comfortable asking. She likes people who say what they want. She also likes being a person who says what she wants. You will too.

Dos, Don'ts and Tips Skill # 16:
Prepare to ask

Before you ask, prepare. Once you have the habit of saying what you want, you won't need so much preparation, but even then, you'll be a more effective asker if you prepare first.

1. Use complaints as a signal you want something and as a clue of what

Don't: get stuck complaining.

    Why not? Complaints don't get you anywhere.

Do: translate your complaints into requests.

    Why? It shifts your focus from problems to solutions.

Example: Jody regularly complained about a traffic light near her house that took a long time to change. On reflection, she decided her complaining was a signal of something she should ask for — adjusted timing on the light.

2. Determine why you want what you want

Don't: say what you want without understanding why you want it.

    Why not? You'll miss potential ways to get your desire satisfied.

Do: determine underlying needs behind what you want and consider multiple ways to get your underlying needs met.

    Why? You're more likely to get your true needs met if you have a variety of options.

Example: Clara wanted a raise. Why? So she could afford tuition to go back to school. When her boss understood what she wanted, he was able to arrange tuition credits instead of a raise.

3. Determine what's in it for them

Don't: focus on your needs alone.

    Why not? Your needs matter most to you; their needs matter most to them.

Do: consider how helping you can benefit them.

    Why? People are motivated by self-interest.

PowerPhrase/What to say: I'd like your help going to school. What I'm studying will make me more valuable here because...

Poison Phrase/What NOT to say: I want to go back to school because I...

4. Help others get what they want

Don't: expect people to give in ways you've been unwilling to give.

   Why not? People keep score on some level.

Do: practice consistent giving.

   Why? What goes around comes around. Because we have different needs and skills, something that is easy for you to give might have a high value to someone else. Your gift could inspire reciprocity that will have a high value for you.

Examples: When Kristi makes labels, she asks around to see who else could use some. When she reads an article that is related to a project a coworker is working on, she passes it on. It's easy for her to do those things, and quite helpful to others.

When Kristi wants something, the people she has supported for years are delighted to reciprocate.

5. Consider taking what you want without asking

Don't: assume you need permission for everything.

   Why not? "It's easier to ask forgiveness than permission."

Do: take action on things you probably don't need approval for.

   Why? Asking focuses the ask-ee on reasons to say no and highlights obstacles. Action assumes reasons to say yes.

Example: Nancy suspected, but wasn't certain, that the boss would approve her order for a new keyboard to replace her keyboard that had a stuck key. She went ahead and ordered it without asking, and the subject never came up.

Know what you want and say what you want

A conversation worth having is worth planning for. Before you ask, prepare. Then, when you do ask, you'll be able to Speak Strong…and you'll be likely to get the response you want.

A conversation worth having is worth planning.

MERYL RUNION

You could help me by...

Skill #17: Ask so you will receive

You gotta start somewhere

I wanted to teach seminars, so I did. I created my own, put posters around town and conducted my classes for the handful of people who registered.

Eventually I sent a trainer application to the top national seminar company in the United States. I suspected I was unqualified, but I figured it didn't hurt to ask. I was elated when they flew me in for an audition. I was deflated when they turned me down after the audition.

One year later I called the same seminar company and asked for a do-over audition. I was elated when they agreed (if I came at my own expense) and I was more elated when they hired me after the audition.

Was I better at my second audition than I had been at my first? A little. Truthfully, I believe they hired me because I showed enough determination to ask twice. The head of faculty joked ironically that they should hire someone else who "really wanted the job," but they'd go with me.

I had a huge learning curve, but a few years later that company would agree that I was high among their better hires and trainers.

If it's a stretch — ask anyway

I expect there were many more qualified individuals who didn't bother to ask for the job once, let alone twice. You may not be the best qualified for things you want to ask for. But you may be the best qualified person who is willing to ask two, three or even four times. You won't know unless you try.

My former assistant Kjersti tested the power of asking. She asked me if I'd like her to update my website. Although it hadn't occurred to me I needed my site updated, and she had never done web design before, I agreed. She created a lovely site, and in the process, she was paid to develop web design skills.

The people who get what they want are the people who are willing to ask. Often the people they ask are glad they did.

Dos, Don'ts and Tips, Skill # 17:
Ask so you will receive

There are ways to ask for things and ways not to. Here's how you ask in a way that is likely to get results.

1. Be clear
Don't: use hints, vague statements and complaints, thinking you've made a request.
 Why not? Your listener might miss the request. Or your listener might catch your request and pretend they don't.
Do: be specific and precise about what you want.
 Why? Powerful requests are clear.
PowerPhrase/What to say: Will you pick up my printing for me this afternoon?
Poison Phrase/What NOT to say: Are you too busy to fit anything in to your schedule this afternoon?

2. Pleasantly persist beyond the first signs of resistance
Don't: think resistance means no.
 Why not? Resistance can be an automatic response based on incomplete understanding.
Do: inquire into the resistance, provide more information, and ask again in different ways.
 Why? Most sales happen after seven requests. When you ask for what you want, you're making a sale.
Example: In my early twenties, I asked my parents to pay for training I deeply wanted. They declined. I asked again and they agreed. It was one of my better requests and one of their better decisions.

3. Let them know what's in it for them
Don't: focus on your needs alone.
 Why not? Your needs matter most to you; their needs matter most to them.
Do: indicate it benefits them to help you — including the benefit of your gratitude.
 Why? Self-interest is a great motivator.
PowerPhrase/What to say: If you were able to do this for me, I'd be happy to…
Poison Phrase/What NOT to say: I want this because I…

4. Invite them to explore alternatives with you

Don't: ask for one option and give up when they say no.

Why not? There might be other ways they can help besides your original request.

Do: invite alternatives.

Why? They might come up with something you hadn't considered.

PowerPhrase/What to say: I need to focus on meeting my deadline and the phones are ringing constantly. I appreciate your not wanting to answer these calls. Is there any other way you can help me meet my deadline?

Poison Phrase/What NOT to say: I need you to answer the phones for me and if you say no and I miss my deadline, it's your fault.

5. Make it easy for them to give what you want

Don't: ask people to do things you could easily do for yourself.

Why not? You come across as demanding and/or lazy.

Do: take care of details to make it easy for them to give you what you want.

Why? It makes the best use of their time, skills and good will.

PowerPhrase/What to say: I have enclosed your contract with a self-addressed stamped envelope.

Poison Phrase/What NOT to say: Please print this out, sign it and overnight it.

6. Ask big

Don't: limit your requests to what you think you can get.

Why not? You could be surprised.

Do: ask for what you want — or even extra.

Why? You might surprise yourself. The more you ask for, the more you are likely to get.

PowerPhrase/What to say: Here's what I want.

Poison Phrase/What NOT to say: I want X but all I dare ask for is Y.

Example: Deidre thought $18 an hour would be too much to hope for, so she asked for $16. Her employer agreed to $16 immediately, leaving her wishing she had asked for $20.

7. Explain why you want what you want

Don't: omit your reasons for asking.

Why not? It helps people understand the importance of your request.

Do: explain what it would mean to you to get what you want.

Why? The word "because" is one of the most persuasive words in the English language.

PowerPhrase/What to say: Could you help me get X? I need X because…

Poison Phrase/What NOT to say: I want X.
Example: Joey asked his web developer Willa to immediately post an article to the website but didn't explain why it was urgent. It was urgent because Joey's client was ready to move on a contract and wanted to refer her boss to the article that afternoon. Willa would have given Joey's request a higher priority had she known why it mattered.

Know what you want and say what you want
Ask and ye shall receive. Ask well and ye shall receive well. Asking is an important Speak Strong skill.

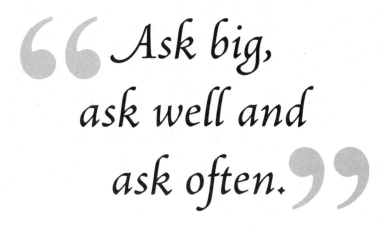

*Ask big,
ask well and
ask often.*

MERYL RUNION

Have I got a deal for you

Skill #18: Persuade, don't manipulate

What you want when you want it

Imagine you just decided to change financial advisors when a financial advisor calls telling you how great his services are, or you just decided to landscape when a landscaper calls seeking work, or you decided to get new photos when a photographer calls to tell you about her specials. Would you listen?

If you would, you'll understand why I wanted to hear what Jim had to say. I had committed to increasing my web site traffic, and Jim worked for a web traffic company.

A shark or a service professional?

Jim's enticement seduced as his pressure repelled. I wanted what he said he could do for me, but I wasn't convinced he could deliver. I felt uneasy. Should I believe him? Was he using persuasion or manipulation?

Jim described his "incredible opportunity," put me on hold while he checked with the "big guy" to see if he could lower the price, and came back in under a minute to tell me the boss approved a better offer. He warned that I needed to act fast because the offer wouldn't stay open long.

Which was it… persuasion (however clumsy) or manipulation? I couldn't be completely sure without knowing if it truly was a great opportunity, if he really did check with the boss for the price approval and if the offer really would expire. If (as I suspected) none of his claims were true, it was a manipulative trick.

There's more. Jim asked me: "If I could bring thousands of paying customers to your web site, would you be mad at me?"

Which was it… persuasion or manipulation? That too depends on the reality behind the words. It sounded like a transparent manipulative sales tactic to me. I thought it was a set up to get me saying yes to an obvious question based on a not-so-obvious assumption. Jim never actually claimed he could bring me thousands of paying customers, but his question implied he could. I suspected he wanted me to assume he could without actually making the claim. When I objected to his sales approach with me, he acted affronted and called me rude and unpleasant.

Was Jim using manipulation?

Whether it was manipulation or not, I assure you, it wasn't persuasion. I remained and remain unconvinced.

Persuade, don't manipulate
There's nothing wrong with persuasion. There's nothing right with manipulation. Don't back off from persuasion because you're afraid you'll come across manipulatively. Read on to learn the difference so you can Speak Strong persuasively.

> *Persuade*
> *with words*
> *that sizzle*
> *without*
> *creating*
> *smoke.*
>
> MERYL RUNION

Dos, Don'ts and Tips, Skill # 18:
Persuade, don't manipulate

Use the power. Don't abuse the power. Here's how you can be persuasive without being manipulative.

1. Use your skills to promote win-win
People often use manipulation to get others to do things that are not in their self interest.

Don't: use your ability to trick an unskilled or vulnerable person into agreeing with something that is not in his or her interests.
   Why not? It's unethical, and has long-range cost.
Do: skillfully design your message to favorably and accurately promote ideas that have mutual benefit.
   Why? It's ethical and builds long-range influence.
Example: After completing the call with Jim, I researched his website company and found a plethora of complaints. It was clear that his company did not deliver what he suggested they did. There were tales of many people who knew (even) less than I about web traffic who imagined he held keys to their success — and discovered he did not. I concluded that Jim had tried manipulation to trick me into investing in services that he couldn't tell the truth about.

In contrast, a blog coach contacted me once to tell me my blog needed upgrading. She convinced me she could help, and she delivered on her promise. (Thanks, Shonnie! *www.speakstrong.com/newsletter/*)

2. Be credible
Don't: argue a position or use a point you personally distrust.
   Why not? It's unethical and it makes you less credible.
Do: pass your points and words through your own credibility meter.
   Why? If you don't believe your own arguments, you're manipulating. Your listener will sense your personal disbelief. One insincere argument can discredit your credible points.
Example: Phyllis knows that multi-level marketing is hard work and that most people who attempt it fail. Yet she promotes her business opportunity as easy and certain. Her over-simplification is manipulative.

3. Make your emotional appeals to the higher emotions

Don't: stir base emotions.

　　Why not? Base emotional appeals bring out the worst in others. They also flood the brain and overshadow the intellect. People often regret decisions motivated by a base emotional appeal.

Do: include noble emotion in an appeal that elevates the dialogue.

　　Why? It's ethical and the results are positive and longer lasting.

PowerPhrase/What to say: This technique will help your client base understand the vision of your service and motivate them to buy.

Poison Phrase/What NOT to say: This technique will seduce your customers and help you separate them from their money without ever know what happened.

4. Balance emotional appeal with logic

Don't: appeal to emotion alone.

　　Why not? If you deliberately overpower reason to get the listener to ignore better judgment, you're manipulating. Persuasion uses both reason and emotion.

Do: communicate a congruent balance of emotion and reason.

　　Why? It allows people to reflect realistically on your perspective.

PowerPhrase/What to say: The firefighters lost their lives because they did not have the proper equipment. It's outrageous that the mayor knew they were under-equipped and did nothing.

Poison Phrase/What NOT to say: The mayor murdered the firefighters.

5. Take responsibility for your implicit as well as explicit meaning

Don't: make false implications.

　　Why not? Deliberate false implications are dishonest even when you don't overtly lie.

Do: take responsibility for the literal meaning of your words and for likely interpretations.

　　Why? As a communicator, you are responsible for the perceptions you generate.

PowerPhrase/What to say: I project a 50% increase in your web traffic in thirty days with this program.

Poison Phrase/What NOT to say: If I got thousands of paying customers to your website, would you be mad at me?

6. Ask: am I putting my best foot forward or a false front?

Don't: put an image forward or project an impression that does not stand up to scrutiny.

Why not? That's a false front and is manipulative.

Do: Make sure close inspection supports rather than discredits your claims.

Why? Persuasion is about presenting information in a convincing way, not a deceptive one.

Example: When I show up for events and people don't recognize me from my pictures, I'll know it's time to update my photos.

If you need to manipulate to persuade, it's time to rethink your point

Why would you need manipulation to bring someone around to your way of thinking? I can think of two reasons. One is that the point itself lacks merit. Another is you haven't developed the skills of ethical persuasion. Make sure you really believe in your stand and then get the skills to encourage others. You can't Speak Strong without knowing how to persuade.

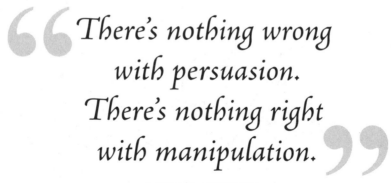

There's nothing wrong with persuasion. There's nothing right with manipulation.

MERYL RUNION

> **❝** *Speak from your heart and others will respond from theirs.* **❞**
>
> MERYL RUNION

This one's for your inner reptile

Skill #19: Talk to all three brains (including the one that really makes the decisions)

Man does not live by intellect — or broccoli — alone

"Some men are like chocolate cake," I said, holding up a slice that made my audience salivate. "You see them, and you drool. You know you shouldn't, but you do. And then you say you'll just have one more bite, but before you know it, you've eaten the whole thing and you've got a stomach ache."

"Now, some men are like broccoli," I continued, displaying and examining a stalk with some trepidation. "I mean you know they're good for you, so you try to include them in every meal. But they're kind of…boring. I mean, you wouldn't cruise the town 2 AM looking for broccoli, would you?"

I had my audience's full attention. My humorous speech entry didn't win me first place for the Iowa Toastmaster's competition, but it did win me second.

The topic was addictive relationships. I could have made my points with flip charts and data. (Excuse me while I yawn.) But because man (and woman) does not live by intellect alone, I made my point in a dramatic way that hit all three brains. As a result, I almost walked away with first prize.

Run on all cylinders

Your intellectual brain relates to thinking. Your emotional brain relates to feeling. Your reptilian brain relates to action. Different words affect different parts of your brain — and your listener's brain. Why not use all three? You'll be Speaking Strong when you do. Plus your words will be more persuasive.

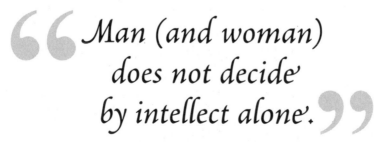

> *Man (and woman) does not decide by intellect alone.*

MERYL RUNION

Dos, Don'ts and Tips, Skill # 19:
Talk to all three brains (including the one that really makes the decisions)

We like to think we're so rational. But your reptilian and your emotional nature motivate you as much or more than your intellectual mind. Here are some tips to help you talk to all three brains: the one that thinks, the one that feels and the one that controls the will and action.

1. Never use a $10 word when a $1 word would do
Don't: use words that are more complicated than you need.

Why not? "Fancy" words engage the intellectual brain and switch off the emotional and reptilian brain.

Do: use the simplest word that will get the job done without actually dumbing the message down.

Why? The decisive primitive brain responds best to simplicity.

PowerPhrase/What to say: Use simple words.

Poison Phrase/What NOT to say: Utilize elementary verbiage.

2. Repeat, repeat, repeat
Don't: pack in more points than you can emphasize.

Why not? You'll overload your listener's thinking process and shut it down.

Do: repeat and elaborate on two to three important points.

Why? The reptilian brain responds to repetition. Shall I say that again?

Example: "Say what you mean and mean what you say without being mean when you say it" is simple enough for the reptilian and the emotional brains. I repeat it often in my presentations and people remember it.

3. Get concrete
Don't: dwell on abstractions.

Why not? The reptilian brain understands concrete words and images.

Do: use examples, illustrations, props, and simple concepts that make your message tangible.

Why? These tools create visceral responses that grab your listeners.

PowerPhrase/What to say: Some men are like chocolate cake, and some women are chocoholics.

Poison Phrase/What NOT to say: Obsessive and pathological relationship tendencies activate a pervasive aversion to solitude and abandonment anxiety in women resulting in an irrational attachment to inappropriate and narcissistic men.

4. Use contrast
Don't: downplay distinctions.

    Why not? The reptilian brain loves contrast.

Do: emphasize differences.

    Why? It makes your point in a way the reptilian brain appreciates and understands.

PowerPhrase/What to say: I am the only one who...

Example: This book uses "dos and don'ts" to create contrast. Political campaigns create contrast by saying, "My opponent wants X, and we want Y."

5. Use reptilian brain language
Don't: overemphasize intellectual words.

    Why not? The intellect speaks indirectly to the reptilian brain. When you include words that speak to the reptilian brain more directly, you will be more effective.

Do: address the reptilian brain's concerns including: self-interest, security, competition and action.

    Why? This is what the "decision" brain responds to.

PowerPhrase/What to say: YOU, guarantee, secure, support, safe, assurance, gain, control, enemy, threaten, collapse, mastery, dependable, preserve, provide, depend.

6. Use emotional brain language
Don't: be afraid to address and evoke feelings.

    Why not? The emotional brain plays an important role in decisions.

Do: communicate the emotional component of your message and pick words that evoke that emotion. Use a language of feeling.

    Why? All communication has an emotional component, so make sure yours sends the emotional message you want.

PowerPhrase/What to say: Imagine, dream, mother, community, country, endear, envision, inspire, ideal, care, share, heart, vision, connect, children, dog, heart.

• How would you feel if...

Example #1: A credit card debt settlement ad says, "We're not here to judge you. We're here to help you." This appeal not only addresses what they do for their clients: it addresses the shame some people feel about their debt.

Example #2: My *World of Truth* video starts with the words: "Imagine a world where…" *www.speakstrong.com/video/worldoftruth.swf* The visionary language engages the emotional brain.

7. Be playful

Don't: think playfulness undermines your message.

> **Why not?** Playfulness accesses the emotional brain and helps your listener connect to your message.

Do: have fun communicating.

> **Why?** Play, laughter and fun open your listener's heart and mind to your message.

Example: Some men are like chocolate cake…

For complete persuasion, speak to the complete brain

If you talk to one brain when you can talk to all three, it's like talking to an agent when you could talk to an agent, editor and publisher. It's like talking to the nurse when you could talk to the nurse, doctor and chief of staff. It's like, well you get the picture. Make sure your listener gets the picture you paint with your words. Speak Strong to all three brains.

> " *It's important to be honest and it's important to be right and it's essential to be both.*
>
> MERYL RUNION

But wait, there's more

Skill #20: Supercharge your message with persuasion

More persuasive than a plate full of cookies

Sandra Dale loves sugar in all shapes and forms. She loves soft drinks, she loves ice cream and she loves the cookies by the registration desk at the Hampton Inn. One bite of sugar propels her into a binge that leaves her nursing a sugar-swollen belly and a deflated sense of self.

Sandra Dale and her friend Katy have a pact to persuade each other to resist the first seductive bite. They call each other whenever the allure of sugar beckons.

That's why Sandra Dale was on the phone to Katy as she entered Carbondale, IL where she would be staying at a sugar-providing Hampton Inn.

"I'm almost at the Hampton Inn and they're going to have cookies out and I'm going to want to eat them all," Sandra Dale confessed.

"You can eat them all if you want to," Katy wisely conceded. Katy knew better than to resist Sandra Dale's craving. She aligned herself with Sandra Dale's inclination and continued with a question that had a carefully chosen verb.

"How will you feel if the cookies defeat your resolve?"

"I'll feel horrible," Sandra Dale said.

"Will it be worth it?" Katy queried. Sandra Dale admitted it wouldn't. Then Katy went in for the close. She asked Sandra Dale for a commitment.

"What are you going to do?" she asked.

"I'm going to check in and go right to my room without eating any cookies," Sandra Dale replied.

Katy kept Sandra Dale focused on a successful outcome with follow-up instructions. "Great," she confirmed. "Call me when you get there, and we'll celebrate your win." Sandra Dale's vision of being successfully on the other side of temptation was now stronger than her image of indulging her sugar lust. She did exactly as she and Katy agreed.

How hard was that?

If Katy's techniques can get Sandra Dale to walk right past a plate of cookies, they can get meeting planners to hire me to speak, your boss to promote you, and your credit card vendor to waive your late payment fees. That's why I listened to Sandra Dale's story with pen and paper in hand. I develop my Speak Strong techniques by studying the masters. Katy is a persuasion master and a role model for the rest of us. Read on for seven techniques to Speak Strong persuasively.

> " *Any point worth making is worth making well.* "
>
> MERYL RUNION

Dos, Don'ts and Tips, Skill # 20:
Supercharge your message with persuasion

Whether you're persuading someone to change a habit, invest in your services or provide a favor; the techniques below will help you make your point effectively.

1. Ignite your verbs

Don't: use bland verbs that lack content and energy.

   Why not? Verbs are your greatest source of action.

Do: illuminate your sentences with verbs that sizzle.

   Why? Colorful verbs have persuasive muscle.

PowerPhrase/What to say: Provoke thought with stimulating verbs.

Poison Phrase/What NOT to say: Utilize verbs to make people think.

Example: Terri promotes a keynote she gives that "electrifies" audiences.

2. Employ imperatives

Don't: use imperatives if the conversation is adversarial.

   Why not? When you're in an adversarial stance, your listener doesn't want you to tell them what to do. When you're aligned with each other, they're more open to it.

Do: embed and directly express positive imperatives once you have rapport.

   Why? When there's trust, people are open to suggestion.

PowerPhrase/What to say: Call me when you get to your room.

Poison Phrase/What NOT to say: Don't eat cookies.

3. Show, don't tell

Don't: describe something when you can illustrate it.

   Why not? Illustrations bring your points to life.

Do: use examples, stories, illustrations, props, and word pictures.

   Why? It makes your point concrete and communicates with the mammalian and reptilian brain.

PowerPhrase/What to say: Do you walk into the next room and forget why you went there?

Poison Phrase/What NOT to say: Have you been distracted lately?

4. Call to action

Don't: make your case without indicating what you want them to do with the information.

   Why not? Knowledge isn't power. Action based on knowledge is.

Do: sum up your points with clear action steps.

Why? So people know how to implement your suggestions.

PowerPhrase/What to say: My newsletter reinforces the information in this book. Register now at www.speakstrong.com.

Poison Phrase/What NOT to say: You'll like my newsletter.

5. Focus on them

Don't: focus on what you need and expect people to care.

Why not? Your listener is wants to know how things affect them.

Do: reframe your points in terms of what it means to them.

Why? To clarify self-interest.

PowerPhrase/What to say: How would you feel if you ate the cookies?

Poison Phrase/What NOT to say: Don't eat those cookies because as your Overeating Anonymous sponsor I want you to be one of my successes.

6. Lead with questions

Don't: make statements when questions will serve you better.

Why not? Questions draw your listener out.

Do: translate some of your statements into questions.

Why? Questions get people thinking…and considering your ideas.

PowerPhrase/What to say: What are you going to do?

Poison Phrase/What NOT to say: Here's what you should do.

7. Tease to tantalize

Don't: answer every question immediately.

Why not? I'll tell you later. (Wink)

Do: use intrigue, foreshadowing and curiosity to hook your listener's interest.

Why? I'll tell you that later too.

PowerPhrase/What to say: Survey assessments were never like this before. We were stunned when we started our totals. What we found was…

Poison Phrase/What NOT to say: This survey assessment has more interaction than most.

Any point worth making is worth making well

Are you suspicious of persuasion techniques? Take another look. Any point worth making is worth making well. Take the time to learn the Speak Strong points of persuasion and make your point so your listener gets your point. It's just good communication. So say what you mean persuasively. Then, it's time to be sure you mean what you say.

Speak
STRONG

STEP 3:
MEAN WHAT YOU SAY

Mean What You Say Skill Set #1:
Protect the Power

Mean What You Say Skill Set #2:
Play It Big

Mean What You Say Skill Set #3:
Be Resolute

Mean What You Say Skill Set #4:
Retrain to Respond

Introduction to Step Three:
Mean What You Say

Saying what you mean is an essential Speak Strong step. But even the best-worded communication will be ineffective if you don't back your words up with action. That's why it's just as important to mean what you say.

Mean What You Say Skill Set #1:
Protect the Power
If you don't protect the power of your words, no one else will. You're probably not aware of things you do that undermine the most perfect of words. This skill set will help you speak and behave in ways that protect—and enhance—the power of what you say.

Mean What You Say Skill Set #2:
Play It Big
Humility is great, but diffidence isn't. It's useful to acknowledge your limits, but it's counterproductive to hide your strengths. It's smart not to overplay your hand, but it's stupid to underplay it. This section takes a look at how you can step into your power and become a person to be reckoned with in an effective and appropriate way. When I say play it big, I don't mean to pretend you're bigger than you are. I mean be your most influential self.

Mean What You Say Skill Set #3:
Be Resolute
Are you a pushover? If you don't take your words seriously, no one else will. You teach people whether you mean what you say or not. Be resolute, and send a message to others that what you say, you mean.

Mean What You Say Skill Set #4:
Retrain to Respond
If people habitually discount your words, you've got some retraining to do. I'm talking about retraining yourself—not them. This section tells you how to break destructive communication habits that teach people your words have no power, and to replace them with constructive new habits that teach people that they do.

How many times do I have to tell you?

Skill #21: Say it so they know you mean it

It's almost a ritual

When I head out for my hike, Otis — the dog next door — enthusiastically runs to greet me. Otis' owners shout commands that Otis ignores. They try to get him but Otis prances away, oblivious to all instruction.

Otis knows it, I know it and Otis' owners know it. Otis' owners' words are empty. They shout commands to look like they're doing something, they go through the motions, but we all know Otis isn't going to suddenly pay attention to the same words he previously ignored.

Otis is like Sharon's kids who know if they don't behave their mom isn't really going to give them socks for Christmas. He's like Julie's manager who knows Julie isn't really going to leave on time today at the expense of his last minute project. He's like Krystal who knows that Carl isn't really about to go tell the boss she stole his idea.

So what's going on?

These are every day garden-variety examples of individuals who have taught others they don't mean what they say. They may talk a good game, but their words have no meaning, no impact and no power. They substitute show for effective action– and everyone knows it. The people in their lives have learned they can ignore what they say.

Sound familiar?

Joan used to be like Otis' people, but not any more.

Joan worked unsuccessfully to get her boss to assign work to her early so she could leave on time at 4:15. Day after day her boss promised he would "try." Day after day her boss asked her to stay late for some emergency or another.

Then Joan got in an accident that totaled her car. Joan was fine, but for two weeks her car was in the shop and she needed to catch a ride home at 4:30 each day. Since she was scheduled to leave at 4:15, 4:30 seemed quite reasonable. However, the first day, Joan's boss was shocked when Joan left (almost) on time. By the second day, her boss started to adjust. By the third day, the boss factored Joan in to his planning and got her assignments to her early enough for her to complete them before she left.

Why was the boss suddenly able to organize when he had previously not been able to? Because Joan's boss knew that now when Joan said she needed to leave on time, she meant it.

Joan had to learn to back her own words up without an external imperative (the car pool) to add power to her words. She rose to that challenge.

I hope Otis' owners rise to Otis' challenge too. But that's another conversation.

> ## If you don't mean it, don't say it.
>
> MERYL RUNION

Dos, Don'ts and Tips, Skill #21: Say It So They Know You Mean It

"They never listen to me." "They only pay attention when I yell." "I keep telling him but he doesn't hear me."

If people don't take your words seriously, look in the mirror. You probably signaled you don't mean what you say through your word choice, through your body language, and/or through your actions.

It's difficult going through life or even just a day when people don't take your words seriously. Say things so people know you mean them. Here's how.

1. If you don't mean it, don't say it

Don't: throw out promises, threats or consequences that you don't expect to act on.

> **Why not?** People learn your words are empty.

Do: make sure you take your own words seriously before you speak them, and if you don't take your own words seriously, stay silent.

> **Why?** That protects the power of your words by teaching people you mean what you say.

PowerPhrase/What to Say: I expect to be there by 2:00 but it will be no later than 2:30.

Poison Phrase/What NOT to say: I'll be there at 2:00. (And show up at 2:20.)

2. Be willing to take a risk

Don't: expect people to automatically appreciate your assertiveness. Don't back off when they don't.

> **Why not?** People will test your resolve.

Do: be willing to take some hits and even lose some things you value when you stand up for yourself.

> **Why?** The more you risk, the more you stand to gain.

Example: Fred finally got his raise when he decided he would quit if he didn't. It was risky, because had he not gotten his raise, he would have faced the choice of backing down or quitting.

3. Differentiate between empty words and action

Don't: say things you don't mean and pretend you've done something.

> **Why not?** Empty words mask inaction.

Do: either stay silent or speak words you mean.

> **Why?** Silence forces you to see reality behind tempting empty words.

PowerPhrase/What to Say: If we can't resolve this on a peer level, I will raise the issue with management.

Poison Phrase/What NOT to say: If we can't work this out on a peer level, I'm getting you fired and destroying your career. (I HOPE you don't mean that.)

4. Avoid weak language that broadcasts weak intent

Don't: water down your wording when people need to know you're serious.

> **Why not?** People hear weak words as suggestions to consider instead of mandates to honor.

Do: choose words that match the strength of your meaning.

> **Why?** So people understand your seriousness.

PowerPhrase/What to Say: "I expect…" "I know…" "The agreement is…"

Poison Phrase/What NOT to say: "I was wondering if you might be able to…" "I kinda think…" "It would be good if you could…"

5. Avoid body language that undermines the strength of your words

Don't: look apologetic with fake smiles, tilted head and pleading gestures while you make strong statements.

> **Why not?** When words and body language conflict, people believe your body language.

Do: adopt and even practice gestures and expressions that reinforce your message.

> **Why?** People will be more likely to believe what you say.

Example: A lovely Jamaican woman once asked me why I thought people didn't take her seriously. She avoided my gaze the entire time she spoke with me. While I understood her limited eye-contact was a cultural habit, I explained that her averted gaze appeared passive and I advised her to work to develop the habit of looking her listener in the eye.

7. Avoid body language that overstates your intent

Don't: put your hands on your hips, cross your arms, wave your finger, have a stare-down or wear a stern expression.

> **Why not?** It creates defensiveness and reactiveness.

Do: Have a neutral, friendly face.

> **Why?** You come across as serious but not serious to the point of being scary.

Example: I was shocked when I watched a video of myself speaking. I came across as very stern. I intended to look strong and determined, but I came across as severe.

8. Speak with knowledge

Don't: speculate and pretend you know what you're talking about when you don't.

Why not? People won't believe you when you talk about the things you do understand.

Do: State fact as fact and opinion as opinion.

Why? It protects your credibility and the power of your words.

Example: When talk show hosts interview military experts, they often go beyond asking military questions into asking political questions. The wise military experts refuse to speculate, or if they do, they make it known they are speculating in areas beyond their expertise.

9. Select your words for accuracy

Don't: exaggerate or dramatize for effect.

Why not? People will learn to discount or dismiss your words.

Do: stay factual.

Why? It teaches people to trust the accuracy of your words.

PowerPhrase/What to Say: I have been waiting 3 hours.

Poison Phrase/What NOT to say: I've been waiting forever.

Don't blame others if they miss a message you're not sending

If your listeners don't believe you mean what you say, you might not be sending the message you think you are. If you want people to take your message seriously, send a serious message. Protect the power and use these tools to help you mean what you say.

> *Avoid weak language that broadcasts weak intent.*

MERYL RUNION

Do as I say, AND as I do

Skill #22: Match your talk and your walk

Now you tell me

Labor is no time to discover that the designated midwife's talk doesn't match her walk — but that's when *Gone With the Wind's* Scarlet O'Hara discovered that her housemaid, Prissy, fabricated her claims to midwifery competence. It would have been nice to have known the truth earlier, before Scarlet decided to rely on Prissy in that crucial moment.

And it would have been nice for me to have known *before* the book was released that the man I hired for Public Relations was too disorganized to manage my book launch. It would have been nice for Ken to have known *before* he married her that Kathy's wealth was an illusion funded by $75,000 of debt. It would have been nice for many adjustable rate mortgage customers to have known *before* they signed on the dotted line that their mortgage broker couldn't anticipate pending rate hikes either.

It's called congruence

People form impressions and expectations based on your words. When you talk a good game and walk a poor one, you lose credibility.

If there's a gap between your talk and your walk — if you lack congruence — people will learn you don't mean what you say. Who would believe a thing Prissy said after the labor fiasco?

If you say it like you mean it, people are more likely to believe what you say. However, no amount of powerful wording and body language will undo the damage that comes from not matching your walk to your talk. To paraphrase Stephen Covey, you can't talk your way out of something you walked your way into.

She walks her talk

My "Official Blog Evaluator," Cindy, promised me an email by Monday afternoon. When I hadn't heard from her by Tuesday, I knew something was wrong. I later learned she had injured her back and was laid up in bed.

On the other end of the spectrum, there's Hank. If he says he'll call and he actually does, I'm surprised.

You can sweet talk for a while, but ultimately, people determine the power of your words based on the congruence between your words and actions.

Oversell can get you a short-term advantage, but consider the long-term cost. Protect the power of your words and match your talk and your walk.

> ❝ *People don't care about what you're going to TRY to do. They want to know what you ARE going to do.* ❞
>
> MERYL RUNION

Dos, Don'ts and Tips, Skill # 22:
Match your talk and your walk

A perfect match

You can talk a promise in a few seconds. You can walk for days, weeks and even months and still not catch up with your talk.

You can walk your way into disgrace in a few seconds. You can talk for days, weeks and even months and still not exonerate your walk.

Talk matters. Walk matters. Talk indicates walk. Walk validates talk. Put them together and you have powerful communication.

That is: you have powerful communication if your talk and your walk match. Here are some tips to help you match your walk and your talk.

1. If you can't walk it, don't talk it

Don't: indicate you are something you're not or that you will do something you're not sure you can.

> **Why not?** If you don't deliver on expectations your words create, your words lose their power.

Do: refrain from saying anything that might create false impressions or expectations for your listener.

> **Why?** To make your walk match your talk.

Example: Mike is the perennial optimist. He expects things to go easily. He used to commit based on his optimistic expectations. That changed when his over-commitment led him to keep his daughter waiting at daycare for an hour after it closed. He developed the new habit of waiting to make commitments until he could be certain he could deliver. It took him a while, because Mike likes to say yes. But he found it works much better to promise realistically.

2. If you wouldn't want to talk it, don't walk it

Don't: do anything you wouldn't want to fess up to.

> **Why not?** Unspeakable walk encourages deceptive talk.

Do: make sure you'd be willing to openly discuss what you're considering doing before you do it.

> **Why?** It will elevate your behavior and your word power.

Example: Clara wanted to stay longer at the sale, but decided not to. She didn't want to explain why she was late to her boss, and she was unwilling to make up an excuse.

3. Take responsibility for the ways people interpret your words

Don't: ignore possible unintended implications and interpretations.

Why not? Just because you know what you mean doesn't mean they do.

Do: ask yourself, "What expectations do my words create?"

Why? If those expectations don't match what actually happens, people will feel let down, whether those expectations are the ones you intended or not.

Example: Marla thinks aloud. She suggests get-togethers, talks about how she can help people, and floats ideas in the spirit of brainstorming. She discovered that other people take her words more literally than she intends. That sets them up for disappointment and undermines her credibility.

4. Examine misunderstandings for talk that didn't match the walk

Don't: blame others when they misinterpret your words.

Why not? It's your job to be clear.

Do: ask yourself—and them—"Did I create false expectations by something I said?"

Why? So you can speak more precisely in the future.

Example: Emily was upset when Ralph did not get the web edits to her by start of business as he suggested he would. Ralph was irritated because it wasn't his job to do the web edits anyway, and he thought it was unreasonable for Emily to expect him to get to it so quickly. On reconsideration, he decided she did have the right to expect prompt delivery for the simple reason that he had implied he would have them by start of business. He decided to be more careful about his promises.

5. Acknowledge discrepancies

Don't: ignore or dismiss un-walked talk.

Why not? 1) If you do, people will conclude you don't mean what you say. 2) If you do, you will continue to under-deliver on your talk.

Do: verbalize the (presumably occasional) gap between your words and your actions.

Why? 1) If you acknowledge where your walk falls short of your talk, others would be more likely to trust your words in the future, and 2) It will make you more likely to speak accurately in the future.

Example: Ralph apologized to Emily for not delivering as promised.

PowerPhrase/What to Say: I committed to getting your edits to you and didn't follow-up. I apologize.

Poison Phrase/What NOT to say: I may have promised to get them to you, but it wasn't my job anyway.

6. Warn your listener if you're thinking aloud or when your words are tentative

Don't: assume your listener knows when you're thinking aloud.

> **Why not?** Not everyone thinks aloud, and even those who do don't know when you are.

Do: tell your listener if your words are tentative.

> **Why?** So they won't form expectations based on words you never intended as commitments.

Example: When Kurt asked Debbie for help, she started talking about how it might be possible for her to do what he asked. She paused to let Kurt know she was thinking aloud to see if she could make it work, and she wasn't committing yet.

PowerPhrase/What to Say: I'm thinking aloud here about whether and how we can make it work.

7. Under-promise and over-deliver

Don't: make promises you can't keep.

> **Why not?** Your promises will lose their power.

Do: be conservative about what you commit to.

> **Why?** People will know that you mean what you say and they can count on you.

Example: Joy thought she could make a 3:00 meeting, but scheduled it for 3:15 because she was more certain that she could make it on time.

PowerPhrase/What to Say: I might be able to make it by 3:00, but to be sure I don't keep you waiting for me let's set it for 3:15.

Protect the power

Big talk can be cheap and seductive, but when the walk doesn't match the talk, your words lose their power.

Shortcuts can be easy and seductive, but when your walk contradicts your talk, your words lose their power.

If you can't walk it, don't talk it. If you wouldn't want to talk it, don't walk it. That's how you protect the power of your words.

> " *Noble words fall flat without corresponding action.*

MERYL RUNION

I'll have it for you by start of business Wednesday, June 16th

Skill #23: Specify and see it through

Zig Ziglar says: "You cannot make it as a wandering generality. You must become a meaningful specific." Zig Ziglar is right. But if being specific is so great, why isn't everyone specific?

Specific sets a higher bar

Many people deliberately avoid being specific. After all, generalizations are safe. Specifics are risky. It's easy to deliver on a generalization. It's harder to deliver on a specific. It's easier to fake a generalization. It's harder to fake a specific. It takes more clarity, conviction and courage to specify and see it through.

Let me be more specific about being specific

Carl is a tax accountant who likes to keep things open. He prefers not to commit to a return delivery time. When Julie pressed him, Carl gave a vague response. He said, "I've got a couple of clients ahead of you."

When Julie called to check on the progress, Carl's secretary said, "He'll call you back soon."

Julie switched her business to David. She thought she had died and gone to heaven when David told her, "I'll be starting on your return by the end of next week. If I have everything I need here, I'll have it ready for your review no later than two weeks from today."

Julie realized she had forgotten to mention a deduction and left a message with David's assistant, who told her, "He'll call you back by end of the business day." He did.

Julie was impressed when David actually had her return ready before he said he would. He said what he'd do and did what he said.

Sure, specific is riskier, but it sure creates clarity and builds trust when you make good.

A vendor who uses specifics to her advantage — and mine

My blog coach, Shonnie Lavender, solicited my business by being specific. She let me know how long she had been reading my blog, told me what kind of upgrades she thought I needed and provided details of how she works.

I hired her.

Shonnie continues to be specific throughout our professional relationship. I always know what to expect from her, and she always delivers what she led me to expect.

She's no wandering generality. She's a meaningful specific. It's worth it to get specific. *www.speakstrong.com/newsletter/*

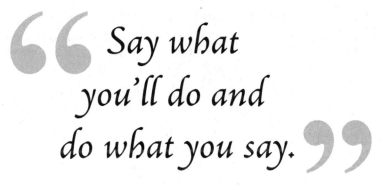

Say what you'll do and do what you say.

MERYL RUNION

Dos, Don'ts and Tips, Skill # 23:
Specify and see it through

Dare to be specific. Sure, being specific sets a higher bar — but why should that be a problem?

Here are some tips about how you can specify and see it through.

1. Create a policy to: Say what you'll do and do what you say

Don't: expect your actions alone to speak for you.

    Why not? In the absence of spoken expectations, you'll get assumed expectations.

Do: talk the walk upfront.

    Why? It creates clarity — and when you deliver as promised, you'll increase the power of your words.

PowerPhrase/What to Say: I like to make expectations clear up front. Here's what you can expect from me.

Poison Phrase/What NOT to say: We'll see how it goes.

2. Include: who, what, when, where, why and how

Don't: think these guides apply to journalism alone.

    Why not? These parameters make useful guides for communication in general.

Do: use these points to make sure you've touched all the bases in your message.

    Why? It will help you be more thorough.

Example: Before Kyle hit "send," he checked his email for the six parameters and realized he omitted a few essential recipients from the distribution list. Once he added those people, he further realized he needed to add more detailed information.

3. When you delegate or commit to something, specify the triple constraints

Don't: leave deadlines, money or specifications to chance or interpretation.

    Why not? While it might give you wiggle room, omitting that important information opens the door for misunderstanding.

Do: detail each of the triple constraints: time (deadlines), budget (money) and standards (specifications.)

    Why? Without the constraints, expectations are fuzzy.

PowerPhrase/What to Say: I'll have this to you Friday at 2:00 PM. I expect it will take six hours of my time so it will cost between $425 and $515. It will be three pages double-spaced, proofread but not edited.

Poison Phrase/What NOT to say: I'll get something to you soon. Shouldn't take me long.

4. Paint concrete pictures

Don't: speak in abstractions without providing concrete examples and illustrations.

Why not? Abstractions are subject to interpretation.

Do: Illustrate your points with concrete examples that paint word pictures.

Why? It's more "real" and easier to understand.

PowerPhrase/What to Say: The SpeakStrong Library contains six books, three DVDs, and fourteen CD's. You'll find it in my SpeakStrong store at: *www.speakstrong.com/store/*

Poison Phrase/What NOT to say: There's a variety of items in the SpeakStrong Library. You can get it on my website.

5. Notify people if/when things change

Don't: leave people out of the loop when projections change.

Why not? People are more forgiving when they are involved in the process.

Do: alert people to delays that invalidate your original projections.

Why? People are more willing to be flexible when you keep them in the loop.

PowerPhrase/What to Say: I ran into some unanticipated problems. I have to reinstall your blog software. I'm calling to update you on time and cost and to get permission to proceed with the extra time.

Poison Phrase/What NOT to say: I know I told you I'd have it last week, but I ran into problems I hadn't anticipated. No one could have anticipated this. Sorry it's late — here's the bill. It's more than I expected, but it isn't my fault.

Be as specific as the situation allows

No one can accurately project the future. No matter how well intended, at times you'll say what you'll do and be unable to do what you said. Sometimes you won't even be able to take a wild guess at how things will unfold.

Sure, there will be exceptions. But exceptions prove the rule. If you live by the guideline to specify and see it through, you will add to the power of your words.

Excuse me, your consciousness level is showing

Skill #24: Get real but not raw

When Scarlet O'Hara was in danger of losing Tara (her plantation) after the Civil War, she went to Atlanta to con Rhett Butler into marrying her. Wearing a green velvet dress made from the living room drapes, Scarlet presented her life as prosperous and herself as a lady of leisure. Her charade succeeded until Rhett took her hands in his and observed — "What have you been doing with your hands? You've been working with them like a field hand. Why did you lie to me and what are you really up to?" Rhett saw through Scarlet's false front, knew she was scamming him and rejected her.

Scarlet's personal presentation almost matched her words, but the part that didn't match betrayed her. If your words don't match your reality, it will undermine your credibility too. Don't put a false front forward. It's not only dishonest, it's risky. "It's not the crime, it's the cover-up."

False fronts, raw reality and best feet forward

A false front can backfire, but raw reality can backfire too. Like Scarlet, you lose credibility if you *deny* your limitations, but that doesn't mean you need to *broadcast* them. Polish your personal presentation and put your best foot forward, but don't let it degenerate into a false front. Use promo pictures that flatter you but still look like you. Describe your work in complementary terms, but not falsehoods. Explain your errors in ways that make them understandable but don't disguise them. Get real without getting raw.

For example, here's how Scarlet O'Hara could have approached Rhett. She could have worn her beautiful curtain dress to meet Rhett and still been up front about her conditions and her intent. Just like you can polish your presentation and put your best foot forward without slipping into a false front.

A question of balance

Life is about balance. It's about balancing too little and too much. It's about balancing form and content. It's about balancing presentation and substance. You'll pay a price if you focus too much on one to the exclusion of the other.

Lipstick doesn't disguise a pig, but it might bring out the finer qualities in a woman's smile. If you are trying to make an impression by putting lipstick on a pig, upgrade your product first. But if what you have is a picture that needs a frame to enhance it, by all means, find a frame you like and put your best face and foot forward.

Dos, Don'ts and Tips, Skill # 24:
Get real but not raw

Scarlet's hands told the truth her words denied. What exposes your unspoken reality? How can you polish your personal presentation to frame the truth, without distorting or overshadowing it? Let's look at some options.

1. Wipe that smile off your face

Don't: smile when you address sensitive issues.

   Why not? It suggests you aren't as serious as you sound.

Do: practice a neutral, friendly face that is serious but not scary.

   Why? If your words suggest a serious discussion and your face minimizes it, people will believe your face.

Example: Heidi smiled her way through the first meeting of the SpeakStrong Retreat. I encouraged her to allow her pain to show. She was surprised to realize she couldn't hide her pain behind her smile. She tells her own story on my blog at: www.speakstrong.com/newsletter/2007/02/21/owning-her-own-life-after-incest-2/

2. Put a smile on your face

Don't: scowl when you can authentically smile

   Why not? It puts people off and shuts them down.

Do: practice and employ a pleasant expression.

   Why? To create safely and put people at ease.

Example: Jeff looks very serious when he's thinking. It sends a message to others that he's unhappy even though he isn't. He practices a pleasant expression when he thinks at home in an effort to make it a habit at work.

3. Look 'em in the eyes when you say that

Don't: avoid people's gaze.

   Why not? People will discount your words.

Do: maintain steady eye contact (without staring)

   Why? Your eyes are the windows to your soul.

Example: President George W. Bush often spoke of how he would look foreign leaders in the eyes and know whether or not they could be trusted.

My husband used to look away as he spoke to me. We discussed it, and he recognized that he looked away because he does one thing at a time, and looking me in the eyes distracted him from his thoughts. He has since learned to look me in the eyes when we talk, which is much more personal and satisfying.

4. Stand straight, walk tall, don't shrink or play small

Don't: slouch.

Why not? It makes you look weak and downtrodden.

Do: pay attention to posture. If you habitually slouch, visit a physical therapist to get exercises to correct your posture.

Why? Posture indicates stature. Poor posture undermines powerful words. Good posture underscores them.

Example: People told me I slouched but I didn't take it seriously — until I saw an embarrassing picture of myself in the paper. Since then, I've been systematically developing my posture. My photos don't scare me as much anymore. (Except for the wrinkles, but that's another story...)

5. Keep all hands on deck

Don't: fidget or hide your hands.

Why not? Fidgeting is distracting and makes you look nervous. Hidden hands seem closed.

Do: use your hands to emphasize your words rather than undermine them.

Why? It reinforces your message.

Example: While watching a video of myself, I was shocked to see how often I used my hands to push my hair out of my face. I was also surprised to realize how distracting it was. My hands undermined words. I cut my hair.

6. Listen for the swing of things

Don't: use an upswing in your voice that makes your statements sound like questions.

Why not? It undermines your message.

Do: end statements on a down swing.

Why? To sound like you have conviction.

Example: If you saw the movie American Pie, you'll remember the girl with the irritating upswing in her voice. Who can forget: "One time? At band camp?..."

7. Videotape yourself

Don't: think you know what you look like if you haven't watched a video.

Why not? Seeing is believing.

Do: study your personal presentation for conflicting messages.

Why? You might contradict yourself without realizing it.

Example: Watching my promotional videos has done more for my speaking skills than anything else I've done, including expensive coaching.

What they see is what they get

If there is a conflict between what people see and what they hear, they will believe what they see. If you talk big but present small, you will send a message that you don't mean what you say. If you're playing small out of habit, practice playing big. If you're playing small because you're being deceptive, either tell the truth or change the situation, so you can get real without being raw.

> " *No one can blow your cover when you don't have a cover to blow.* "

MERYL RUNION

It's um, uh, you know, kinda important to, like, pick your words well

Skill #25: Don't let weak speak sneak in

Every word counts

You can tell when a presenter at a Toastmaster's club meeting has had their "filler words" counted recently. They are painfully aware of their "ums" and "uhs" and "kindas" and "sortas," but they haven't learned to eliminate them yet. As soon as the weak speak slides out of their mouths, they catch themselves, apologize, and stumble on until another weak comment slips past their fledgling weak speak filters. The most confident of speakers can slip into self doubt while they learn to overcome the "filler word" habit.

If you've never had someone count your filler words, you probably don't know how often you use them. You are probably unaware how your word habits undermine your message. Every word you use that doesn't add to the power of your message weakens it. Filler words are one form of weak speak.

A peek at weak speak

Weak speak cost US Senate candidate "Rodney Hale" at least one vote, and possibly the election. Missy planned to vote for Hale until her friend Owen pointed out something she had missed.

"He doesn't mean what he says," Owen complained. "He doesn't speak convincingly."

"You're kidding!" Missy objected. "He speaks with absolute conviction."

"Yes," Owen replied, "He speaks with conviction when he talks tough. When he talks about confronting the enemy. When he talks about protecting the right to bear arms. When he talks about being tough on crime. But listen to him when he talks about families and values and civil rights. All of a sudden, his smooth talk gets choppy. He stumbles over his own words, and he uses all kinds of filler words. He ums and uhs and all his bravado disappears. He talks strong about punitive things, but his conviction disappears when he talks about social issues."

Missy paid closer attention to her candidate and realized Owen was right.

Tough or tender, but never weak

Owen and Missy decided Hale's speak got weak because he didn't mean what he said. They might have been right. If you speak weak because you don't believe your own words, realign your talk with your true beliefs. But if your speak is weak because you're afraid to Speak Strong, or because you have a habit of speaking weak, read on.

You can't play big and use weak speak.

> *" Sometimes Speaking Strong is tough. Sometimes Speaking Strong is tender. But Speaking Strong is never weak. "*
>
> MERYL RUNION

Dos, Don'ts and Tips, Skill # 25:
Don't let weak speak sneak in

Whether you need to talk tough or talk tender, don't talk weak. Play big and eliminate words, habits and expressions that weaken your message.

1. Eliminate filler words (um, uh, etc.) one by one

Don't: try to eliminate filler words all at once.

Why not? You're unlikely to succeed.

Do: pick a filler word to eliminate. Once you master that, pick another one.

Why? It's easier and more likely to lead to success.

Example: Crystal followed most of her points in her speech with, "You know?" An audience member (that would be me...) observed that it sounded like she was soliciting the audience's approval. Crystal picked "you know" as her first words to eliminate.

2. Embrace silence and "pregnant pauses"

Don't: try to fill every moment with words.

Why not? You're likely to fill them with weak speak.

Do: practice deliberate pauses after making poignant and powerful points.

Why? For emphasis, and to eliminate the temptation to fill the pause with weak speak.

Example: As a professional speaker, I've delivered the same material as often as 1000 times. (I know, I know. I needed a life and I'm working on getting one.) I learned that my timing, including pauses, matters as much as my words. For example, a joke I make might go unnoticed until I've paused long enough for it to sink in — and once it does, the room responds. If I neglect the pause, I don't get the laugh.

3. Don't choose to excuse your words

Don't: apologize for what you're about to say.

Why not? If you're going to be sorry about saying something, don't say it.

Do: state your point with confidence.

Why? If you believe what you say, others are more likely to.

Example: Mary started her presentation by explaining she didn't have much time to prepare. By excusing what she had to say in advance, she indicated that what she had to say might not be worth hearing.

4. Interrupt interrupters

Don't: think it's rude to interrupt those who interrupt you.

Why not? Your words matter too.

Do: let people know you want to finish what you have to say and once you make your point, you'll listen to them.

Why? If you consistently allow yourself to be interrupted, you seem weak.

PowerPhrases/What to Say: Excuse me, I wasn't done yet.

5. Replace passive voice with active voice

Don't: talk like the subject is the object—unless the subject really is on the receiving end.

Why not? It makes you sound like a victim.

Do: structure your sentences as subject/verb/object—or—someone does something to someone.

Why? It's more powerful. Passive voice is appropriate for messages that suggest a weak subject but not for general usage.

PowerPhrases/What to Say:
- I opened the meeting.
- Critics believed.

Poison Phrases/What NOT to Say:
- The meeting was called to order.
- It is believed…

6. Monitor your apologies

Don't: habitually say you're sorry.

Why not? It makes you sound like you're a sorry person.

Do: eliminate inappropriate apologies.

Why? Passive people over-apologize. Aggressive people under-apologize. People who Speak Strong apologize when they do something that causes harm that they would never deliberately do again.

Example: Roger arrived at the appointment so late that Misty had to cancel. Out of habit, Misty was about to apologize for canceling, but she refrained. After all, it was Roger's responsibility to be on time, his lateness inconvenienced her, and if anyone should apologize, it was him. She scheduled another appointment and asked him to be on time.

Play big

No matter how big your ideas, they'll sound small if you present them in weak speak. Eliminate communication habits that make you sound small.

You wouldn't want to help me, would you?

Skill #26: Expect to be taken seriously

It ended before it began

I'm sure he was a very nice man, but he talked me out of meeting him as he attempted to talk me into it. He dissuaded me with comments like — "I don't suppose you want to meet me, do you?" "I bet what I'm saying doesn't interest you." And "You're probably already regretting answering my single's ad."

He was right. I did regret answering his ad. He was a new widower with small children, and my heart went out to him. Clearly he was shattered. But I didn't see how meeting him could lead to anything constructive for either of us. He sounded like a rejection waiting to happen. I suspected that he would set up whomever he dated to rebuff him. I didn't want to play that role in his life.

If you expect to fail, you probably will

It's hard to take someone seriously who doesn't expect to be taken seriously. It's hard to see the value in a job candidate who doesn't expect you to see their value. It's hard to be persuaded by an argument that the advocate assumes you'll reject. It's hard to want to buy a product the sales presenter apologizes for recommending.

For many years I sub-contracted training for a seminar company that expected trainers to offer books, videos and audios for sale during the program. When I was new, I fearfully described these products. I was afraid attendees would object to hearing a "sales pitch" during training they paid for. I was afraid they would give me bad evaluations at the end of the day. I was afraid they wouldn't respect my recommendations.

I didn't expect to be taken seriously.

I wasn't.

As my skills rose, so did my expectations. As my expectations rose, so did my sales...AND my evaluations. I came to trust my attendees would want to continue their learning after the training was over, and therefore want to take advantage of the resources. Attendees met my emerging expectations and took me seriously.

Realistic expectations

Sure, it's true that some requests, assertions and endeavors will be better received than others. Don't confuse positive expectation with blind optimism.
If a realistic assessment suggests that your listener will resist your words,
prepare for that resistance. Acknowledge and address anticipated objections.
Go in with your eyes open — and with the expectation that you will be taken
seriously.

> " *No one will take your words seriously unless you do.* "
>
> MERYL RUNION

Dos, Don'ts and Tips, Skill # 26:
Expect to be taken seriously

In a debate between a charlatan who expects to be taken seriously and a legitimate expert who doesn't, my bets would be on the charlatan. No, I don't suggest you emulate the charlatans. I do suggest you both earn and expect respect, and let your talk reflect that. Here's how.

1. Anticipate possible objections and prepare to address them

Don't: think that listing their possible objections is defeatist.

Why not? It's realistic to prepare by anticipating objections and planning to counter them.

Do: prepare by playing a "yeah but" game. Ask yourself what reasons they would give to dismiss you (if they were honest).

Why? Preparedness works better than blind optimism.

Example: Juan didn't want to think of all the reasons why Melissa would reject his recommended policy change, because he thought his point should be self-explanatory. He equated preparing for objections with expecting rejection. He later decided that considering possible reasons to dismiss his argument was a realistic way to prepare.

2. Think long term

Don't: let initial resistance undermine your expectation to be taken seriously.

Why not? Objections and resistance often indicate people are listening to you—which means they take you seriously.

Do: expect respect to grow over time, even when people initially dismiss you.

Why? If you continue to expect people to take you seriously, you more likely will be.

Example: It took over a year and two attempts at auditioning for me to get a national seminar company to take me seriously as a candidate for trainer, but eventually they did. I worked for them for eight years.

3. Emphasize apparent support

Don't: let dismissals blind you to areas of common ground.

Why not? The areas of common ground are your keys to progress.

Do: observe and accentuate support that you do get, and the areas where those who dismiss you actually do take you seriously.

Why? What you put your attention on grows.

Example #1: In the movie *Pirates of the Caribbean*, Captain Sparrow was undaunted when Commodore Norinton said "You're the worst pirate I've ever heard of." Captain Sparrow responded, "Ah, but you have heard of me."

4. Address dismissive attitudes

Don't: ignore when someone is categorically dismissive.

Why not? You'll be swimming upstream. They may be unconscious of their attitude until you draw their attention to it.

Do: mention if your listener seems predisposed to reject your words before hearing you out.

Why? To make them aware of their predisposition so they can factor that in. It might motivate them to be open, just to prove you wrong for suggesting they are closed.

PowerPhrases/What to Say:
- I ask that you stay open to what I say until I've finished.
- Your initial reaction may be to reject this. Please hear me out and stay neutral until I've made my point.
- Please consider how this could work before concluding it can't.

5. Reinforce possibility thinking

Don't: let the restrictions of "what is" define your vision of what could be.

Why not? Many things that seem impossible are only impossible because people think they are.

Do: persist in sharing your vision.

Why? You could generate a critical mass that creates new paradigms or ways of thinking.

Example: Martin Luther King, Jr. had a dream, and before long, much of America shared the same dream. President Barack Obama ratified that dream on November 4th, 2008.

6. Create your own standard of what ideas deserve to be taken seriously

Don't: let mainstream public opinion determine what's credible.

Why not? Mainstream lags behind "early adopters."

Do: support your own dreams and visions.

Why? That's what early adopters and other leaders do. It's how they make things happen.

Example: Jack Canfield thought a book of inspiring stories could be a big seller. 32 different publishers disagreed. Canfield couldn't find a publisher for his book, *Chicken Soup for the Soul,* so he published it himself. The rest is history. That history was profitable for Canfield.

People do what you expect them to

I remember what my sales coach, Bill, said when he taught me how to sell books at seminars. He said, "People do what you expect them to. If you expect them to buy, they will."

He was right. Not everyone, but enough to make me successful in sales as well as training. I just had to get out of my own way and expect my audiences to take me seriously when I made my recommendations.

Your words are
as powerful as
your own
commitment
to them.

MERYL RUNION

> ❝ *Commit to walking your talk. It will make you careful about what you say.* ❞

MERYL RUNION

I don't do windows

Skill #27: Establish boundaries

Unbounded love

His youthful vitality lost its charm when I realized his child-LIKE-ness was really child-ISH-ness. Like a child, he didn't distinguish between his wants and needs. His desires were immediate and intense. Tom was my first love after my husband's death, and Tom had poor boundaries.

My boundaries were lacking too. I'll spare you the details except to say that I catered to Tom's wants and Tom's needs at the expense of my own. Until a therapist taught me about boundaries.

A useful metaphor

Dr. Trieloff was a friendly, enormous, bearded therapist who introduced me to boundaries, gave me permission to set them, and provided me a metaphor that gave me a vision of what healthy boundaries look like. Here's what he said:

"Think of your time and property as items in a cupboard. You are happy to share what's in that cupboard. But you and only you get to decide what you share, when you will share it and how you share it. You can go into your cupboard and pull items out to distribute when you choose to. But you hold the keys. Others can't go in and take what they want without your consent. They don't get to pressure you into giving items you don't want to give."

I loved the metaphor. I became the keeper of my own cupboard, and I set the policies of who got what from that cupboard. I became a fledgling boundary setter.

Boundaries: they're not just for relationships anymore

Boundaries aren't just for relationships — they're for every aspect of life. Not doing windows is a boundary. Limiting the number of hours you will spend on the phone with a client is a boundary. Not letting someone else's lack of planning become your emergency is a boundary. Boundaries are the "walls" you create around yourself. They are limits you set around time, activities and your attention.

Well-written job descriptions establish clear boundaries that allow management and employees to determine priorities and agree to what they can and can't expect from each other. Like all good boundaries, job descriptions help people invest their time and energy wisely.

Boundaries also help you to mean what you say.

> " *You teach people*
> *how to treat you.*
> *Are you teaching them*
> *what you want them*
> *to learn?* "
>
> MERYL RUNION

Dos, Don'ts and Tips, Skill # 27
Establish boundaries

Boundaries define you

Boundaries define what you value and how you prioritize those values. If you have fuzzy boundaries, you'll have a fuzzy, undefined identity.

Boundaries set you free. They set you free from constant decisions about what you will and won't do. They set you free from undue influence from others. They set you free from going down paths that you don't belong on.

So establish your boundaries. Here's how.

1. Examine your boundary beliefs

Don't: just look for limiting boundary beliefs.

> **Why not?** You may have some healthy beliefs that you can build on.

Do: examine what you tell yourself about your rights or lack of rights to set boundaries.

> **Why?** To reconstruct your boundary beliefs into healthy ones that will make you your own advocate.

Example: I used to hold beliefs about female submission that kept me from setting limits with the men in my life. Many people hold beliefs about bosses and other authorities that limit their willingness to set needed boundaries.

2. Affirm your boundaries

Don't: be apologetic about setting boundaries.

> **Why not?** It's in everyone's interest for you to stay in balance. Boundaries do that.

Do: Honor your right and need to set good boundaries.

> **Why?** They're not selfish. They're necessary.

Example: I learned a lot about boundaries from a friend who was clinically diagnosed as manic depressive. She never pushed herself because she couldn't push herself. If she honored her boundaries, she stayed in balance. If she didn't, she fell apart. I found it inconvenient for her to be unavailable when I wanted her to be, but it meant she didn't crash and burn like she used to before she learned to honor her boundaries.

3. Set goals
Don't: leave your intentions undefined.
>   **Why not?** You'll find yourself serving those who do have clearly defined goals.

Do: clearly and realistically decide what you intend to accomplish.
>   **Why?** To keep your focus and to understand what you sacrifice if you relinquish your agenda for someone else's.

Example: Macy was disappointed with her slow progress writing her book. Then she committed to completing two chapters each month. Once she had that commitment she found it easier to say no to distractions such as coffee dates and helping people with their projects at the expense of her own.

4. Commit to yourself
Don't: assume others' requests are more urgent than your own agenda.
>   **Why not?** If you don't honor your own interests, no one else will.

Do: make promises and pledges to — and appointments with — yourself in the same way you do with other people you value.
>   **Why?** Most people consider promises to others as more binding than the ones they make to themselves. If you commit to yourself, you'll show up for yourself.

Example: Macy decided she would finish her book by writing for two hours each morning before she did anything else — besides waking her daughter for school and drinking her coffee. She let the phone ring, skipped her morning news and when her daughter missed her bus to school, she told her daughter she would have to walk. Macy realized how many distractions she normally allowed to interfere with her writing.

5. Differentiate between can do and should do
Don't: assume that because you can do something that you should or are somehow obligated to do it.
>   **Why not?** You don't need an external reason to set a boundary.

Do: give yourself permission to decline requests that you could accept.
>   **Why?** It respects your power of choice.

Example: Phil's afternoon was unscheduled — he could have covered the phones for Stella. But Phil had hoped to catch up on his paperwork. Sure, he could do his paperwork later, but he also knew the reason Stella needed help was because she didn't plan ahead. It was something Phil "could do," but he decided that didn't mean it was something he "should do." Phil honored his own boundaries and declined the request.

6. Inventory and prepare for your boundary busters

Don't: overlook anyone or any part of your life.

Why not? You may have good boundaries in all but one life area.

Do: review what people and situations challenge your ability to set boundaries, and prepare for them in advance.

Why? Forewarned is forearmed.

Example: Kathleen had no problem setting boundaries with her direct reports, but it was her kids who wore her down every time. She studied their exchanges and prepared for how she would honor her own boundaries in the future.

7. Brainstorm a boundary "wish list"

Don't: leave anything out no matter how unrealistic it is.

Why not? You may assume you can't set a boundary that you actually can.

Do: write out every boundary you would like to set, and consider establishing each one.

Why? To define who you are and what you stand for.

Example: Years ago I set a boundary that I would not accept sarcasm. No one uses sarcasm with me any more.

Fran made her list and decided she would stop taking last minute changes on printing jobs. She was pleased to find out that most of her clients were able to plan ahead once they knew of her new policy/boundary.

She wanted to set a boundary requiring full payment up front, but decided that was unrealistic and backed down.

Do windows if you want to

Boundaries exist to serve you. You can set boundaries where ever you want. They can be flexible or rigid, narrow or broad. You get to decide. And once you decide on and commit to your boundaries, you will be able to mean what you say.

> **You get the relationships you deserve... or at least that you tolerate.**
>
> MERYL RUNION

Perhaps I wasn't clear

Skill #28: Implement boundaries

Boundary woes

"Boundaries don't work," Wally reported. "I told him I wasn't going to put up with his being late, but he came late anyway."

"What you suggested didn't help," Carolyn complained. "My employee turned her reports in on time for a week, but then she started turning her reports in late again."

"I decided a long time ago that I wasn't going to tolerate cursing," Tamara objected, "but my kids and I have a different definition of what cursing is. When I object to what they say, they tell me there's nothing wrong with their words."

Okay, there's more to setting boundaries than sitting in your office and creating them. There's more to setting boundaries than standing on a platform and announcing them. The challenge of boundaries comes when you walk the talk.

When you announce a boundary, everyone should just fall in line, right? You wish!

A question of balance

You have equilibrium with the people in your life. When you set a new boundary, you upset that equilibrium. Chances are good that others will attempt to reestablish the old order of things. And to make it worse, you probably will too. Even a norm that doesn't work for you is comfortably familiar.

Boundary back-up

If you have trouble implementing boundaries, it may not be the boundaries' fault. Your boundary-setting may be similar to sending a platoon in for a mission that requires a division. If the mission fails, you can't blame the soldiers—especially if you don't back them up with proper support and supplies.

And it may be like pouring a glass of water on a raging house fire. You can't blame the water for not working.

When setting boundaries, going to war or putting out fires, a half-hearted effort won't work. If you're not willing to see the mission through to the end, don't set yourself up for failure. Reconsider the mission.

Both Wally and Carolyn need to back their boundaries up with action to support their "boundary mission." Tamara needs to redefine her mission and "redeploy." To continue the war metaphors, "no good battle plan ever outlives first contact with the enemy." Mobilize for resistance and give your mission the firepower it deserves — or call your "boundary troops" back.

> ## *If it were easy to Speak Strong, everyone would do it.*
>
> MERYL RUNION

Dos, Don'ts and Tips, Skill # 28
Implement boundaries

Well begun is half done

It would be great if everyone fell in line with your newly established boundaries. You should be so lucky. Those who took advantage of your former wavering nature won't like it a bit when suddenly faced with someone who has discovered how to be resolute. Here's how to implement boundaries in a way that is more likely to get results.

1. Assume cooperation

Don't: present boundaries in a way that signals they have reasons to resist.

    Why not? If you assume resistance, you're likely to get it.

Do: prepare for resistance, but open communication in a way that suggests acceptance.

    Why? To avoid creating resistance where there is none.

PowerPhrase/What to Say: I need to limit interruptions to focus on my proposal. Please keep your interruptions to a minimum.

Poison Phrase/What NOT to say: Would it be possible for you to limit your interruptions?

2. Provide options

Don't: set boundaries that keep others from getting legitimate needs met.

    Why not? You're not an island. Your decisions affect others, and they will battle your boundaries.

Do: offer options that will meet your needs and theirs.

    Why? To get stable arrangements others can live with instead of walls that others resist.

PowerPhrase/What to Say: Please compile your questions and bring them to me once a day.

Poison Phrase/What NOT to say: Deal with it.

3. Present new boundaries respectfully

Don't: condemn existing behavior when you set new boundaries.

    Why not? It keeps the attention negative and in the past instead of focusing on the future and possibilities.

Do: talk about what you want and how things will be rather than how "bad their behavior" was.

Why? If you allowed bad behavior, it's your responsibility too. And, old bad behavior is like a sink hole you may never get out of. New possibilities are inspiring.

PowerPhrase/What to Say: I've come to realize that I don't enjoy participating in gossip, so please don't gossip around me.

Poison Phrase/What NOT to say: This gossip is despicable and I'm not lowering myself to your level anymore.

4. Clarify your boundaries

Don't: assume boundaries are self-explanatory.

   Why not? What's clear to you is not clear to others.

Do: prepare to answer the questions "does that mean that...?"

   Why? To make your boundaries concrete.

PowerPhrase/What to Say: Some of the words I won't listen to any more are...

Poison Phrase/What NOT to say: Everyone knows what curse words are.

5. Establish follow-up

Don't: lay down the new law and forget about it.

   Why not? They'll forget it too, and you'll lose credibility.

Do: set times for follow-up when you set a boundary.

   Why? To demonstrate that you mean what you say.

PowerPhrase/What to Say: Let's check in and review how it's going in a week. How's Tuesday at 2:00 look for you?

Be resolute

When you implement boundaries, you proclaim your intent to be resolute. Do it in a way that is likely to work. That way you won't have to mobilize so many forces to show that you mean what you say.

Don't make me come back there!

Skill #29: Communicate consequences (not disguised threats)

In case she forgot why she left him...

Cynthia's ex-husband ignored her boundaries when they were married, and once they were newly divorced, that pattern didn't change any.

When Cynthia moved out of their house, she asked Mick to take the utilities out of her name. He said he would but didn't follow through. A month later Cynthia reminded Mick to take the utilities out of her name. He said he would but didn't follow through. A month after that, Cynthia insisted that Mick take the utilities out of her name. He said he would but didn't follow through. A month after that, Cynthia demanded that Mick take the utilities out of her name. He said he would but didn't follow through. A month after that, Cynthia advised Mick that if he did not take the utilities out of her name within a week, she would close the account and switch the utilities off. He said he would but didn't follow through. Cynthia did follow through. Mick was furious when he came home one day to discover he had no water.

Cynthia felt bad, but I thought it was one of her proudest moments. She wasn't punishing her ex, nor was she taking pleasure in triumphing over him. (Well...not much anyway — and it wasn't her motivation.) She took action to enforce her boundary that her ex take his service out of her name.

Cynthia's marriage had failed (in part) because she was unable to establish boundaries with Mick. (Of course, had she set boundaries before they married, the marriage might never have happened. Which probably would have been a good thing, but I digress.) Finally, months after their divorce, Cynthia set her foot down and took decisive action.

Actions have consequences

Consequences add muscle to your requests, appeals and demands. They address the ever-popular consideration — why should I do what you want?

Consequences can resemble threats, but there's a subtle — and vital — distinction.

Here's the definition of a threat: a declaration of an intention or determination to inflict punishment, injury, etc., in retaliation for some action or course.

Here's the definition of a consequence: an act or instance of following something as an effect, result, or outcome.

Note the difference?

Threats are about punishment and retaliation. Consequences are about outcome.

When Cynthia informed Mick she intended to close out the utilities if he didn't transfer them himself, she wasn't threatening him. She was letting him know what the consequences of inaction would be.

You threaten when you put pressure on someone so they will do what you want.

You explain consequences when you inform someone of what you will choose to do based on what they do. That information allows them to decide based on an accurate assessment of the consequences of their action (or inaction.)

Use the tools in your tool box
It took Cynthia years to use the tools she had in her tool box, but once she did, she got results. Consequences, properly used, are powerful resources, and an important part of resolutely meaning what you say.

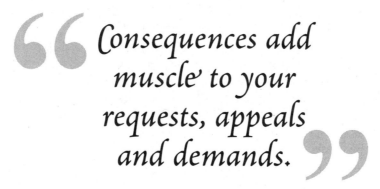

Consequences add muscle to your requests, appeals and demands.

MERYL RUNION

Dos, Don'ts and Tips, Skill # 29
Communicate consequences (not disguised threats)

I walk the line
The line between consequences and threats is a fine one that is well worth learning to walk. Here are some tips to help you.

1. Share consequences on a need-to-know basis
Don't: express consequences for crossing your boundaries if: 1) you think they are likely to respect your boundaries without consequences and 2) you can afford to wait to see if a simple request will work before you up the ante.
   Why not? Unnecessary consequences sound harsh and imply distrust.
Do: communicate consequences if 1) you have reason to believe they will disregard your boundaries and 2) non-compliance would result in immediate consequences.
   Why? To: 1) add needed muscle to your words and 2) provide the information they need to make an informed decision.
Example: As Mike and Ronnie made plans to drive to the convention, Mike told Ronnie that if she was more than ten minutes late, he'd go on his own. Ronnie was habitually late, and Mike thought it only fair to warn her instead of leaving without a warning.

2. Claim your consequences
Don't: blame them for the choices you make.
   Why not? It muddies the waters.
Do: explain intended consequences in terms of your own choices.
   Why? It treats you both like responsible adults.
PowerPhrase/What to Say: If this continues I will…
Poison Phrase/What NOT to say: You're going to make me have to…

3. Evaluate your consequences
Don't: use consequences that are inconsequential, bluffs or extreme.
   Why not? People will learn your consequences are empty or unreasonable.
Do: express consequences you reasonably intend to implement.
   Why? To be taken seriously.
Example: Jill told her mother that the next time she took a pot shot at her, she would leave. It was Thanksgiving and they hadn't even sat to dinner when

her mother sniped at her for "using the wrong size pan." Jill was conflicted because it was Thanksgiving—but she told her husband and kids she was leaving anyway. When her husband and kids told her they didn't want to go, she gave them the choice of staying without her or leaving with her. They stayed, and although Jill missed a family Thanksgiving dinner, she made a strong point that led her mother to behave better in the future.

4. Enforce consequences neutrally

Don't: dramatize.

    Why not? It's manipulative and punitive.

Do: be matter-of-fact about taking the action you said you would.

    Why? To send the message that you are in control of yourself and your consequences are reasonable.

Example: Jill was calm and uncomplaining about implementing her consequence with her mother. She didn't get angry and she didn't pressure the rest of the family to leave with her or punish them because they didn't. Her calm resolve made it difficult for her mother to fault her.

5. Risk for reward

Don't: play it too safe.

    Why not? You'll stay stuck in a situation that doesn't honor you.

Do: consider risking it all to gain it all.

    Why? The more you risk, the more you stand to gain.

Example: Communication is important to Helen. Her love interest, George, shut down when she tried to discuss sensitive issues. Helen informed George that she needed to be able to discuss important issues if they were going to continue as a couple. George realized it was a deal-breaker for her, and decided to work on their communication. Helen risked it all and gained it all.

Go for it

When you need to up the ante, do it right. Walk the line, communicate consequences that are not disguised threats, and let people know that you are a force they should reckon with. Oh, yes, and that you mean what you say.

That that was my evil twin

Skill #30: Meet and greet your communication devil

You and your Communication Devil

React…respond…what's the difference? For some, the difference is about three seconds. For others, it's about three days. For others still, it's about three years — three decades — or some might say three lifetimes — but don't quote me on the last one.

If you regret things you said, you probably reacted in the situation instead of responding. If you say "I don't know what got into me," "I couldn't control myself," or "That was my evil twin," it's time to meet and greet your Communication Devil.

I know, I know, you'd rather not. I know that because if you did want to meet your Communication Devil, you'd have done it already.

You could wait until things get pretty bad. Like they do for Brie, who gets emotionally volatile from time to time. Brie can rein in her reactions for a while, but then something will trigger her and she goes unconscious. After a few hours or sometimes days, when she returns to normal, she's faced with some serious damage control.

Everyday unconsciousness

If you ever forget what you did two minutes ago, you know what it's like to go unconscious. You might wonder where you just put your keys. You might have to check the bowl to know if you fed the cat. And you might not recall what you just said. There are times when your unconscious mind takes over your actions and your conscious mind has no clue what you're doing.

If you have good habits, in those unconscious moments, you put the keys on the rack instead of in the freezer, you fed Fluffy cat food and not Cheerios, and you said something reasonable. But if you don't have good habits, you may never find your keys again, Fluffy's not a bit happy with you, and you said something that would get you censored had you been on prime time television.

Rude awakening

When you shine the light on your unconscious habits, you may be shocked at what you find. You can go from being a reasonable person and a good communicator into being a communication kindergartener seemingly over-night.

Surprise — unless you are exceptional, you always were a communication kindergartener. You're just now figuring it out. You were operating in the dark, and now that the lights are coming on, you get to see the good, the bad and the ugly.

Ouch! Why would you want to do that? Because that's how you grow.

No fun, I know, but do it anyway. It's a lot of work to retrain to respond. It's also rewarding work.

> " *React…*
> *respond…*
> *what's the difference?*
> *It's about three seconds.* "
>
> MERYL RUNION

Dos, Don'ts and Tips, Skill # 30
Meet and greet your communication devil

Who are you and what have you done with the me I know and love?

It's amazing how many people don't know themselves. After living with themselves their entire lives, they think they are good communicators and in complete control, when even a casual observer knows they're not. They haven't met and gret — uh — they haven't taken the time to meet and greet — their communication devils.

Of course, you're different. Or are you? Everyone I've ever met has a communication devil. Some have gotten to know theirs, which is an important step in learning to respond, not react. Here's what you can do to meet and greet yours.

1. Review childhood lessons

Don't: think your habits came from nowhere.

Why not? They didn't. You learned them from people in your early life.

Do: inventory how your parents communicated, noting what they did that you do too.

Why? Even if you don't like your parents, you're probably much more like them than you admit. And if you didn't pick up their habits, you probably formed habits in reaction to them.

Example: Nick's mother would sulk if his father criticized her, and Nick learned to sulk too. It wasn't pretty, and it held him back at work. People would avoid him when they could, because they found him to be unpleasant.

2. Invite feedback on your communication skills

Don't: think that your intentions are reliable indicators of how you come across.

Why not? You may not be as well-intended as you think, and even if you are, your words might not accurately reflect your intentions.

Do: ask people how you come across to them.

Why? To get an objective — or at least external — perspective of your Communication Devil.

Example: Bill had no idea his words implied subtle discrimination when he acted surprised by minority members who perform well, referred to minority groups by names they don't prefer and flirted inappropriately with professional women. He thought his words were innocent at worst and possibly benevolent. He learned otherwise when he solicited feedback.

3. Videotape and audiotape yourself

Don't: trust your memory of conversations.

> **Why not?** We delude ourselves. Just like we can falsely "remember" putting our keys where they belong, we can also falsely "remember" having been polite when we asked for help.

Do: record sensitive discussions (with permission) and study them.

> **Why?** You'll be surprised by what you hear. And you'll hear it more objectively than you would from memory.

Example: Rachael thought she was reasonable in her negotiations with her brother, but when she listened to a recording, she realized she came across as aggressive.

4. Debrief derailed discussions

Don't: disregard disappointing conversations, arguments and misunderstandings without garnering their messages.

> **Why not?** "Thar's gold in them thar hills." (Hills = conversations.)

Do: consider where and how you lost your cool — and perhaps went on unconscious automatic pilot.

> **Why?** To get a clue about what you do.

Example: John lost his temper with his boss. Fortunately he didn't blow up often, so his boss was willing and able to overlook this incident. But John knew he couldn't afford too many explosions. John decided to decipher what happened and why he reacted so intensely.

5. Explore and embrace the automatic-alternate-you

Don't: beat yourself up.

> **Why not?** Torture results in unreliable intelligence. ;-) Be gentle with yourself.

Do: fearlessly explore the you that takes over when you go unconscious. Consider naming that you, work to understand his/her motivations, and show interest in understanding that part of yourself.

> **Why?** So you can work with that part of your psyche.

Example: John observed that things went south for him when his boss rolled his eyes at him. He also realized his boss' eye rolls were a habitual trigger for him. He dialoged with the part of himself that got triggered (no, that's not weird) to understand his dynamic.

6. Take my SpeakStrong Online Communication Style Quiz
www.speakstrong.com/inventory

Why? It will highlight your communication characteristics which, taken to an extreme, become communication devils.

There are no perfect people — not even you

We all have our angels and our devils. If you pretend you're all angels, it actually gives your devils more power in your life. Once you examine your darker nature and take the time to untangle and educate it, you'll find it's not so scary after all. You'll also find that you will be less inclined to say things you don't mean. It pays to retrain to respond.

Courageous communicators feel fear; they just don't let it stop them.

MERYL RUNION

*" There's power
in the things you'd
rather not say. "*

MERYL RUNION

Open mouth and extract foot

Skill #31: Stop, drop and purge bad habits

The grip of addiction

Have you ever tried to break an addiction? Whether it's an addiction to recreational drugs (including sugar and alcohol), codependent relationships, to shopping, approval, or to work, breaking addictions is hard.

Speech habits are also addictive. You hear people around the water cooler getting their "fix" of gossip. You hear the pundits on television providing viewers with their daily dose of negativity. And you probably know at least one person who can't go for ten minutes without apologizing for something, or exaggerating something or bragging about how exceptional they are. If they haven't met their communication devils, they probably don't know they have a problem. It would surprise them to consider that they have a speech addiction. But challenge them to stop and they'll find all kinds of excuses not to. That's what addicts do.

Try refraining from a destructive speech habit, be it a passive or an aggressive habit, and see how tough it is. See how tempted you are to get your fix. You could even give up one of these habits for Lent. Good luck making it until Easter.

When a habit is an addiction

Mary decided she wanted to break her habit of interrupting. She didn't know she was addicted to interrupting until she tried to stop. She asked me to help by calling her attention to every interruption she made. At first Mary interrupted me when I tried to point out her interruptions. Mary's speech addiction alienated a lot of people.

You know you're addicted when something you do costs more than the payoff, but you keep on doing it. You know you're addicted when you feel compelled to continue, even when the payoff is negative. You know you're addicted when you can't stop.

Mary still interrupts me, but she usually catches herself right after she does it. It would be nice if Mary just let me talk, but at least now I don't have to fight her to make a point. I can live with that.

Retrain to respond

No, it's not easy to break an addiction. But you can do it if you set your mind to it. It helps if you have the right tools and techniques. It's all about retraining—retraining to respond.

> *The Chinese definition of insanity is doing the same thing and expecting a different result. Are you insane?*
>
> MERYL RUNION

Dos, Don'ts and Tips, Skill # 31
Stop, drop and purge bad habits

Are you a slave to communication habits? Break the bonds. Here are some tips to help you.

1. Pick a single habit to work with
Don't: try to change everything at once.

Why not? That would be like trying to quit drinking, smoking, sugar and television at the same time. Please warn me before you invite me over the week you decide to do that!

Do: set yourself up for success by eliminating a single communication habit.

Why? Your success will encourage you to continue.

Example: Robby knows that when he gets irritable, he tends to get hypercritical of his editor. He set a goal to stop picking on her when he feels irritable. That does mean staying silent at times — but that works better than the verbal attacks.

2. Charge your friends to catch you when you slip
Don't: get defensive when friends point out your transgressions.

Why not? They're doing you a favor. Don't punish them for that.

Do: tell them exactly what you want help with, and thank them for their input. If their feedback isn't exactly what you're looking for, clarify later rather than in the moment.

Why? To reinforce their effort to help.

Example: Tangents were so natural for me that I'd go off on them without realizing it. Other tangential talkers understood me just fine, so I didn't understand why my logical listeners didn't. I studied how logical communicators think, and started warning my logical thinkers when I was about to make a tangential point. I invited my logical husband to point out my tangents to help me be more aware when I went off on one.

3. Reward your success
Don't: think you have to be perfect to earn a reward.

Why not? Every step forward is progress, even when you're far from the goal.

Do: promise yourself a reward once you go for a designated period without indulging in your habit.

Why? It makes your commitment more concrete and minimizes the likelihood of backtracking

Example: Mindy celebrated going a week where she waited for 30 seconds before she yelled at her sister. It may have been a minor achievement in the minds of many, but it was progress deserving of reward to Mindy.

4. Overindulge the habit

There are two powerful ways to change habits. One is to stop it, but another is to overindulge. That exaggerated behavior breaks your old habitual behavior. Sometimes the best way to make a positive change is to make any kind of change at all.

Don't: overindulge with people you haven't enlisted to support you.

Why not? They'll think you've gone off the deep end.

Do: safely "overdose" on a communication habit to the point of absurdity in safe environments.

Why? It will make you conscious of what you do in a relatively painless way.

Example: Frank habitually exaggerated, so he decided to exaggerate to an absurd level. He solicited the cooperation and understanding of some of the people in his life and went full tilt boogie. He didn't just inflate his sales by 10%; he inflated them by 500%. He didn't just add fifteen minutes to how long he waited for his wife, he added five hours. He didn't just say his client was inattentive, he said his client put his fingers in his ears and sang *Row, Row, Row Your Boat*. After a couple of days, he and his associates were laughing at the silliness of it—and Frank became aware of his normal tendency to exaggerate.

Frank's wife liked the idea of the technique and decided to use it with her habit of apologizing. She started apologizing for the weather, inflation and not anticipating Frank's every need. That shined a light on her habit and helped her to overcome it.

Kiss your habits good-bye

Are you insane? The Chinese definition of insanity is to do what you've always done while expecting a different result. I therefore admit to being a bit crazy, but not to being as crazy as I once was.

Where do you react instead of respond? How often do you confess—"I didn't mean what I said. It just came out of my mouth"? If you say that at all, stop, drop and purge your bad habits. Then, read on to create some new ones.

New and Improved!

Skill #32: Out with the bad habits, in with the good

Stop, drop and ask

I'm developing the habit of asking more questions. That means overcoming the habit of ignoring doubt and responding without complete understanding. I'm replacing it with a reflex I call: stop, drop and ask.

I forget to practice my new approach sometimes. When I review a conversation that didn't go as well as I would have liked and discern what I could have done that would have been more effective, nine times out of ten, questions are my answer.

My old habit was to assume understanding. My new one is to stop, drop and ask. That's one of many habits I'm working with. I invite you to join me on this journey.

New trumps old

I like skill #32, the skill of developing new habits, better than skill #31, of eliminating bad habits. It's more fun to practice something new than to stop something familiar. And when you start something new, familiar old habits often drop off automatically.

When you start addressing issues directly, sarcasm drops off. When you start listening better, interrupting drops off. When you start being more logical in your delivery, tangents drop off. It's like changing your diet by adding all kinds of culinary delights that nourish you and discovering you don't eat so much junk anymore. Yum!

For example, Nina started saying "yes and" when she differed, and in the process she stopped saying "yes but." Mona started focusing on what employees could do differently and in the process she focused less on what they were currently doing wrong. Zeb added potent pauses and in the process, stopped using filler words like "um" and "uh."

Sometimes you only need to introduce a new habit and for the old one to drop off.

I don't suggest it's easy. I do suggest it's worth it. Take the time to retrain yourself to respond in a new way that works.

Dos, Don'ts and Tips, Skill # 32
Out with the bad habits, in with the good

The success gurus are right
It's a success principle as old as time – what you put your attention on grows in your life. So put your attention on what you want – good communication habits. Here's how.

1. Educate yourself
Don't: stop studying and learning.
   Why not? You can make life-changing advances at any age.
Do: become a student of the communication habits you want to develop. Read articles, books, and ask people who seem to have a handle on them. Become an expert in the topics.
   Why? When you have the skills to handle situations effectively, you won't even consider communicating the old way.
Example: I used this approach to eliminate my sarcasm habit. I studied sarcasm, irony and mixed messages. I researched diligently to develop an understanding of why I used these approaches and what would work better.
Resources: I have an article about sarcasm at www.speakstrong.com/articles/ workplace-communication/sarcasm.html

My book *PowerPhrases!* offers phrases to counter sarcasm. *www.speakstrong. com/store/*

2. Replace, replace, replace
Don't: ban ways of communicating without selecting an alternative.
   Why not? You'll frustrate the heck out of yourself and be ineffective.
Do: find and implement a positive alternative to every negative habit you uncover.
   Why? It's easier to drop a bad habit when you have a clear substitute – even if you haven't mastered the alternative yet.
Example: Replace gossip with legitimate substantive discussion. Replace threats with consequences. Replace labels with accurate descriptions of the behaviors that lead you to want to label. Replace emotional manipulation with honest appeals.

3. Interact with conscious people
Don't: overlook what you can learn from people who already have the skills you seek.

160

Why not? Skilled communicators are a great resource for learning excellence in action and communication.

Do: interact with people who already practice the communication habits you want to develop.

Why? You'll learn by osmosis…or at least by association.

Example: Kelly overheard her boss speaking directly and clearly with a hostile vendor. She took inspiration and instruction from her boss' mastery.

4. Be human while building acumen

Don't: expect immediate perfection or purity of motive.

Why not? You'll never take action.

Do: be willing to bungle, be awkward and look foolish as you practice.

Why? Like learning to walk, as you practice, you fall.

Example: In retrospect, Melinda could think of a thousand better ways she could have worded her feedback to Joe. She almost wished she had given him a pass on his performance review as she used to do. She also felt guilty about the pleasure she felt letting him know he wasn't the model employee he thought he was. But Melinda is human, and that means she makes mistakes as she practices new behaviors. Give it your best and let yourself be human – even if you inadvertently harm others by your lack of acumen.

Who are you and what have you done with the ineffective me?

Changing habits is a challenge, but there is great joy in discovering you've remade yourself. When you look back and realize you automatically spoke up, listened, asked clarifying questions or practiced whatever communication habit you worked so hard to develop, you'll thank yourself.

The ability to change habits is an important skill. And if you have habits that signal others that you don't mean what you say, it's worth the time, discomfort and energy to make the change.

So retrain to respond. Learn to mean what you say with communication habits that enable you be who you want to be.

> " *People change*
> *when the pain*
> *gets bad enough,*
> *the possibilities*
> *get appealing enough,*
> *and the steps*
> *for change*
> *are clear enough.* "

MERYL RUNION

Speak
STRONG

STEP 4: DON'T BE MEAN WHEN YOU SAY IT

Don't Be Mean When You Say It Skill Set #1:
Check Your Attitude

Don't Be Mean When You Say It Skill Set #2:
Assert, Don't Aggress

Don't Be Mean When You Say It Skill Set #3:
Give up the Games

Don't Be Mean When You Say It Skill Set #4:
Purge the Poison

Introduction to Step 4:
Don't Be Mean When You Say It

Clarity and resolve are excellent communication components. But there's one more component that is as essential as clarity and resolve: kindness. A PowerPhrase is as strong as it needs to be and no stronger. Speaking Strong means saying what needs to be said clearly, directly and **kindly**. This Speak-Strong step helps you find the perfect amount of strength.

Don't Be Mean When You Say It Skill Set #1:
Check Your Attitude

If you're angry, resentful or impatient, it's difficult to not "be mean when you say it." If you're negative, cynical or dismissive, it's difficult not to "be mean when you say it." Even if you carefully choose to respect the dignity of your listener, chances are your attitude will seep through. This section helps you work with your attitude as a foundation for communicating in ways that don't create avoidable resistance.

Don't Be Mean When You Say It Skill Set #2:
Assert, Don't Aggress

Most people confuse assertiveness and aggression. For some, that confusion makes them reluctant to be appropriately assertive. For others, that confusion causes them to be unnecessarily harsh, and to excuse aggression by calling it assertiveness. This skill set helps you find the balance between passive and aggressive. That balance is effective assertiveness.

Don't Be Mean When You Say It Skill Set #3:
Give up the Games

People play many communication games. This skill set helps you unlearn communication games and replace them with effective communication strategies that say what you mean, and mean what you say, without being mean when you say it. The line between a game and a strategy is a subtle one. Learn to recognize it so you can walk on the integrous side of the line.

Don't Be Mean When You Say It Skill Set #4:
Purge the Poison

Good intentions are great, but if you're full of communication poison, the poison will undermine your intentions. This skill set helps you purge the poison of common negative communication habits and replaces your poisonous habits with healthy ones.

My head is a war zone

Skill #33: Elevate thinking to elevate speaking

Check your attitude

Is your head a war zone? Do you ever:
- ☐ Mentally conflict?
- ☐ Condemn yourself or others?
- ☐ Battle with yourself?
- ☐ Explode mentally?
- ☐ Think like your own worst enemy?
- ☐ Need a mental cease-fire?
- ☐ Sabotage yourself?

If you answered yes, don't kid yourself that you can keep your inner war your little secret. You can read hundreds of pages about powerful communication, but if your head is a war zone, your words will sound like a battle cry. That battle cry could easily trigger resistance in someone who might have been willing to cooperate.

If your attitudes don't serve you, make the change. A Cherokee elder explains how.

The Two Wolves

The Tale of Two Wolves tells the tale of inner conflict. Although I didn't write this story and I've used it in my other books, I offer it here again because it's so useful.

An elder Cherokee Native American taught his grandchildren about life, explaining, "A fight is going on inside me… it is a terrible fight and it is between two wolves. One wolf represents fear, anger, envy, sorrow, regret, greed, arrogance, self-pity, guilt, resentment, inferiority, lies, false pride, superiority, and ego. The other stands for joy, peace, love, hope, sharing, serenity, humility, kindness, benevolence, friendship, empathy, generosity, truth, compassion, and faith."

"This same fight is going on inside you, and inside every other person, too."

The children thought about it for a minute and then one child asked "Which wolf will win, Grandfather?"

The old Cherokee simply replied… "The one you feed."

What do you feed?

The Cherokee elder was wise indeed to say that the part of yourself you feed grows stronger in your life. John Nash discovered that his life went from disaster to success when he went on a 'mental diet' and chose which of his thoughts he should feed with his attention. *(A Beautiful Mind)*

Check your attitude. Feed your higher nature by feeding your high-minded thoughts. That feeds high-minded speech and will help you avoid being mean when you say what you say. It's all about Speaking Strong.

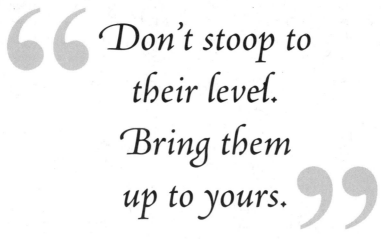

> *Don't stoop to their level. Bring them up to yours.*

MERYL RUNION

Dos, Don'ts and Tips, Skill # 33
Elevate thinking to elevate speaking

What do YOU feed?
Every thought you have feeds one mindset or another. Here's how to elevate your thoughts beyond the war zone. When you do that, it will elevate your words.

1. Observe your low-minded thoughts
Don't: pursue, resist or ignore low-minded thoughts.
> **Why not?** You feed thoughts when you pursue or resist them. When you ignore thoughts, you allow them to feed themselves.

Do: observe your fearful, angry, envious, sad, regretful, greedy, arrogant, self-pitying, guilty, resentful, inferiority, dishonest, prideful, superiority, and egotistical thoughts.
> **Why?** Observing thoughts and feeling the corresponding emotions dissipates them. (Perhaps not as quickly as you'd like, but it does dissipate them.)

Example: Rob would wake up angry in the early morning and focus his anger by making a case against his wife. One critical thought led to another. When his wife woke up, he was ready to unload on her.

When the sun came up, Rob's perspective on his early AM train of thought changed. In the light of more sanity, he saw the absurdity and unproductive nature of his thinking.

Rob decided not to feed his thoughts, but to simply observe them and to feel the corresponding emotion. Gradually his morning mental battles subsided.

2. Avoid low-minded conversations
Don't: gossip, complain, listen to divisive communicators or otherwise participate in low-minded discussions.
> **Why not?** It feeds negativity and divisiveness.

Do: speak up or leave when a conversation turns unbecoming. If you can't remove yourself, observe the words and corresponding emotions in the same way I recommend you observe your own low-minded thoughts.
> **Why?** To make your lower mind conscious.

Example: Nick listened to a virulent political radio show daily. He burned with anger after the show. Eventually he decided to stop listening to it (he did go through some withdrawal) and found a more balanced commentator to get his political commentary.

3. Practice elevating self-statements

Don't: feed thoughts that drag you down.

Why not? It perpetuates low-mindedness.

Do: create a collection of self-statements that raise your thinking level. Deliberately select your phrases to defuse the things your lower mind tells you.

Why? To feed the higher-mind.

Example: When Rob was thinking with his higher-mind, he created a series of statements to repeat to himself when he slipped into his AM low-mindedness. Here are a few of his phrases: 1) This will look different to me when the sun rises. 2) My mind is trying to trick me. 3) I am bigger than this thought. 4) God guides everything.

4. Listen to uplifting materials and read elevating books

Don't: indulge in input that drags you down.

Why not? It perpetuates low-mindedness.

Do: bathe your mind and senses in input that leaves you positive, optimistic and at peace.

Why? To elevate the way you think.

Example: I listen to inspiring tapes and CDs every evening as I go to sleep. It reminds me to see beyond the illusions of the world and think beyond the limits of my mental conditioning. That reinforces an elevated way of thinking at a very impressionable time.

Make your head a comfortable place to live

Check your attitude. What's the environment like in your head? Would you leave a small child alone in your head? (Metaphorically speaking.) Do you need to clean up your mental neighborhood?

You clean up your mental neighborhood one thought at a time, one book at a time and one affirmation at a time. Elevate your thinking to elevate your speaking.

"Do be a Do-Bee"

Skill #34: Turn your negatives into positives (that get results)

Magic words

Imagine your life if every word you said manifested. Boy, would you ever pick your words with care! You sure wouldn't say things like "I wish you were dead," "You'll never amount to anything," or "That's a dress to die for." (I hope not, anyway…) If every word became reality, you couldn't afford to be negative.

Here's a News Flash: even though the laws of manifestation are more abstract than what I described in the paragraph above, you still can't afford to be negative. You might not strike anyone dead with your words, but your words still have impact. You and your listeners record every word you say, even if just unconsciously. Be careful what you invoke. You just might get it.

Don't do don't

But wait—there's more. When you negate something, you actually invoke it.

Let's test that assertion. Don't think of an elephant.

You just thought of an elephant, didn't cha? You missed the 'don't' and heard the elephant and did the very thing I told you not to do.

No, you're not being ornery. It's not your fault. When you hear the word elephant, you naturally think of one.

Okay, we'll survive. There are worse things than thinking of elephants…

Consider what my husband said to my son David as he left for a motorcycle ride: "Don't get killed." Take away the 'don't', and what have you got? A suggestion I would prefer my son's subconscious mind not hear. I reinforced the positive intent of the remark by saying: "Be safe."

Do-Bee

It comes down to what my more senior readers and I learned in *Romper Room*. "Do be a Do-Bee. Don't be a Don't Bee." Put the emphasis on the Do-Bee. (Not to be confused with a doobie. If you don't know what a doobie is, good for you…)

I'm not suggesting you go overboard on this. Obviously I'm not advocating eliminating "don't" from your vocabulary. If I was, I would be violating my own advice with my "don't" category in the tips sections. Just be aware of the balance of your words. Put your emphasis on the positive.

Optimists live longer

Negative communicators complain about what's not working, what they don't want and how bad things are. Positive communicators talk about what works, how to fix what isn't working, what they do want, and how to make things better.

It's the difference between a problem and an opportunity, an obstacle and a challenge, a mistake and a learning experience.

I've heard it said that pessimists may be right, but optimists live longer. They're also much nicer to talk to. So turn your negatives into positives and Speak Strong.

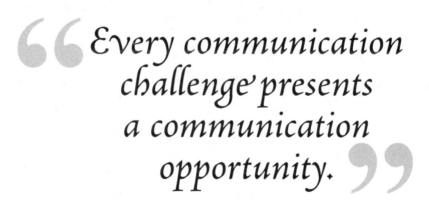

> *Every communication challenge presents a communication opportunity.*
>
> MERYL RUNION

Dos, Don'ts and Tips, Skill # 34
Turn your negatives into positives (that get results)

Don't-Bees are wet blankets

It's the perennial question: is the glass half empty or half full?

Do you want your assistant to stop constantly interrupting with questions, or do you want her to try to find her own answers first before she asks you? Do you want your manager to stop micromanaging or do you want her to start trusting you? Do you want your employees to stop giving vague work estimates or do you want them to give more accurate estimates?

These aren't really either/or questions. Chances are you want both. You're more likely to get what you want if you turn your negatives into positives. Here's how.

1. Track your negatives

Don't: omit negatives that seem unavoidable.

    Why not? 1) It's grist for the mill and 2) You might be surprised how often you can turn a negative into a positive.

Do: write down when you use words like stop, don't, can't, won't and other negatives when you write, speak and listen. (That should keep you busy.)

    Why? To become aware of how often you negate. To collect examples you can work with to develop the skill of turning things around.

Example: If you tell your child that he can't go to a wild party, put that on the list. If you tell your boss you can't get your work by Friday, put that on the list. If you tell your mother you can't afford to fly home for Christmas, put that on the list.

2. Find the positive behind the negative

Don't: worry about wording yet.

    Why not? This is a process. We'll get to that later.

Do: ask what your payoff is for negating.

    Why? You negate in order to create some kind of positive.

Example: You want your kid to pass on the party so he will be safe. You decline your boss' deadline because you know the only way to meet it is to drive yourself and to do a bad job. You prefer to stay home for the holidays because you want to stay within your budget. Sounds positive to me!

3. Look for positives your listeners will value

Don't: focus excessively on the positives for you.

Why not? Others care more about their own interests.

Do: communicate in terms of what others care about.

Why? It takes the sting out of any negation and is more motivating.

Example: Why would your mother benefit by you not flying home for the holidays to stay in budget? Well, in addition to your own financial well-being, it might mean you'll be able to go back to school sooner, and most mothers love it when their kids get more education. If that's true for you, say so.

4. Rephrase your tracked negatives into positives

Don't: expect to be able to express every idea or desire affirmatively.

Why not? At times you'll need to detail what's wrong.

Do: seek a positive rewording of every negative.

Why? To find the positive value behind the negative.

PowerPhrase/What to Say:

• I have committed to stay in budget this year, and that means staying here for Christmas. If I keep within my budget I'll be able to get my credit cards paid down by next fall and start saving for grad school.

• I want to keep you safe.

• I want to do a great job for you, and a Friday deadline won't allow that.

5. Determine if you need to include negation in your communication

Don't: sacrifice clarity for positivity.

Why not? At times you need to detail what's wrong.

Do: speak about the positive if possible (what you want/can affirm), and speak about the negative (what you don't want/denounce) if you must.

Why? To make your point in as positive a way as possible.

Example: I want you to be safe, and a party with older kids doesn't seem safe. I won't let you go, but I will…

What would you rather have?

Many years ago, I received counseling that highlighted a lot of my flaws. After some years of that, I went to a different kind of counselor who asked me the simple question, "what would you rather have?" Every time I pointed out one of my limitations, she encouraged me to turn it around into what I wanted. I learned two very interesting lessons from that. The first lesson was how challenging it is to turn negatives into positives. The second was how rewarding it is.

If wishes were horses, beggars would ride

Skill #35: Express positive realism (not delusional fantasy)

Jenny, the magical thinker

"What's going on with your headaches?" Monty asked.

"I don't want to talk about it," Jenny responded. Monty was taken aback. He was a nurse practitioner, Jenny was his patient and she was in for a check-up. Or at least she was supposed to be in for a check-up.

"Why don't you want to talk about it?" Monty asked.

"I don't want to put any energy into it," she replied. "I just saw the movie *The Secret* about manifesting what you want, and I don't want to put my attention on negative things."

Monty resisted the temptation to roll his eyes, took a deep breath and asked, "Okay—what can we do to improve on your health today?"

"I'd like my head to be pain-free," Jenny replied.

Cynthia, another magical thinker

"I'm marrying Mick," Cynthia told me. My heart sank.

"Why?" I asked. "He doesn't treat you well."

"That's because I've been resisting him. He'll treat me better once we're married."

Joe, yet another magical thinker

"We're launching the website on Friday," Joe said.

"Are you sure the shopping cart will be ready?" Richard asked.

"Nathan promised me it would," Joe answered.

"But Nathan hasn't met a single deadline on this project yet," Richard countered.

"Don't be so negative," Joe scolded. "He said he would. People change."

Don't kid yourself
The positive realist

Positive realism is not the same as delusional fantasy. Wanting something to be so doesn't make it so. Picturing something happening and ignoring evidence that it won't doesn't get results. If wishes were horses, beggars would ride. They aren't and they don't.

The positive realist sees things as they are AND as they could be. Based on what they want, they take the necessary actions to promote the best outcome. The positive realist knows the glass is half full AND half empty. The positive realist doesn't suggest that the glass will magically fill itself. He/she enjoys the half glass and/or takes action to fill the glass, pitcher or even a reservoir.

Check your attitude. Is it negative, delusional fantasy, or positively realistic? Your attitude affects your word choice.

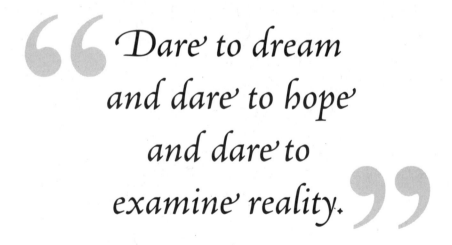

Dare to dream and dare to hope and dare to examine reality.

MERYL RUNION

Dos, Don'ts and Tips, Skill # 35
Express positive realism (not delusional fantasy)

Get smart, get real and get positive

If you think being real and being positive are mutually exclusive, you would be wrong. There is a fine and important distinction between realism and cynicism. There also is a fine and important distinction between positivity and delusion. So — get real, positive and smart. Here's how.

1. Apply the Serenity Prayer

Don't: think the Serenity prayer is sectarian.

Why not? The wisdom is universal.

Do: accept the things you cannot change, change the things you can and develop the wisdom to know the difference.

Why? That's positive realism.

Example: Mindy thought Clarence should be fired and management agreed, but they were afraid he'd sue. Once Mindy accepted that Clarence was there to stay, she adapted to having him in the office. She started CCing people on her emails to him in order to put her requests on record. She got her own fax machine so she didn't have to count on Clarence to deliver her faxes to her in a timely way. She created a drop-off box outside her office so she didn't have to interact with Clarence when he made deliveries. While other people in her office kept complaining about Clarence still having his job, Mindy accepted the things she couldn't change, and changed the things she could.

2. Test the limits of what's possible

Don't: accept that you can't change something without making a clear effort.

Why not? It's defeatist

Do: look for reasons and ways that things can work before you look for obstacles.

Why? To gain "the wisdom to know the difference" between what you can and can't change.

Example: The long-standing employees "accepted" that they couldn't get the company to upgrade the operating system — but no one had actually asked. When David came on board, he thought the argument for changing the operating system was so strong that management would have to make the change once they understood the reasons why. He pitched the idea up three levels

175

before he got the support he sought. He tested the limits of what was possible beyond what his coworkers thought was possible, and made a change.

3. Review with impartiality

Don't: let your desires delude you.

> **Why not?** It's easy to kid yourself into thinking what you want to be possible is.

Do: consider how your words would sound to you if someone else made the same case you are.

> **Why?** To determine whether your positivity is realistic.

Example: Herb wanted to start a multi-level marketing business. He planned how to approach the subject with his wife. He then imagined how he would respond if the tables were turned and his wife told him that she wanted to start a multi-level marketing business. That opened his eyes! After having turned the tables around, he modified his goals to better match what seemed realistic to him.

4. Drop your complaints about things you can't change

Don't: complain about things you can't change.

> **Why not?** It's a waste of time, and negative.

Do: catch yourself when you complain about things you can't change, and reinvest your energy into acceptance or what you can change.

> **Why?** To direct your energy in ways that get results.

Example: After three years of nagging her cube-mate to clean his desk, Fawn decided she was wasting her energy. She angled her desk slightly (she couldn't move it more than a little) so she didn't see his desk as readily.

Sweet serenity

There's nothing quite like serenity. The path to serenity is contained in the Serenity Prayer — have the strength to accept the things you cannot change, the courage to change the things you can, and develop the wisdom to know the difference. Check your attitude and Speak Strong — from a serene platform.

Speak softly enough for them to hear you

Skill #36: Embrace true power

Unexpected power

Yolanda is one powerful lady. You might not notice at first glance. The room doesn't light up when she walks into it. She's not the life of the party. She doesn't have an impressive title. But if you want something done, Yolanda can make it happen. Yolanda doesn't make excessive demands, but when she does ask for something, she gets it. Yolanda doesn't get aggressive, but she is quite willing to assert herself. Yolanda is short on show, but she is long on results.

Covert clout

Yolanda's power flies under the radar, but it's there when she needs it. She builds and exercises five kinds of clout.

Yolanda has personal power. You can't yank Yolanda's chain, ruffle her feathers or get under her skin. She knows who she is and she upholds her own value. She takes care of herself and stays in balance. You won't see her in an emotional display — except for the occasional incident where she deems it appropriate, effective and prudent to let it fly.

Yolanda has knowledge power. She's a life-long learner who constantly expands and develops her skills. She completes her computer tutorials, reads the policy and procedures manuals (really!) and listens to her managers and colleagues, not just to support them, but to learn everything she can. As a result, she has become the go-to person for her department and in many ways, her organization.

Yolanda has vision power. She has a career plan to guide her, and she follows it. Her career plan is integrated with her organizational and departmental mission. She helps her colleagues see their day-to-day activities in terms of their long term plans. Yolanda's vision guides her and inspires others. She comes across as high-minded — because she is.

Yolanda has people power. She takes care of her employees, employers and colleagues as she would her best of friends. She celebrates their achievements, takes a genuine interest in their progress and helps them make things happen. People like Yolanda, and they value their relationships with her. They feel good about supporting her.

Yolanda has persistence power. She knocks on doors until she finds the one that opens. She gives things time to work. She succeeds when others fail because she's more committed than they are. She doesn't need to win her argument TODAY, she doesn't need to persuade you TODAY and she doesn't need to get what she wants TODAY. She's not about immediate gratification. She knows it takes time to build things of value, and she is willing to do what it takes, even if what it takes is time.

True power is worth having

If you see parents scream at their kids, managers threaten their employees or customers badgering cashiers, you are probably seeing someone who doesn't have real power. Yolanda has true power. It's not power over anyone. It's not control of anyone. It's not power she took. It's a power with others, a power of influence, and a power freely given to her. Take a cue from Yolanda and embrace your true power. That's the kind of power that enables you to say what you mean and mean what you say without being mean when you say it.

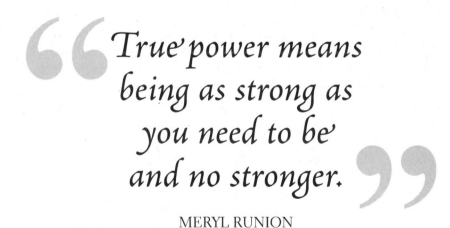

True power means being as strong as you need to be and no stronger.

MERYL RUNION

Dos, Don'ts and Tips, Skill # 36
Embrace true power

Competence, capacity, control and clout
What is true power?

Search the word "power" on thesaurus.com and the first definition you'll find is competence. The second is capacity. The third is control. I like the first two definitions, and I like the third definition as long as the control is self-control. Here are some tips to help you develop clout and embrace your true power.

1. Become unflappable
Don't: confuse a strong reaction with power.

Why not? If someone can provoke you, they have power over you.

Do: master your own emotions, reactions and choices.

Why? Power begins at home — with you personally. If you allow people to upset you emotionally, pull you off your center and provoke behavior that is outside your better judgment, you're powerless.

Example: When the opening keynote speaker cancelled an hour before the conference, Misty's colleagues argued about who was to blame and fretted over what a disaster it would be. Misty calmly suggested they bump the closing keynote speaker to the opening to give them time to locate a replacement. They found an inspiring speaker from the attendees list who was able to close the conference successfully.

2. Commit to life-long learning
Don't: think you're done learning just because you finished school.

Why not? You'll become irrelevant — not powerful.

Do: read at least a half hour each day, explore developments in your field, take your tutorials and otherwise be a continuous learner. Then, share your knowledge to help others achieve their objectives.

Why? Most people don't actively improve their skills. If *you* do, you'll have an advantage. If you don't, younger people will usurp your influence.

Example: Randy became a self-taught web developer while working as an assistant. After months of developing his skills, his boss mentioned his plans to hire an outside vendor for a website redesign. Randy raised concerns about necessary safeguards for a site transfer. The boss was impressed and asked Randy to take charge of the redesign. Randy became his boss' authority on web development.

3. Be a visionary

Don't: limit yourself to the confines of other people's thinking, what has already been done, and what's wrong.

> **Why not?** Powerful people spend more time talking about possibilities than limitations.

Do: consider and communicate new perspectives, things as they could be, and possibilities.

> **Why?** It will elevate every conversation to the broader context.

Example: I interviewed several publicists for my book launch and hired the one who understood and addressed my vision. She saw what I had, saw what it could turn into and convinced me she was the one who would make it happen.

4. Curry favor

Don't: think it's unethical or "sucking up" to seek to win the hearts, minds and support of colleagues and supervisors.

> **Why not?** It's only unethical if you are insincere in your efforts.

Do: deliberately speak to build alliances, connect and bond.

> **Why?** People like to support people who support them.

Example: When Jena needs copies, she asks her colleagues if they need some. It doesn't take her much longer to make copies for her colleagues along with her own, and it predisposes them to want to do things for her. That adds to her power. Jena also takes every opportunity to acknowledge her colleagues directly and to others — especially to people in power. That creates trust. She also makes notes of important events in people's lives and acknowledges them. That creates a personal connection.

5. Practice patience

Don't: think you need to win every battle.

> **Why not?** The battle you win could cost you a war.

Do: consider long term objectives when choosing what to say.

> **Why?** True power is built over time.

Example #1: Bernie treated everyone with respect — including the janitor at his company. Imagine his surprise years later when he went for an interview for a job he wanted, and the HR Director was the former janitor. The Director said, "I know you. You're in."

Example #2: Grace had a three point plan that she thought would enhance interdepartmental communication. Her boss agreed, but then dealt her a blow by suggesting someone else implement it. Grace stared to resist, but backed off when she realized what a win it was that her boss heard her idea and was willing to implement it. It was one step of many toward positioning herself for success at work.

True power means being as strong as you need to be and no stronger

Melissa learned about power from her teenage son. When she yelled at her son, he said: "Mama, the louder you talk, the less I hear." That phrase captures the essence of true power. It's not about throwing your weight around and making a lot of noise. It's about getting results. Go for true power. It's the foundation of Speaking Strong.

The louder you talk, the less they hear.

MERYL RUNION

> " *Don't have a knee-jerk reaction to knee-jerk reactions.* "

MERYL RUNION

Nice girls (and boys) don't

Skill #37: Assert yourself (without inviting one of the "B" labels)

Is there a double standard for communication that penalizes women?

My Fair Lady has a song that asks: "Why can't a woman be more like a man?" Well…it might be because when she is, she is disparaged for it. Are the communication cards stacked against women?

Think about it. You've heard this…"What do you call a man who takes a stand? Strong. What do you call a woman who takes a stand? Well…it starts with B and rhymes with itch."

If that's true, what's a girl to do?

Sure, men have a B label too. But clearly the itchy label women contend with is more pervasive and damaging. Women often speak out at their own peril because they risk being evaluated more harshly than men for strong words.

Of course, the power structure is changing, and even without this shift, there are exceptions to every rule. For example, minorities and non-alpha males often find themselves faced with a double standard too. And some alpha females are members of the Good Old Boys Club (GOBC) or might as well be.

You know better than I do whether your assertiveness is condemned as aggression. You know whether you're a member of a GOBC, which allows stronger expression, or are a non-GOBC'er, who is held to a higher standard of assertion.

If you think this double standard is not an issue for you, bookmark this page. Regardless of gender, you might come face to face with a GOBC you didn't know existed until you crossed it. I did.

I encounter the club — and not as a member

The Good Old Boys Club was something of a legend to me until I met it face to face in 2002. The legend became reality when a vendor I used had over-promised and seriously under-delivered. I heard he was speaking at a conference and I wondered if he would mention his work with me in his presentation. He did. He took credit for results he had nothing to do with, and when he ran out of those, he invented successes that never happened. His claims sounded like his original promises and they sounded like what I had paid him to do. But his claims did not resemble what he actually did for me.

I called the vendor to complain about falsely representing his work for me. He accused me of "ragging on him." If he wouldn't even acknowledge the offense, I figured he was likely to repeat it in the future. I raised the issue to the meeting planner who had arranged for him to speak. The meeting planner threatened me, and implied that I complained because I was a bitter former client taking revenge by trying to "destroy a man's career." I raised the issue to the association president. The association president did acknowledge the egregiousness of the offence, (I am grateful for that much) but recommended I let it go.

The vendor, meeting planner and association president were male, knew each other and protected each other. They circled the wagons to protect their own.

During the process, I sought support from female friends who were association members. I was stunned by the contrast in how my female colleagues responded. They gasped, groaned and…sighed with recognition. They had been down roads like mine before. They too had come face to face with the Good Old Boys Club.

While my relationships with men are overwhelmingly positive, I realized in 2002 that the Good Old Boys Club isn't an urban legend. It helps to know what you're up against. And if the GOBC you face has some women in it, the dynamics are the same, and the tips every bit as helpful.

> " *The Good Old Boys Club doesn't willingly surrender power because it's the right thing to do. The good news is you don't need them to. You have sources of power they haven't dreamed of.* "
>
> MERYL RUNION

Dos, Don'ts and Tips, Skill # 37
Assert yourself (without inviting one of the "B" labels)

Here's how you can be an assertive woman (or an assertive non-alpha man)…
without inviting a label.

1. Differentiate between resistance to strength and legitimate issues
Don't: assume gender issues.
> **Why not?** Even though the term "b%^#*" has obvious gender connotations, the person who uses the term might be objecting to not getting what they want, rather than objecting to a strong woman.

Do: consider if the resistance you experience might have less to do with your gender and more to do with the issue.
> **Why?** If you know what you're dealing with, you can respond more appropriately.

Example: Janie complained that Kyle employee resisted her management because she was female. The fact was, he objected because she didn't understand his job description, and she gave him inappropriate and ill-advised assignments. If Kyle prioritized her assignments the way she wanted him to, important projects would fail and he would fall short at the performance review.

Janie's assumption kept her from dealing with the genuine issues.

2. Consider possible differences in how you show strength and how the most effective men (or women) show it
Don't: think toughness or emotional displays equate with power.
> **Why not?** The more powerful you are, the more likely it is you won't have to put your strength on display.

Do: scan your communication for victim language, overkill or uncontrolled emotional undertones.
> **Why?** Effective men (and women) *tend* to be calm and composed about setting boundaries or asserting themselves. That ease sidesteps unnecessary resistance or gaming.

Example: When I first started my career as a trainer, I was more strident and forceful than I eventually became. Once I became more confident in my effectiveness, I backed my tone down a bit — and got more powerful results.

3. Explore your sensitivity to gender labels
Don't: let gender labels provoke or trigger you.
> **Why not?** You lose your footing and react instead of respond.

Do: notice when gender labels take you out of power and into reaction. Learn to stay calm.

Why? If someone can push your buttons with gender slurs, they have control. Awareness will keep the reins in your own hands.

Example: Rob used gender slurs to get Debbie to back down. For a while she tiptoed around him to avoid his labels. Once she had enough, she decided to stop letting herself be manipulated that way. She called him on his gender slurs and prepared phrases to repeat mentally when Rob went on the attack. Those phrases helped her to be able to respond instead of react.

4. Stop personalizing others' reactions and opinions

Don't: assume if someone objects to your behavior it's your problem.

Why not? People are responsible for their own reactions and opinions.

Do: speak according to your own communication standards and let the chips land where they will.

Why? You limit your own power when you take responsibility for others' reactions.

Example: Liz's husband was raised by a controlling mother, and Liz made a point of not being like her. She backed off at her husband's first implication that she was dominating.

Eventually she decided his interpretation of her assertion wasn't her problem. She stopped tiptoeing around his gender-based accusations.

5. Search your communication for undetected aggression

Don't: assume all gender labels really are about gender.

Why not? The accusations might have some kind of non-gender-based foundation.

Do: monitor what you say for aggression you're not aware of.

Why? To see if you play a gender card without realizing it. To see if you ignore inappropriate aggression in your own behavior.

Example: Tammi thought her board had gender issues with her until she watched a video that showed how aggressive she truly appeared.

Tammi's own frustration aggravated her aggressive stance. She had been a victim of gender bias in the past which left her hypersensitive in the present.

6. Embrace and celebrate assertiveness in other women

Don't: expect people to embrace assertiveness in you that you reject in other women.

Why not? Women need to be in it together to bust gender discrimination.

Do: make sure you don't display the same bias you complain of.

Why? To pave the way for others—and yourself—in the future.

Example: When I was in the 5th grade, I ran for VP of the Student Council. Had I won, I would have been the first girl to hold that position. I lost by one vote. That was highly ironic because I voted for the boy who ran for President instead of the girl...because "boys make better leaders." The girl who ran for Student Body President also lost by one vote. (I'm over that kind of discrimination now.)

7. Get mentored

Don't: try to make it up on your own.

> **Why not?** It's like raising yourself up by your bootstraps.

Do: find a strong woman to mentor you—one who has found her way.

> **Why?** She can show you what it looks like, sounds like and feels like to be an empowered woman (or minority.)

Example: Women's networking groups are flourishing in the US in recent years as women help each other to become strong in business.

8. Adjust expectations by educating and moving on

Don't: blast people or judge too harshly for displays of sexism.

> **Why not?** It will polarize conversations. Attitudes are unconscious and people often don't know what they're doing.

Do: educate offenders about the bias they display and move on.

> **Why?** To give them the skills rather than complaining that they don't have them.

PowerPhrase/What to say: Are you aware of how that remark sounds to women?

Poison Phrase/What NOT to say: You're a biased SOB to suggest that.

Redefine the B labels

If you follow these steps, you still might be called the "B" name, but you won't be inviting it. And once you're standing your ground, you just might find the sting goes away from the labels.

I once told a therapist that my boyfriend accused me of being controlling. The therapist noted, "It sounds to me like he doesn't want you to be in control of yourself, because he wants to be in control of you." That fascinating observation desensitized me to the "controlling" label. It also provided me with a foundation to appreciate Oprah's definition of the "B" word. She calls it: **B**eing **I**n **T**otal **C**ontrol of **H**erself.

By that definition, I say, go for it!

*Let your words
build bridges,
not barriers.*

MERYL RUNION

If I smile while I stick a knife in your back, will you still like me?

Skill #38: Purge passive-aggressive habits

A spoonful of sugar

Cheerful viciousness. Lipstick on a pig. Passive-aggression. A spoonful of sugar just might make the medicine go down. Sweetness might make poison go down too. It may even go down "in the most delightful way." But it's still medicine and it's still poison, and no matter how good it tastes, you should think long and hard before you dish it out or swallow it.

When you hide an unpleasant dig in a joke, you're being passive-aggressive. When you land a hit and run attack, you're being passive-aggressive. When you smile while you stick the knife in someone's back while hoping they feel the pain but don't notice where it came from, you're being passive-aggressive.

If you act like you're "helping," but create more work so they don't ask for your help again, you're being passive-aggressive. If you give someone the manual they asked for but deliberately "forget" to provide the password, you're being passive-aggressive. If you offer a lame excuse for being late (again) and act offended when someone lets you know your lateness is an issue, you're being passive-aggressive. If you tell someone you love their hair and ask if they cut it themselves, you're being passive-aggressive.

Passive-aggression can be subtle

Barbara uses passive-aggressive communication. She's a very sweet woman, and you probably wouldn't think of her as passive-aggressive. But if you hurt her feelings, she won't tell you. She'll just stop returning your calls or suddenly be less personal than she had been.

Randy uses passive-aggressive communication. He's a very dear soul and you probably wouldn't imagine him that way. But when his wife didn't put things away in the exact place he wanted them, he hid them where she wouldn't be able to find them.

David is passive-aggressive. When his sister didn't understand his instructions about how a computer software program worked, he expressed his irritation with sarcasm.

A disguised attack is still an attack

I'm a recovering passive-aggressive. I still occasionally catch myself landing a side swipe or veiled attack. Not often, but it happens. And I understand why and how people justify passive-aggressive behaviors. After all, if you think someone is way out of line to expect your help, it's easy to justify putting forth a half-hearted effort. If the person you shared your manual with should have created their own, it's easy to justify sabotaging their efforts to use yours. Basically, if you believe that someone deserves to be clobbered, and you merely inconvenience them…if you want to attack someone in a full frontal assault but you merely land a side punch…if you're pulling the punch you want to give…it's easy to excuse yourself for being passive-aggressive.

And if you do excuse passive-aggressive behavior, you cut yourself off from your true power.

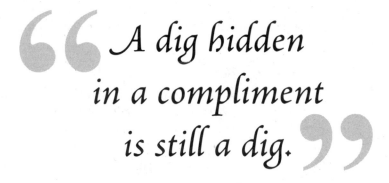

> *A dig hidden in a compliment is still a dig.*

MERYL RUNION

Dos, Don'ts and Tips, Skill # 38
Purge passive-aggressive habits

Changing habits
If you have passive-aggressive habits, take steps to purge them.

Of course, if you read my earlier chapters, you'll already know how to begin. Chapter 31 provides tools for changing habits. You can apply those guidelines to passive-aggressive behavior.

But to save you time and for the sake of clarity, I'll provide the steps here.

1. Give up your excuses
Don't: think passive-aggression is noble, justifiable or inevitable.
> **Why not?** That belief will keep you excusing a weaker behavior.

Do: use your temptation to be passive-aggressive as a signal you need to be assertive.
> **Why?** If you don't allow yourself to be passive-aggressive, you will be forced to find more honest and constructive ways to communicate.

Example: Lisa used sarcasm with her colleagues. When her manager confronted her about her sarcasm, Lisa said it was innocent humor. When her manager challenged that excuse, Lisa suggested that sarcasm was the only way she could make her point without triggering people. When her manager challenged that excuse, Lisa said her colleagues deserved much worse and she was being kind. Finally, Lisa gave up her excuses and acknowledged that her sarcasm was a coward's aggression. Lisa agreed to learn assertiveness.

2. Set boundaries
Don't: invent boundaries and limits as you go along.
> **Why not?** You won't recognize violations as they happen, so you'll be less likely to address them. If you don't address violations on the spot, chances are you'll either not address them at all or will do it indirectly.

Do: set boundaries of what you will and won't do, and what you will or won't accept.
> **Why?** Your clarity will allow you to be assertive with others on the spot.

Example: Pam's colleague Dave consistently wiggled out of commitments. His unreliability angered her, and she reacted by shutting down to subtly punish him. Pam decided to set a boundary of expecting people to honor their commitments to her and to speak up when they didn't.

Dave tested her resolve by turning in a report with numerous errors. In the past, Pam would have fixed the errors herself and behaved coldly toward Dave in the days to come. Instead, Pam returned the report to him and asked him to rework it himself. The conversation was uncomfortable, but she felt clear afterwards and did not feel a need to punish him.

3. Make it safe to talk to you

Don't: be threatening and/or invite someone to talk with you and then attack them for telling you the truth.

Why not? You need to make it safe to be direct.

Do: stay calm and create safety.

Why? You'll get more truth and reduce the need for indirect expression.

Example: Dave agreed to correct the errors, but explained to Pam that he believed part of the report was actually her responsibility. They were able to work out solutions.

4. Be honest

Don't: allow yourself to avoid truth with indirectness.

Why not? Indirectness gives the illusion of having addressed an issue.

Do: say what you mean and mean what you say without being mean when you say it.

Why? Telling the truth is the antidote to passive-aggressive behavior.

Example: Pam started by telling the truth to herself. She really wasn't okay about taking her time to correct Dave's sloppy work. She was uncomfortable admitting that, but she knew if she didn't admit it, her frustration would come out indirectly.

Go direct

It's time to come out of hiding and go direct. Drop passive-aggressive behavior. Once it's gone, you'll be amazed at how powerful you become. You might be scared of your own power, but eventually it will inspire you. It will inspire others, too.

You're with me or you're against me

Skill #39: Be a uniter, not a divider

I never set out to be a diversity trainer. I'm a communication trainer and I include the topic of communication between diverse groups as part of my training. The HR director on an army base liked what I did. So they hired me for intergenerational training. I called my seminar: *Walk in My Generation's Shoes.*

Generational training, like other kinds of diversity training, aims at uniting dissimilar groups. Unfortunately, the training doesn't always work that way.

Insults, injury and targets
I broke my seminar class into generational groups, and had each group discuss their shared generational experiences. Each group then addressed the class as a whole.

The discussion was lively and insightful, but when the Boomers shared their issues with their younger coworkers, the discussion heated up. The Boomers laid the issues a little too bare. It wasn't just the neutral "this is what's not working, so how can we resolve this?" discussion I had sought to initiate. It turned into: "this is what's wrong with you and your kind." We got through it, but some residual discomfort remained. I left wondering — does it have to be like this? Can't we lay ourselves bare without targeting each other?

My evaluations were as mixed as my own feelings about the day. They were positive overall, and people found the training useful, but clearly the less-than-gracious exchanges left some scars. The younger employees felt particularly targeted — and they had been.

If I thought I was bad...
As part of my quest for a better approach, I attended an intergenerational training session presented by another trainer whom I'll call Curt. I wanted to see if Curt had found the key to address hot-button issues without exploding land mines. He hadn't.

Like me, Curt broke his class into small groups for dialogue according to their generation. (He thereby destroyed my illusions about the uniqueness of my methods.) While I had my groups address several questions in my training, Curt simply instructed the groups to list the things they liked and didn't like about other generations. I joined my Boomer group and learned a lot about how not to structure discussions.

My Boomer group was lively and pleasant, but when we started to put our elders and juniors into the + and - column, there was a distinct shift in demeanor. It was as if someone had taken my good-natured colleagues and replaced them with hostile variations of themselves. They turned into fault-finding machines — in others — and self-congratulating machines — toward themselves. The younger generations bore the greatest brunt of the critical focus.

Curt had each group present their results to the class as a whole. Each group highlighted the flaws of the others.

People did enjoy the training, but a young woman told me later she thought her generation was picked-on. She was right.

Curt tapped into generational animosity. It was a lively time, but it divided more than united. People enjoyed airing their grievances, but the format burned bridges instead of building them.

Learn from someone else's mistakes

I learned from my own errors, and I learned even more from Curt's mistakes. I restructured my diversity training, and my subsequent sessions were unifying, not divisive.

I figured out how to be a uniter, not a divider. Read on, and learn from my mistakes, just like I learned from Curt's.

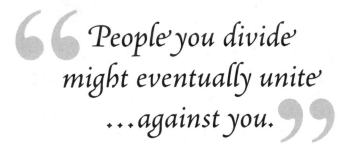

> ❝ *People you divide*
> *might eventually unite*
> *...against you.* ❞
>
> MERYL RUNION

Dos, Don'ts and Tips, Skill # 39
Be a uniter, not a divider

"Divide and conquer" works...but at what price?

Sure, you can create factions and fuel divisions and disempower others and stir people up and manipulate them. And it might work as long as you can maintain control. Lose control, and all that divisiveness you stirred up could be redirected at you.

Being a uniter takes greater skill, but doesn't have the same risks. It takes more savvy to motivate through understanding than to polarize. But if you develop that skill, you can harness the full power of people working together, not the tenuous power of factions.

Here are some tips for you.

1. Think and talk "we," not you and me
Don't: emphasize distinctions and differences to the exclusion of similarities.
   Why not? That makes the walls appear less penetrable than they are.
Do: speak about being in different parts of the same boat.
   Why? It gets you thinking as a team.
Example: Rachael is Larry's assistant. Larry often leaves without letting her know when he'll be back. That makes Rachael sound uninformed and incompetent when people call.

Instead of complaining about how inconsiderate Larry is, how his being the boss doesn't entitle him to be dismissive of her or how she has needs too, Rachael spoke of their need to function and present as a team. Her team-talk united them. Had she spoken in terms of "you and me," it would have framed them as being in opposition to each other. In fact, their individual success depended on mutual cooperation.

2. Explore with an open mind
Don't: jump to conclusions.
   Why not? Quick conclusions come from being entrenched in your own perspective. Until you can walk in their shoes, you don't have the full story.
Do: be curious. Listen, learn, consider and explore.
   Why? People like people who show interest. It draws them in and...unites you.

Example: Ollie discovered that her new friend hunts. Although Ollie is very opposed to hunting, she restrained her condemnation and asked questions to learn about her friend's hobby. Ollie learned a lot about her friend's sport and actually discovered that her friend was more humane than she had imagined. Ollie has no plans to become a hunter herself. But she left the discussion far more informed and less judgmental than she started.

3. Lose the labels

Don't: refer to people in different groups or with different beliefs using language or labels they wouldn't apply to themselves.

> **Why not?** It's dismissive to be so ignorant of cultures you define them in ways that disregard how they define themselves.

Do: err on the side of caution when you apply labels and characterizations.

> **Why?** To avoid landmines and unintended insults, and to stay open to others.

Example: It bothers Michelle when her boss refers to her as Oriental. Michelle prefers the word Asian, and is insulted that her boss hadn't taken the time to figure out how she likes him to refer to her.

4. Speak of common goals

Don't: let the trees blind you to the forest.

> **Why not?** You'll overlook the common ground that can unite you and get you working cooperatively.

Do: seek out shared goals and desires and emphasize those.

> **Why?** It gets you moving forward and working together.

Example: Kelly and Ray argued over policies for their child welfare agency. Kelly paused and said, "I'd like to take a step back and remember that we both want to serve the best interests of the kids who come here. We just have different ideas about how to do that. Do you agree?"

Ray agreed and it helped them to work together.

5. Acknowledge when you learn

Don't: let an insight go unacknowledged.

> **Why not?** People like knowing they've have an impact.

Do: allow others to influence you, and let them know when they do.

> **Why?** It establishes give and take.

Example: The 2008 US Presidential election inspired a lot of discussion about feminism. Randy asked many women how they defined feminism. His interest created bridges and made him popular with the ladies. He also learned a lot he didn't know about women from the experts — women.

6. Avoid binary, "either/or" thinking and speaking

Don't: speak as if there are only two alternatives.

Why not? That ignores differences and forces people into alternatives they might not fit into well.

Do: include shades of gray in your options.

Why? It allows for options and ways of working together.

PowerPhrase/What to Say: I ask you to stay open to what I say, and if you have questions, we can discuss them at the end of my presentation. Then you can decide what's useful to you and what isn't.

Poison Phrase/What NOT to say: You either believe me or you don't. You trust me or you doubt me. You're with me or you're against me.

It's all about us

Years ago I watched a hilarious episode of *Malcolm in the Middle* where Malcolm's younger brother managed to get everyone around him fighting, while coming across as innocent himself. Eventually people caught on, and became unified…against him.

Divide-and-conquer tactics work for a while, but unite-and-concur leads to a more stable and lasting success.

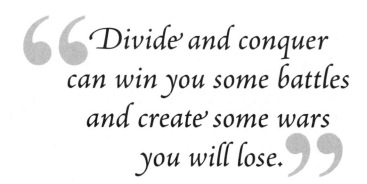

> **Divide and conquer can win you some battles and create some wars you will lose.**
>
> MERYL RUNION

" *Just say it.* "

MERYL RUNION

Pay no attention to the man behind the curtain

Skill #40: Drop the distractions and the deceptions

Toto blows Oz's cover

Remember the Wizard of Oz? He hid behind a curtain and inspired awe by projecting a grand video image of himself that he claimed was him. It took a tiny dog named Toto to blow his cover. The exposed Oz tried to get everyone to ignore what their eyes told them and to "pay no attention to the man behind the curtain." Oz sought to distract his visitors so they wouldn't see the truth of who he was.

Of course, the humble man behind the curtain turned out to be more effective than the scary manufactured Oz. And chances are excellent that if you drop your own deceptions and distractions, you'll be more powerful too. I think of a recent presidential election where it sure seemed to me that some candidates were more concerned with image than reality. Sometimes it works but recently those efforts failed.

If you think who you are is not enough, you might be tempted to create a distraction so no one will see you as you are. That's no way to run Oz, an election or a life. It's also no way to Speak Strong.

Misdirection

Magicians use sleight of hand to hide their tricks. They create a distraction to draw the attention away from the trick itself. The trick takes place right in front of the audience's eyes, but they miss it because they're paying attention to what the magician wants them to.

A pick pocket does the same thing. (As do politicians, of course.)

Here are a few tools in a communication mis-director's toolbox. They talk about things that don't matter, they express false outrage and they turn the tables to control conversations and to deceive. If the mis-director is smooth, the listener doesn't know he…or she…has been fooled again.

Like Barbara, who gets fooled every time her boss changes the subject when she tries to talk about a promotion. She realizes it later when she reflects on their conversation.

And Grace, who tries to address her employee Gary's lateness and finds herself promising him more supplies and agreeing to reassign one of his clients.

She's back in her office before she notices the conversation about lateness never took place.

Or Sandy, who watches the news and learns all about what celebrities are up to without wondering if there is something going on in the world besides actors going on trial.

Or Sam, who kept meaning to ask about the radiator on the used car he was buying, but ended up buying it without ever asking the question. He did have some great conversations about the fabulous paint job.

You probably distract and detour in your conversations too. Let's go over a few distraction techniques and see which ones you employ.

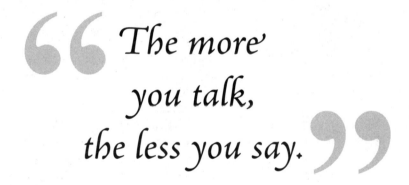

> **"The more you talk, the less you say."**
>
> MERYL RUNION

Dos, Don'ts and Tips, Skill # 40
Drop the distractions and the deceptions

Ditch distractions

Get that beam out of your own eye first. End your own distractive communication habits before you tackle the other guy's behaviors. Not that it's easy to do that. It's amazing how hard it can be and how long it can take to end a distraction habit. Once you get a handle on how often you "pull an Oz," you can speak up when someone tries to "pull an Oz" on you.

Here are some pointers to break your own distraction habits.

1. Listen first

Don't: switch the topic from them and their issue to you and yours until you (and they) know you've heard them.

> **Why not?** Changing the subject is a major distraction technique.

Do: be willing to talk about their perspectives and issues first.

> **Why?** To be sure you don't create distractions to avoid hearing what they have to say.

PowerPhrase/What to Say: That reminds me of something I need to discuss with you, but I want to stay focused on your concerns first.

Poison Phrase/What NOT to say: Yeah, but you…

2. Be open to their perspective

Don't: assume you already know everything.

> **Why not?** That assumption makes a great excuse to block and distract.

Do: encourage and make it safe for people to initiate crucial conversations.

> **Why?** To foster openness and honesty.

PowerPhrase/What to Say: If that's important to you, let's discuss it.

Poison Phrase/What NOT to say: Let's not talk about that.

3. Ask yourself: "Are we talking about the real issues here?"

Don't: talk around an issue.

> **Why not?** Hints don't substitute for directness.

Do: review to ensure you keep the true focus.

> **Why?** To keep you from kidding yourself about your honesty level.

Example: Danny argued with Renee about her wording when she asked him a question. Renee started to quote exactly what she had said, but she stopped herself. She realized her wording wasn't the issue. The issue was the fact that she felt unsafe asking questions. Arguing over details distracted her from the real issue. She redirected the conversation to the crucial conversation.

4. Be willing to be vulnerable

Don't: go for comfort.

Why not? Genuine issues are often uncomfortable to discuss.

Do: notice how you protect yourself, and be willing to step out of your comfort zone.

Why? The desire to avoid being vulnerable is a primary motivator for distractive behavior.

PowerPhrase/What to Say: I'm tempted to pretend I'm perfect here, but the reality is I sometimes make mistakes.

Poison Phrase/What NOT to say: If there's a problem, it's your fault.

5. Separate communication strategies from games

Don't: confuse a well thought out strategy with a communication game.

Why not? Strategies help you Speak Strong, games keep you from it.

Do: review strategies to make sure you use them to increase understanding, not decrease it.

Why? Strategies and games can look alike, but they're very different.

Example: If Karen thought her boss was harshly critical of her, she shut down to punish him. He noticed her silence, felt guilty, and tried to make it up to her.

When Karen decided to give up the game, she initially thought that meant she had to address the issue immediately, regardless of circumstance. She later concluded that waiting to respond until she had composed herself wasn't gaming. It also wasn't gaming for her to time her response and wait until her boss had more time to listen. In fact, it was a good communication strategy.

6. Realign your games into strategies

Don't: throw your games out without examining them first.

Why not? You play your games for a reason.

Do: uncover your reasons and equip yourself before you drop your distraction games.

Why? Your games show you where you need to grow.

Example #1: Jennifer was afraid to disagree with Nina. When Nina pressed her to agree, Jennifer changed the subject.

Jennifer decided she wanted to give up that kind of distraction. But before she did it, she figured out how she could word her disagreement to be clear but gentle.

Come out from behind the curtain

When Toto exposed "The Great Oz," the "man behind the curtain" went through a myriad of gyrations to keep his distraction going. He fumbled with levers and knobs and gave the impression of a juggler trying to keep too many balls in the air. Distraction techniques consume a lot of energy.

Like that, your distraction techniques consume a lot of energy. So get rid of your distractions and come out from behind the curtain. You have nothing to lose but an illusion. Give up the games. Strategies are much more fun anyway.

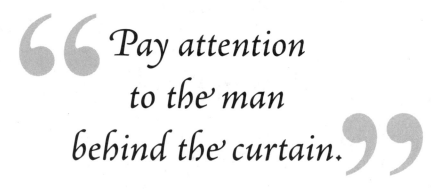

> *Pay attention to the man behind the curtain.*

MERYL RUNION

"Manipulation destroys trust."

MERYL RUNION

Like putty in my hands

Skill #41: Stop manipulating

I walk—and cross—the line

The line between manipulation and skilled communication is so fine that the two can appear identical. That makes this a tough chapter to write. But here we go.

I'll start with definitions. One definition of manipulation is: devious management, especially for one's own advantage. If you're doing that, stop. Another definition is: skillful or artful management. If you're not doing that, start.

This chapter talks about the first definition. And I'll start with a confession. I managed a conversation deviously just last night.

Last night I emailed a friend to tell her I was writing a chapter on manipulation, that I needed an example of manipulative communication, and I hoped she had time to talk on the phone soon. This morning I emailed her again with a confession. I confessed that my request to her was manipulative communication. I really wanted to revisit a discussion we had earlier about a personal issue. I presented one agenda to get her to call, when another agenda really drove my request. My morning email confessed to having had a hidden agenda which amounted to minor manipulation.

You walk the line

How about you? For example, have you ever played stupid or deliberately done a bad job of something so you'd get out of having to do it again? If so, you used devious management for your own advantage—or manipulation. Of course if you really are that dumb or that incompetent, it's not manipulation for you to be your stupid, incompetent self. However, if you faked your stupidity, you manipulated. If you're really good at manipulating, no one will be able to tell the difference. If manipulation is deeply ingrained as your mode of operating, even you won't notice it.

Here's another manipulation example. Have you ever flattered someone to win favors? That's manipulation. But if you shared sincere praise without an agenda, that's not manipulation.

But what if you want something from someone you sincerely respect...because you respect them? Is it manipulation to let them know you're asking this favor out of your respect for them? Nope. It's good communication.

Okay, now we're getting into the finer distinctions. Ken Blanchard's book *The One Minute Manager* suggests supervisors "catch people doing things right." He suggests that when managers systematically acknowledge employees, productivity soars.

If you're a manager and you praise an employee as a management technique, are you manipulating the employee?

Maybe — and maybe not. You could just be practicing smart communication.

So how do you know the difference? Remember the word "devious." It's all about whether you intend to deceive and take advantage of someone's weakness, or are using skill to achieve honest results.

Sounds simple, but in practice, it's easy to fool even yourself. That's why I wrote this chapter.

Dos, Don'ts and Tips, Skill #41
Stop manipulating

The first step to end manipulation is to recognize it. The second is to seek alternatives. Finally, just stop doing it. Let's get started. Here are your tips.

1. Check your willingness to admit to your strategies

Don't: use a communication strategy you'd be afraid to fess up to.

Why not? If you'd be embarrassed for anyone to know how you operate, chances are you're using tactical manipulation, not strategic communication.

Do: use approaches that you're proud to claim—especially to the person you're communicating with.

Why? It's a great test. Most people would not proudly admit to manipulation.

Comment: While I did admit my manipulative effort to my friend as mentioned in the intro to this chapter, I admitted it humbly, not proudly.

Example: Wendy knew that Rod felt guilty about losing her time sheet. She considered referring to it before she asked him for a favor, thinking the reminder would increase the likelihood he would agree. But she stopped herself and asked for the favor without leveling a "guilt trip." She knew that if Rod caught on to her tactic, he would be offended. She saw that as an indication that bringing the time sheet up was manipulative.

2. Make sure your strategies are win-win

Don't: use a communication strategy for unfair advantage.

Why not? If it's unfair, it's manipulation — and perhaps worse — exploitation.

Do: hold the other person's interests at heart.

Why? Might does not make right, and neither does accomplishment through devious methods.

Examples: Misty waited until her boss had her coffee before she asked her for approvals. That was good strategy. Roger waited to ask his boss for approvals until his boss was ready to run out the door, so she wouldn't have time to reflect on the details. Misty's strategy benefited her boss as well as herself. Roger's only benefited himself. Misty used great communication strategy. Roger used tactical manipulation.

3. Check your logic

Don't: use logical fallacies.

  Why not? It's a form of manipulation.

Do: study logic and make sure yours is solid.

  Why? To avoid manipulating by tricking people into thinking things that don't make sense do.

Examples: Ryan asked his employee if she wanted to come in early or stay late. That was a false choice that implied there were only two options. He recognized the flaw in his logic and discovered he was trying to give his employee the appearance of choice in a way that kept her from realizing how many options she really had.

4. Develop skills to get what you want without manipulation

Don't: settle for substandard communication skills.

  Why not? Manipulation is a way to overcome powerlessness. If you have true power, you'll have less temptation to manipulate.

Do: discern why you manipulate and find a better way to accomplish your goals.

  Why? To get results with integrity.

Examples: Ryan used to tell his clients he needed to get the big guy to approve discounts—when there was no big guy who needed to approve anything. He found a way to use discounts as incentives that did not involve lying or manipulation.

5. Be overt

Don't: trick people to satisfy a hidden agenda.

  Why not? It will come back to bite you.

Do: be open about what you want and why.

  Why? The same behavior that is manipulative if you're covert can be non-manipulative when used openly.

Example: Mary wanted Rory to hear her speak at a conference she organized. She also knew Rory was interested in indigenous cultures. So she arranged for a presentation on indigenous cultures right before her own speech. She invited Rory and explained, "I'd like you to hear me speak at the conference and as added incentive, I arranged a talk on indigenous cultures right before mine."

Because Mary's arrangements were out in the open, Rory did not feel manipulated.

6. Develop manipulation-free friendships

Don't: go it alone.

Why not? There are other people who want to purge manipulation from their communication habits too.

Do: develop manipulation-free friendships where you agree to be direct and to admit when you slip.

Why? Supportive environments help you break habits.

Example: In the opening to this skill chapter, I confessed to having asked a friend to call me for one reason when I really wanted her to call me for a different reason.

Manipulation-free zone

There is something wonderfully refreshing and clean about being manipulation-free. Come out of the dark and into the sun, and experience it for yourself.

> " *You can manipulate people into giving you what you want, but you can't manipulate them into respecting you.* "
>
> MERYL RUNION

> *A pit bull
> is influential,
> but poodles
> can win their way
> into your lap*
>
> MERYL RUNION

After all I've done for you …

Skill #42: Get guilt-free in accountability

You made me…

I loved my mom, and she loved me, but that doesn't mean our communication was perfect. I remember many times when she inappropriately exploded at me. I got upset, and she apologized. If it had stopped there, it wouldn't have been highly damaging—but it didn't. After telling me she was sorry, my mother went on to explain that it really wasn't her fault that she came down so hard on me because I had pushed her into it. She compounded the original offense with the guilt of thinking I had forced my mother into behaving so badly. I remember sitting on the bed with tears streaming down my cheeks as my mother admonished me by saying, "I'm sorry but you…" I was in horror over what I had done. Not that I really understood what I had done. My mother packed our bags and took us on a guilt trip. The terrain was ugly.

Guilt: The gift that keeps on giving

If you access someone's guilt, you just might be able to get them jumping through hoops. It sure worked for my mom. I hated feeling guilty, and I did what I could to avoid it. Bosses use guilt, parents use guilt, preachers use guilt, and in fact, some world leaders manipulate entire populations with guilt. Here are some phrases that MIGHT be employed to trigger guilt.—*See what you made me do?—After all I've done for you. — How could you?* And—*Traitor!*

I expect some of you are feeling guilty just from reading those phrases, as if I just called you down for some imagined offense. As master manipulators know, you don't have to BE guilty to FEEL guilty. When master manipulators feel the pain of your guilt, they translate it into opportunity. They lay guilt trips on people to get what they want.

Healthy guilt

It's normal to feel guilt when you do something wrong. It's valuable to acknowledge your own imperfections. It's healthy to apologize for actions that don't live up to standards you aspire to. If I hurt you, the appropriate response is for me to admit my guilt, or role, in what happened, and to make amends if possible. Some call that kind of acknowledgement a healthy sense of shame.

But, as manipulators know (consciously or unconsciously), some people have an unhealthy sense of shame and feel guilty for their very existence. I'm actually not exaggerating when I say that.

Inherent guilt

Inherent guilt creates a fertile field for manipulation. If you're tempted to manipulate others through their guilt, give it up. Guilt-based relationships are unsatisfying, you'll lose respect for the other person and eventually you'll lose respect for yourself.

Here's another benefit of giving up the guilt trip. Once you commit to going guilt-free, you'll become more aware of how guilt trips work. That will make you impervious to the guilt trips others lay on you. Plus it will force you to learn to communicate in honest ways.

It's all about saying what you mean and meaning what you say without being mean when you say it. It's very mean indeed to exploit another's guilt.

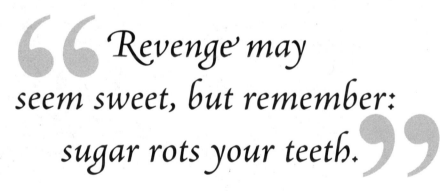

Revenge may seem sweet, but remember: sugar rots your teeth.

MERYL RUNION

Dos, Don'ts and Tips, Skill #42
Get guilt-free in accountability

Like other forms of manipulation, there are plenty of ways to lay a guilt trip on someone while feigning innocence. My mother pretended my behavior left her no choice. Your boss might pretend she's simply providing useful feedback. You might assure your spouse that you're speaking "for his/her own good." (Ever heard that one?) Let's look at what you need to know to give up the guilt trip — without laying one on yourself in the process.

1. Research guilt, shame and blame
There are libraries full of information about where guilt comes from, what healthy shame is, and the role of blame in life. Check them out.

Don't: assume you don't manipulate others with guilt tactics.
  Why not? Most of us do, often unconsciously.
Do: study the literature, attend 12-step meetings, and observe the role of these dynamics in your own life and life in general.
  Why? To learn how to hold people accountable without dipping into meanness or unacceptable tactics.
Example: Once I studied guilt and shame, it became easier for me to understand where my mother was right to call me out on my misbehavior, and where she crossed a boundary into manipulation and meanness. That helped me as a mother, enabling me to teach my son without crossing the boundary my own mother had.

And, of course, it helps you know whether you're in line or out of line when you hold your colleagues accountable.

Resources: *www.speakstrong.com/articles/speak-strong/beyondblame.html* This article identifies the difference between blame and accountability.

2. Examine your expectations
If you're guilt-tripping someone, it's pretty clear they did not meet an expectation you hold. But are your expectations realistic?

Don't: expect others to live by your rules and expectations.
  Why not? You'll set them up to disappoint you. That creates fertile soil for you to guilt-trip them.
Do: ask yourself what expectation their offending behavior violated.
  Why? To determine if unreasonable expectations are the real issue.

Example: Grace referred business to Nancy, and was outraged that Nancy didn't return the favor. She was going to address the issue, but in examining her expectations, she decided it wasn't reasonable.

3. Negotiate relationship agreements

Relationships need a sort of job descriptions — sets of expectations everyone agrees to.

Don't: assume others are in agreement with you about how to relate unless they've told you they are.
   Why not? They're probably assuming a different set of agreements.
Do: teach people how you like to be treated. Ask them about their relationship expectations. Reach agreements about how you will interact with each other.
   Why? To create standards you can implement without doubt.
PowerPhrase/What to say: I sent you an email with a request for information two days ago, and have not heard back. I like to have a 24 hour response policy and wonder if that would work for you, too.
Poison Phrase/What NOT to say: I sent you an email with a request for information two days ago, and have not heard back. Obviously I'm not a priority, even though I've invested countless hours in supporting your project.
Example: Ken thinks when he and a colleague go to seminars and networking events, they should stay together to reinforce and support each other. Kathy thinks they should separate to meet new people and increase their influence. They negotiated agreements about how to interact at events.

4. Hold people accountable

Don't: conflate holding people accountable with laying a guilt-trip.
   Why not? They're not the same.
Do: Enforce agreements, address offenses, and speak up when someone crosses your boundaries.
   Why? To keep relationships honorable, honest, clear and clean — and to remove the main temptation to guilt-trip someone.
PowerPhrase/What to say: When we agree to a deadline, I expect you to honor it or let me know as soon as you can if there's a problem. That didn't happen, so we need to talk about it.
Poison Phrase/What NOT to say: Um, that's okay you didn't get it done on time. It was only a $5500 commission I lost.

5. Focus on what you want

Don't: over-focus on what you don't want or what isn't working in the name of accountability.

> **Why not?** Even a legitimate complaint or concern can be guilt-invoking when overdone.

Do: Touch as lightly as possible on the problem. Talk as much as possible about the solution and where you want to move the relationship.

> **Why?** To avoid slipping from accountability to guilt. To keep the atmosphere positive.

PowerPhrase/What to say: I needed an immediate response to the email I sent you yesterday, and I could lose a client if I don't get the information I need. Will you respond to my email now, and in the future, respond to my requests within 24 hours?

Poison Phrase/What NOT to say: I sent you an email with a request for information yesterday, and you couldn't be bothered to respond. Just because of you, I might lose a client I've been cultivating for months. I can't believe you're so inconsiderate! How dare you! Obviously I'm not a priority, even though I've invested countless hours in supporting your project. (Etc.)

6. Provide appropriate guilt-free consequences for broken agreements

Don't: punish.

> **Why not?** Punishment assumes guilt.

Do: Let people know the results of their behavior without assigning blame or guilt.

> **Why?** So they can make informed choices knowing what the consequences of their actions will be.

PowerPhrase/What to say: I sent you an email with an urgent request for information two days ago, and have not heard back. It's come to the point that I can't count on you to respond to me in a timely way. If I don't hear back within 24 hours, I will move my accounts to a more responsive vendor.

Poison Phrase/What NOT to say: Obviously my account isn't important to you, because I sent you an email with an urgent request for information two days ago, and you couldn't be bothered to respond. After all the customers I've sent you, I expect better. If you don't get back to me now, I'm walking, and leaving your pathetic company behind.

Life without guilt

Some people think that a life without guilt will be hedonistic. And it might be, if there is no *appropriate* sense of guilt for legitimate offenses. It's valuable to acknowledge when we behave inappropriately or badly. It's destructive and counterproductive to wallow in guilt or to apply pressure on someone through guilt. It's also just plain mean, so if you're really committed to saying what you mean and meaning what you say without being mean when you say it, get guilt-free in accountability.

> " *The kinder, gentler, softer way is the smarter, wiser, stronger way.* "
>
> MERYL RUNION

You have a great face for radio

Skill #43: Put sarcasm in its place

Sarcasm versus Irony

Some say sarcasm is the lowest form of wit. I can think of lower forms, but I'll spare you the details. Sarcasm can be extremely clever — and it also can be extremely unkind. It's time to put sarcasm in its place.

Before you moan, groan and complain that I'm taking away your fun, let me explain — I'm talking about sarcasm, not irony. Irony can be a playful release, and a bonding tool among friends. I'm not on a mission to stomp out irony — I'm targeting sarcasm, not irony.

Sarcasm — irony — what's the difference, you ask? The difference is your intent.

Sarcasm is an indirect ironic remark intended to wound. Irony is the use of words to convey a meaning that is the opposite of its literal meaning. Not all irony is sarcasm. By definition, all sarcasm is irony. By definition, sarcasm is destructive.

For example, if you tell me you're on your way to the dentist for a root canal and I respond, "how nice," I'm using irony but not sarcasm. I'm not trying to wound you and I'm not sending an indirect message about how I *really* feel about your root canal.

However, if you tell me you're on your way to the dentist for a root canal and I respond, "You need a root canal? Oh, that explains your sweet breath," chances are I'm being sarcastic. I'm implying that your breath is not so sweet and I'm taking a poke. I'm trying to hurt you with my indirect, ironic message.

Of course, sometimes people use sarcasm to target third parties. Like in: *The 13 Office Rules for My Boss*. I found this on the internet without attribution. I wouldn't claim it if I had written it, either.

13 Office Rules for My Boss
(My title for this is: A Great Example of a Really Bad, Sarcastic Employee Attitude)

1. Never give me work in the morning. Always wait until 4:00 p.m. and then bring it to me. The challenge of a deadline is refreshing.

2. If it's really a rush job, run in and interrupt me every 10 minutes to inquire how it's going. That helps. Or even better, hover behind me, advising me at every keystroke.

3. Always leave without telling anyone where you're going. It gives me a chance to be creative when someone asks where you are.

4. If my arms are full of papers, boxes, books, or supplies, don't open the door for me. I need to learn how to function as a paraplegic and opening doors with no arms is good training in case I should ever be injured and lose all use of my limbs.

5. If you give me more than one job to do, don't tell me which is the priority. I am psychic.

6. Do your best to keep me late. I adore this office and really have nowhere to go or anything to do. I have no life beyond work.

7. If a job I do pleases you, keep it a secret. If that gets out, it could mean a promotion.

8. If you don't like my work, tell everyone. I like my name to be popular in conversations. I was born to be whipped.

9. If you have special instructions for a job, don't write them down. In fact, save them until the job is almost done. No use confusing me with useful information.

10. Never introduce me to people you're with. I have no right to know anything. In the corporate food chain, I am plankton. When you refer to them later, my shrewd deductions will identify them.

11. Be nice to me only when the job I'm doing for you could really change your life and send you straight to manager's hell.

12. Tell me all your little problems. No one else has any and it's nice to know someone is less fortunate. I especially like the story about having to pay such high taxes on the bonus check you received for being such a good manager.

13. Wait until my yearly review and THEN tell me what my goals SHOULD have been. Give me a mediocre performance rating with a cost of living increase. I'm not here for the money, anyway. —*Source Unknown*

Put sarcasm in its place: translate sarcasm and irony into honest requests

WARNING—I do not provide the 13 rules for you to post, no matter how much you relate to it. I provide it to illustrate the true place of sarcasm, which is to alert you to conversations that you urgently need to have. Sarcasm is a signal that you need to Speak Strong.

This employee's challenge…and yours, if you relate…is to write: *13 Office REQUESTS for My Boss.*

While sarcasm has no place for expression in the workplace, it has a great place in alerting you that you need to Speak Strong. So instead of reaching for the wisecracks, reach for your Power Phrases and say what needs to be said.

> *Sarcasm is an ironic remark intended to wound. What's so funny about inflicting pain?*

MERYL RUNION

Dos, Don'ts and Tips, Skill #43
Put sarcasm in its place

Sarcasm has a place, but it's a very limited one. Here's what you do to put sarcasm in that place.

1. Review where you learned to use sarcasm
Don't: think you invented sarcasm.

> **Why not?** You didn't, and figuring out where you learned to use it will help you overcome it.

Do: reflect on your primary caretaker's use of sarcasm, TV shows and other early exposures.

> **Why?** It's easier to see sarcasm in others. You're probably more like your early role models than you know, and you can identify your own use of sarcasm by learning where it came from.

Example: My mother was a queen of sarcasm. By reflecting on how my mother used sarcasm and realizing how I unconsciously imitated her, I was able to identify my own use.

2. Explore why you use sarcasm
Don't: assume it's just for innocent fun.

> **Why not?** That ain't the way to have fun. Innocent fun is never at another's expense.

Do: work to understand why you use sarcasm.

> **Why?** To find other ways to get the results you seek.

Example: May used sarcasm out of habit and because she didn't know how to address issues directly. She had a sense of powerlessness and sarcasm helped her feel like she had some power. It felt safer to hide behind sarcasm than to address issues directly.

3. Admit how destructive sarcasm can be
Don't: pretend that hiding a dig in a joke neutralizes the damage. Don't think sarcasm is a kinder way to tell someone about a problem than directness.

> **Why not?** It's bad enough to wound someone. It's worse to wound someone and pretend you're not.

Do: learn, acknowledge and tell the truth about the destructive nature of sarcasm.

> **Why?** True power and Speaking Strong are based on truth.

Example: I gave some training for a group deeply infected by sarcasm. Nina made a particularly sarcastic remark to Latitha early in the day. At the end of the day, when the subject of sarcasm came up in the workbook, I asked for an example of a sarcastic remark. Latitha offered her example from earlier in the day. We could tell that Nina's dig had made a deep impression on Latitha because she was able to quote Nina's remark exactly.

Nina was stunned that her cutting words had made such an impression. Nina apologized profusely. Habits change slowly—Nina laced her apology with irony, which minimized the impact and put her sincerity into question.

4. Distinguish between sarcasm and irony

Don't: confuse sarcasm and irony.

Why not? Irony is good natured, and sarcasm is not. If you confuse the two, you're likely to excuse bad behavior or avoid innocent irony that actually creates bonding between friends.

Do: study the definitions and elevate the spirit of your communication.

Why? To make sure you're not sticking the knife in when you speak.

Example: Lee and Carol often make ironic remarks like, "Looks like we're stuck working together again." The fact is, they love working together, and because of that, their irony is actually an affirmation of how much they enjoy each other. However, the minute one of them finds their work together tedious, the same remark will cross over into sarcasm and become destructive.

5. Evaluate the trust and confidence level before using irony

Don't: use irony when the trust level is low, no matter how well-intended you are.

Why not? When trust is low, people will be more sensitive to innocent remarks.

Do: review interactions to make sure you share a high level of trust before you risk irony.

Why? To keep interactions positive.

Example: When Debbie walked into the seminar room, Krystal said, "I guess they'll let anyone in here." Krystal meant it as a playful way to greet Debbie. What she hadn't considered was the fact that she and Debbie had experienced some tension recently. Also, Debbie felt underqualified in the topic, was afraid the information would be over her head and was concerned about looking stupid by asking questions. Because the level of trust was not at its usual high, and Krystal's comment tapped into some real fears, her words were hurtful, not enlivening.

6. Translate sarcasm and irony into honest remarks and requests

Don't: think sarcasm and irony have no value.

> **Why not?** Sarcasm and irony tell you what conversations you need to have.

Do: check your temptation to use sarcasm and ask yourself what conversations you need to have.

> **Why?** Sarcasm and irony are warning lights that something is wrong. If you shoot the warning light without addressing the problem, the problem will continue.

Example: Jake was upset when Larry didn't return his call. When Larry eventually did call, he wanted to say, "Nice to hear back from you so quickly." He checked that impulse and said, "Larry, I needed an answer on this last week. How can I get you to return my calls more quickly?"

On this topic, be ruthless.

I'm on a mission to stamp out sarcasm. And I can say that I've done it in my own life. People who are close to me know there are two things you don't do with me—you don't tickle me and you don't use sarcasm. I like having a sarcasm-free life. You will too.

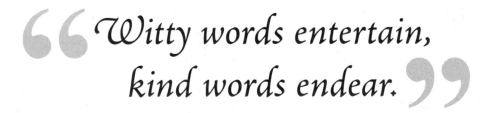

**" *Witty words entertain,
kind words endear.* "**

MERYL RUNION

You're an *$!#% *#

Skill #44: Put labels in their place

Labeling and name-calling

Oh, do I dislike being labeled — and I do have to watch my own communication to avoid doing it myself.

One of my most memorable experiences with labeling was when a business partner labeled me "selfish" because I didn't do what he wanted. It seemed the reverse of reality, but it did get me doing a song and dance for a while to prove his label wrong. (Now I think I should have embraced the label. I could have used some more selfishness.)

I was stunned the first time someone labeled me as belonging to a specific political group. I felt summarized, condensed and dismissed. It was as if everything I had said became secondary to the prejudged label. I also felt misunderstood, because I didn't think I belonged in the box they put me in. It told me they hadn't listened to what I said.

From "wacko" to "pinhead" to "idiot," labeling is rampant in the world of political dialogue, but it also happens at the office and at home. While some people back off from sincerely held political views to avoid the label "out of the mainstream," other people back off from expressing deeply held ethical concerns to avoid the label "not a team-player."

Even when someone seems to have earned their labels, labeling still reduces their victims to one limited quality. Even positive labels can be controlling and reductive. If I label my assistant "supportive," it might inhibit him from taking an action that might seem unsupportive. Okay, this isn't to say you shouldn't call your assistant supportive — just stay open to the idea that even positive labels put people in boxes that could constrain them.

Labels stop thought

A friend of mine is an ordained minister for a very unusual religious group. She tells me she can have a productive religious dialogue with anyone…until she names her religion. Suddenly people stop listening, because they think they know all there is to know about her faith. They're usually completely misinformed. The label stops communication because the label stops inquiry and thought.

Your reptilian brain likes labels (mine does too) because labels take complex realities and reduce them to simple concepts. Your reptilian brain sees in black and white, embraces simple explanations, and revels in simplicity. But life isn't that simple. An accurate label sees the forest instead of the trees. An inaccurate label sees the forest despite the trees. Either way, labels miss some of the trees.

Labels can be useful tools as long as you don't see them as absolute. Use labels when you need to characterize a forest, but stay aware of the diversity of the trees that make the forest up. If you insist that a pine forest is simply a pine forest, you'll miss the hundreds of aspens that decorate the landscape. When you say what you mean and mean what you say, keep thinking and limit labeling.

Labels stop thought.

MERYL RUNION

Dos, Don'ts and Tips, Skill #44
Put labels in their place

A properly-applied label is a tool. An improperly-applied label is a weapon. You can use labels for clarity — or to manipulate, belittle and minimize. Let's talk about how to use labels for clarity.

1. Define the labels you use
Don't: use a label you can't define.
    Why not? If you don't know what a label means, how will they?
Do: make sure you can define a label before you apply it.
    Why? Labels stop thought. By defining your labels, you increase thought.
Example: The phrase "abuse" can mean anything from driving an extra 300 miles before you change your oil to hauling a trailer behind a Ferrari. It can mean physical abuse, from an inappropriate hug to a beating that takes the victim to the edge of death. It can mean verbal abuse, from a word that is a bit too harsh to deliberate, devastating verbal attacks. If you label your ex-boss abusive, I might have a very different interpretation of what that label means than yours.

2. Consider using the definition instead of the label
Don't: use charged labels lightly.
    Why not? They create reactions that trigger the reptilian brain and stop clear thinking.
Do: explain the behaviors and traits that earned someone their label instead of applying the label.
    Why? It's clearer, and it avoids the thought-stopping quality of labels.
Example: Jennifer is new at her job. She's a very capable woman who is experiencing a major learning curve. She cringed when her boss told her that she wasn't ready to deal with a major client because she was incompetent.

Her boss caught her reaction and clarified. He explained that he used the term to mean anyone who couldn't do a specific task regardless of the reason. He explained what he really meant was she wasn't ready for that client because she was still learning and getting up to speed. He then explained that he was quite pleased with her progress, he just wasn't ready to throw her to the wolves.

Her boss could have used the labels "not up to speed" or "in a learning curve." If he had started with his explanation/definition, he probably would have used the more appropriate labels — or avoided labels at all.

3. Keep your eye on the trees that make up the forest

Don't: paint with a broad brush that covers over distinctions.

Why not? You'll miss subtleties.

Do: keep your eyes open for exceptions to your labels.

Why? To see people as they are and to avoid labeling them in a way that restricts them.

Example: Sybil is an artist. She has an artist's nature, an artist's temperament and an artist's style. Some of her friends label her as an artist, but those who know her better recognize her command of logic and her embrace of structure.

William, who didn't know her as well, dismissed her offer to coordinate an event for him by saying, "thanks, but you're an artist. What I really need is someone with management skills."

By characterizing Sybil as an artist, William blinded himself to her management capabilities.

4. Limit labels to behavior

Don't: use a label to characterize a person unless they themselves invite it.

Why not? It reduces them by defining who they are by selective behaviors and qualities.

Do: only apply labels to behaviors and specific qualities — and do that sparingly.

Why? It's more accurate and less offensive.

Example: Ralph confronted Amy about taking credit for his idea. He started to refer to Amy as dishonest, but then switched to refer to Amy's credit claim as dishonest.

5. Examine your reasons for using labels

Don't: use a label without knowing why.

Why not? Words that aren't targeted aren't PowerPhrases.

Do: figure out what you hope to accomplish when you use a label.

Why? To weed out cheap shots and limiting language.

Example: Bob will ask women to hold their questions while he's making notes by saying, "I'm a simple man. I only do one thing at a time." He finds that to be a very clarifying remark, because many men work best when they focus on one thing at a time, and most women have learned that. Bob labels himself to clarify, not deprecate.

Bob's label serves him. However, I would think long and hard first before I would ever refer to Bob as a simple man.

Don't be a labeler

I hope you caught the irony in the above header. If you missed it, I'll explain. I used a label to characterize you as a labeler if you label. I was joking, but usually labeling isn't funny. It's a limiting, disempowering, discrediting communication tactic. So please lose the labels. If you don't lose labels, I won't label YOU a labeler — but I might carefully label your way of communicating.

> **" Never underestimate the power of a single word. "**
>
> MERYL RUNION

" *Don't confront when you can connect.* "

MERYL RUNION

Nothing is the way it seems

Skill #45: Clean up counterfeit communication

Polite, maybe. Nice? Not so much. Politeness disguised as niceness

Steve didn't understand how his client, George, could be so nice and yet Steve felt like he was getting a rotten deal. That's because Steve mistook politeness for niceness. George was very polite, but he wasn't nice. He took advantage of Steve at every turn and did it in the politest of ways.

This kind of confusion is all too common. You think one thing is happening, when in fact another is. That leaves the message muddled and you befuddled. Disguising exploitation with politeness is one face of counterfeit communication. There are many different faces of counterfeit communication that may be familiar to you. In fact, you may use them daily.

Is it love? Or how about neediness? Or even…control?

Andrew told Emily how much he loved her every single day. He brought her presents, seemed deeply interested in how she was doing, and called her throughout the day. Andrew was deeply in love, or so he said. Yet something seemed off for Emily. She couldn't quite put her finger on it, but she consistently felt stifled.

At times it seemed Andrew used his love for her as justification for bad behavior and excessive demands. Was his declaration of love genuine? Or was it counterfeit communication to disguise a less noble agenda? What do you justify in the name of love?

She's opening up and sharing what's in her heart. So why does it hurt so much? Put-downs disguised as sharing.

Daniel was delighted when, after weeks of uncomfortable silence, Emma asked if she could speak with him about their relationship. She told him she was ready to open up and communicate at a more honest level.

He was less delighted when her conversation seemed like a critic's committee. When he protested, Emma told him, "I'm just telling you how I feel." She wasn't – she was bombarding him with put-downs and hiding behind a guise of sharing. When you "open your heart to share," does it feel like a gift? Or do you use sharing as an excuse to unload on someone?

She feels my pain, so why do I feel like a pathetic loser? Pity disguised as empathy.

There's no shame in experiencing hard times. When we do, it's nice to find an empathetic ear. Michelle discovered the value of turning to her friends when she hit a wall. But there was something about the way Ava empathized that left her feeling like a pathetic loser. Ava said she empathized, but it seemed to Michelle that Ava saw herself as above such difficulties. Ava appeared to think less of Michelle because she wasn't above it all.

Are you really empathizing with someone, or are you "pitying the poor fool"?

Anyone who discloses their humanness must be honest, right? Disclosures confused with openness.

Ethan interviewed Hannah for a public relations job. Hannah told him about the many great placements she had made, and Ethan was impressed when she disclosed to him that there was one client she had difficulty placing. She went on to explain why Ethan would be easy to get placements for.

Ethan heard Hannah's disclosure as an indication of openness. He took it to mean she was open about everything else. He was shocked later to realize that her one disclosure did not mean she was honest overall. She had far more skeletons in her PR resume than the one she confessed to.

How about you? Do you feign openness? Are you selective in your full disclosure?

If this is help, what would undermining be like? Shaming disguised as guidance.

Andy's boss, Josh, told him he was interested in his career, and that's why he offered lots of guidance. When Andy made mistakes, Josh went over them with him to track down the source of the errors.

Andy wanted expert guidance, but the way Josh gave it, Andy felt like Josh was rubbing his nose in it. He felt shamed for routine minor errors.

Do you shame people when you offer guidance?

She's so passionate. Why do I feel like I'm running in circles? Drama disguised as passion.

Sarah was exciting to be around, but something wasn't quite right. At first, her passion inspired Gabe, but eventually he felt like he had been taken for a ride. That's because Sarah wasn't so much a passionate person as she was high drama. She wasn't really the caring, enthusiastic person Gabe had taken her to be. She was addicted to drama, but sold her drama addiction as passion.

Are you a drama queen (or king), hiding behind a mask of passion?

So many disguises.
Counterfeit communication can be subtle and it can be overt. Usually there's a little of both mixed in, and it's difficult to sort. If you've discovered counterfeit communication in your repertoire, don't despair. Just consider what the authentic version would be, and favor that.

> " *Is there such a thing as too much truth? Only if it is offered with too little tact.* "

MERYL RUNION

Dos, Don'ts and Tips, Skill #45
Clean up counterfeit communication

It's easy to slip unknowingly into counterfeit communication. It's also tempting to continue the pretense once you become aware of your deceit. Here's how you clean up your act a little bit at a time.

1. Create your own list of counterfeit communication pairs
Don't: limit yourself to my list.
> **Why not?** There are plenty more where these come from.

Do: create a list of disguised-communication pairs that you've experienced.
> **Why?** To become aware of all the possibilities for fake communication.

Example: Threats can be disguised as explaining consequences; blame can be disguised as holding someone accountable – the list goes on and on.

2. Reverse your counterfeit communication list to see if you ever deem authentic communication to be counterfeit
Don't: let this list make you cynical or paranoid.
> **Why not?** There's as much danger in thinking authentic communication is counterfeit as there is in thinking counterfeit communication is authentic.

Do: check your authenticity, and when you give yourself a pass, Speak Strong without doubting yourself.
> **Why?** To avoid limiting yourself and to avoid being overly suspicious of others.

Example: I've met many people who are afraid to warn people what the consequences of certain behavior would be, because they don't want to sound like they're threatening. In fact, it's legitimate and appropriate to let people know what will happen if they continue doing what they're doing.

3. Verify and trust
Don't: assume guilt until proven innocent. Don't doubt your own authenticity unless you have good reason to.
> **Why not?** It's harder to prove innocence than guilt. No one is perfect, and if you look for shreds of insincerity, you're likely to find them.

Do: only use your counterfeit communication list to evaluate something that doesn't look/sound or feel right, or something that causes you to question.
> **Why?** To upgrade your authenticity without getting paranoid.

Example: Danny can get defensive and hear suggestions as criticism. That causes his manager, Kayla, to doubt her own sincerity when she offers suggestions.

Kayla examined her words and intent and recognized that she did, in fact, use suggestions to disguise criticism at times. Once she became aware of that distinction, she was able to offer suggestions more confidently and to be direct when she did need to communicate critical feedback.

Danny still does hear suggestions as criticism sometimes, however. When that happens, Kayla checks herself out and if she gets a pass, she trusts her intent instead of doubting herself.

The gold standard
Once you clean up your counterfeit communication, your words can become the gold standard for others. Then you can more easily detect counterfeit communication in others as well…and be able to respond authentically.

No matter how well intended, if your communication is counterfeit, you're not saying what you mean and meaning what you say without being mean when you say it.

You are responsible for the falsehoods you tell and the falsehoods you allow.

MERYL RUNION

" *If you can't say anything nice, you really need to talk.* "

MERYL RUNION

Speak STRONG

STEP 5:
SPEAK YOUR SIMPLE TRUTH

Speak Your Simple Truth Skill Set #1:
Express Yourself

Speak Your Simple Truth Skill Set #2:
Create, Radiate and Elevate

Introduction to Step 5: Speak Your Simple Truth

Just like the words United States on a US map, simple truth can be easy to miss if you're not looking in the right place. And simple truth can be tough to speak if you're not accustomed to expressing it. Now that you've developed the tools to say what you mean, and mean what you say without being mean when you say it, you're ready to put it all together and give voice to your deepest values, understandings and observations. When you do, the results might surprise you. This section tells you what to expect.

Speak Your Simple Truth Skill Set #1: Express Yourself

There are many ways to grow and develop. I started my personal development journey with a firm commitment to growing from the inside out. When it became painfully clear that I needed to develop my communication skills, I started developing myself from the outside in. It surprised me how much I grew from finding my voice. The skill of expressing yourself isn't just one that will help you succeed in accomplishing the things you want to do. It will also help you succeed in becoming who you want to be.

Speak Your Simple Truth Skill Set #2: Create, Radiate and Elevate

You know words are powerful, but you probably don't realize just how powerful. This skill set enables you to craft words that frame present reality in a positive and productive way, and also invokes a future reality that you gladly embrace. It empowers you to elevate your conversations to their highest potential. Enjoy the ride!

Hear me roar, purr, growl and meow

Skill #46: Communicate all you are

Limited intimacy

Alyssa and Brian work together. They respect and value each other, but on some levels, they don't know each other at all. Brain can be like a bull in a china shop, and when he steps on Alyssa's toes, she won't say ouch. She won't let Brian see the part of herself that questions and doubts. Occasionally, once Alyssa gets her confidence back, she'll tell Brian what she went through. But she won't let Brian see her when she's vulnerable.

She also doesn't tell him when he steps on clients' toes, and she doesn't tell him when she doesn't care for his ideas.

It's a big stretch for Alyssa even to share the vulnerable part of herself with her friends. It's a big, healthy stretch. If you hide a part of yourself from everyone, you're sitting on some of your power. Find places and ways to let your whole self out.

Expanded intimacy

Alyssa's relationship with Brian wouldn't work at all for Rose. She used to have relationships like that—where she toned her genius down to avoid threatening her colleagues, where she pretended to agree when she didn't, and where she didn't argue when her boss blamed his error on her. When Rose interviewed for subsequent jobs, she presented herself exactly as she was so she could be all of who she was at work.

Playing it safe wasn't safe at all

The more authentic and open I became as a speaker, the more effective I became as a speaker. In my early days, I played my cards carefully. I acted like I had it all down. I hid my exuberance. I denied my foibles. I avoided controversy. As I became more confident over time, I became freer in my expression. The freer I was in my expression, the more people liked me, which built my confidence, which…well, it was a good cycle that I was happy to develop. Not everyone liked me, of course, but enough did to keep me successful.

Hiding your light

We all have parts of ourselves we hide from the world. The part you hide just might be a part other people are hungry to know. It could be a part of yourself you're hungry to share. It also could be a part that sets you free and allows you to realize your dreams.

Some of us hide our vulnerable sides. Others hide their passionate sides. Others hide their knowledgeable sides, or goofy sides, or spiritual sides or graphic sides. We wear our masks and hide our simple truths.

Of course, there is such a thing as appropriateness and adapting to the environment. You're unwise to share your graphic side with a small child or the Queen of England. But too many of us take appropriateness so far that no one knows who we are — including ourselves.

I recently asked a dear friend if it would blow her cover if I wrote up a story she had shared with me in my newsletter. She responded by saying,
- I don't have a cover to blow.

Can you imagine going though life without having a cover to blow? Sweet, indeed.

I'm sure it won't surprise you to know that my friend is a very powerful woman. Not only that, but she inspires the rest of us to be more of who we are.

Look out world! We're coming your way! Hear us roar, purr, growl and meow. We're very fun. And powerful!

Dos, Don'ts and Tips, Skill #46
Communicate all you are

1. Journal your heart out
Don't: edit.

Why not? Unedited journaling reveals submerged aspects of your nature.
Do: pick up pen and paper and just start writing. Express your deepest thoughts and feelings — the good, the bad and the ugly.

Why? To get to know yourself.

Example: When Alexa journaled, she was amazed by the good ideas she had about how to solve problems at work.

2. Compare what you told your journal to what you communicated with others
Don't: judge.

Why not? You'll explore why you stay silent later.
Do: juxtapose the you that shows up on paper with the you that shows up in life.

Why? To uncover where you hide.

Example: Wyatt had some very successful friends who knew a lot more than he did about business. He hesitated to offer his own perceptions or insights because he was afraid his friends would think he was arrogant. This exercise helped him realize how much he held back. It inspired him to reveal more of himself.

3. Ask: what would you do and say if you weren't concerned about consequences?
Don't: be practical.

Why not? This is about setting yourself free — at least in your imagination. There's plenty of time to get practical later.
Do: pretend that you can say or do anything you want with impunity.

Why? To identify how much of yourself you hide.

Example: Juan discovered that if he wasn't concerned with consequences he would tell his boss he thought he could do a better job on the restructuring than the manager his boss tasked with it.

4. Find ways and places to express more of yourself

Don't: go right out and confess all your sins and dreams.

> **Why not?** There's a reason why you haven't expressed these aspects of yourself. Sudden honesty without strategy could backfire and send you back into obscurity.

Do: develop the skills to express more of yourself. Find appropriate outlets to express things you can't express directly.

> **Why?** To unblock yourself.

Example: Juan created a strategy for offering input at work. Larry worked with computers, but was also a poet. He found a poetry group to provide an outlet for his poetic expression.

5. Forge new responses

Don't: allow yourself to respond in habitual ways for a given period of time.

> **Why not?** It will force you to forge new habits.

Do: ask yourself: If I couldn't respond to situations in my habitual way, how I respond?

> **Why?** To oblige yourself to engage with hidden aspects of yourself.

Example: Cindi's mother triggered her anger and sometimes rage. When a counselor asked Cindi, "What would you feel if you couldn't be angry," Cindi discovered that she didn't know what she would feel without anger. Eventually she was able to experience other emotions in response to her mother—and to communicate a broader range of her emotions.

6. Hang out with people who meet you at every level

Don't: spend all your time with people who don't relate to you. (Or that you don't relate well to.)

> **Why not?** It causes you to shut down.

Do: meet and spend time with people who share your interests and skill level.

> **Why?** To draw out and nourish aspects of yourself you didn't know about.

Example: I attended a male-oriented conference with a female friend who shared and expanded on my own perceptions of the tone and conference content. We experienced two dimensions to the conference—the presentation content, and the similar way my friend and I experienced the presentations. We were delighted that we both knew what the other was talking about when we spoke of things like places in the talk where the speaker spoke coercively, overly intellectually or dismissively. We discovered that we meet each other at many levels. That means we can express more of who we are with each other than we can with most other people. In fact, I find myself speaking to her with words I rarely use in other circumstances.

7. Revisit childhood qualities and dreams

Don't: forget your hopes, wishes and dreams from childhood.

Why not? They are clues to who you are and what parts of yourself you may want to nurture.

Do: think about whom you were, how you behaved, what you wanted, and what heroes you admired when you were little.

Why? To access more of your nature.

Example: As a child I admired Pippi Longstocking. Can you guess why? I related to her outspoken nature. I'm actually an introvert, but my love for her showed me that I wanted a more outward role in life—which I developed.

All this and more

It's hard for a big person to fit into a small box. So many of us only let a fraction of who we are out. When you learn to speak your simple truth, you'll find that there's plenty of room for more of you. Enjoy!

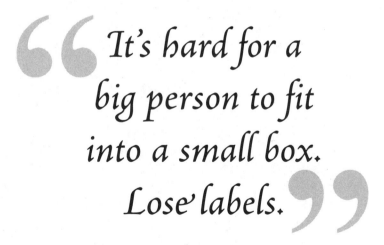

It's hard for a big person to fit into a small box. Lose labels.

MERYL RUNION

> " *Truth*
> *is good*
> *for the soul.* "

MERYL RUNION

I didn't know that until I said it

Skill #47: Talk your way to self-knowledge

I shared a dream with a counselor many years ago, who responded by asking me, "Why are your dreams so clear, but you're so fuzzy to talk to?"

No, I wasn't insulted. I was excited. I knew I was fuzzy to talk to, but I hadn't realized that I was actually quite clear underneath all that static. My job in therapy wasn't as enormous as I had thought it was. I didn't have to build from the ground up because I already had a strong foundation to stand on. That's why therapy was so productive for me, and that's why writing and public speaking have been so valuable for me.

I used to think I had to have all my ducks in a row before I opened my mouth. Now I open my mouth to get my ducks lined up.

You don't have to pay a therapist or become a professional speaker and author to talk your way to self-knowledge. You just have to express yourself.

Have you ever tried to explain something you thought you understood and discovered that you didn't understand it as well as you thought? When you put your ideas into words, it forces you to a new level of clarity that thinking alone won't inspire.

But don't just talk — talk and listen to yourself. Don't just write — write and read what you've written. There's a reason why blogs and social networks are so popular these days, and it's not just narcissism. There's a reason why many women like to call five of their closest girlfriends to share the details of significant events in their lives. There's a reason why self-publishing is a booming industry. It's self-discovery through self-expression.

It's amazing what you can learn from yourself, if you speak your simple truth and talk your way to self-knowledge.

Dos, Don'ts and Tips, Skill #47
Talk your way to self-knowledge

An unsafe assumption

My husband used to assume that when I said something, I had thought about it. He soon discovered that was not a safe assumption. I often think aloud, and evaluate my thoughts after voicing them. I often don't know what I mean until it comes out of my mouth.

When you open your mouth without knowing what will come out, you might feel out-of-control. And that's why it's effective. While I'm a big advocate of preparing PowerPhrases, in the right setting, when you let yourself speak outside of your own control, it can lead to some surprising discoveries.

Here are some tips for you so you can talk your way to self-knowledge.

1. Speak impromptu

Don't: try this everywhere.
> **Why not?** High-stakes situations require preparation.

Do: let yourself explore ideas aloud without preparation in safe environments.
> **Why?** You'll say things you didn't know you meant.

Example: Toastmaster's International is an association that helps people learn skills of public speaking. One practice they offer is impromptu speaking. One member will give the speaker a topic for them to present on the spot. It's excellent training for quick verbal organization — but it's also great training for speaking spontaneously. People are often surprised at what they are able to do in that format.

2. Listen to what you say

Don't: think you can't learn from listening to your own words.
> **Why not?** Deep insights can escape your lips from beyond your conscious mind.

Do: listen to yourself as if you were listening to someone else.
> **Why?** You'll surprise yourself.

Example: People often come up to me on seminar breaks to share an experience that relates to some point I made. If I think the group as a whole will benefit from the story, I ask them to share it with everyone. Almost invariably, when they tell their stories to the group with a little more time to prepare, their stories are much less interesting. If they had listened to themselves when they spoke impromptu, they would have heard and learned what mattered most in their stories.

3. Mine your gaffes and blunders for insights

Don't: distance yourself from Freudian slips, weird comments or words you're not proud of.

> **Why not?** They might reveal the deeper you.

Do: listen to gaffes and blunders to see if there's more truth in them than you want to admit.

> **Why?** "Misspeaks" are often more honest — and potentially powerful — than the things you intend to say.

Example: John meant to report on a decision he had made, but referred to it as a "division" instead of decision. He corrected his error but realized he knew his decision would create a division.

4. Follow the emotion

Don't: back off when your words trigger emotions.

> **Why not?** You've heard of "follow the money?" I say, follow the emotion. That's where the gems of understanding are buried.

Do: use emotion as a compass to indicate that you're on to something and need to keep going in that direction.

> **Why?** Emotion is an indication of caring. You don't feel emotional about things that don't matter to you. If your words trigger emotion, close in and keep talking. You'll be amazed at what you learn.

Example: Emotional processing uncovers layer after layer of masked meanings by following the words that trigger anger, sadness, inspiration, love and joy. We often reflexively run from emotion — which keeps us from self-discovery.

If you don't know yourself, how can you know anything at all?

Have you ever met anyone who didn't know themselves? You know, people who growl that they never get angry? Most of these people are afraid of what they'll find if they make their own acquaintance on an intimate level. While they may seem self-absorbed, in fact they're false-self-absorbed. They don't know who they really are.

There are many ways to get to know yourself, and one powerful way is to talk your way to self-knowledge. Once you have that, you're ready to flaunt the uniqueness of Brand-you.

" If you don't know yourself, how can you know anything at all? "

MERYL RUNION

Brand You

Skill #48: Define and communicate your uniqueness

Branding boom

Branding is a big deal among speakers, authors and others in the information industry. Branding is a big deal in corporations. Branding is a big deal among marketers. If you're in business, it's almost certain someone has told you that you need to find your brand.

Even if you're not in business, someone has probably told you to find your brand. They've told you to write a 30-second elevator speech about who you are and what you're about. They've told you to package yourself.

And if they also told you to package yourself by clarifying who you are, what you stand for, and what your unique contribution to the world is they did you a service. If they told you to package yourself by creating an image to hide behind, to squeeze yourself in to and fake, they did you a disservice. Great brands are clarifications, not covers. Remember my friend who told me she didn't have a cover to blow? She has one great brand.

Your brand may be bigger than you are – or bigger than you thought you were

No brand is a perfect representation of what it characterizes – just the closest possible. You might emphasize certain aspects of who you are to embody your brand. You might ignore a few of the "trees" to highlight the general overall qualities of the "forest" of your brand. You might have to stretch yourself to live up to a brand you aspire to, as I do with the SpeakStrong brand. Trust me – there are times when I would love to pretend everything is fine when it isn't. There are times when I'd like to make up an excuse instead of tell the truth. There are times when I wonder who I am to have the brand that I do. When those times hit, I Speak Strong about them. I confess to being who I am instead of claiming to already be the master I aspire to be. Your best brand will stretch you like mine stretches me.

Vanilla, chocolate or caramel mint mocha?

While the reality of who you are is too complex to summarize in a catch-phrase, you do have your own unique flavor. Discover that flavor and communicate it in a way that shows others who you are.

Dos, Don'ts and Tips, Skill #48
Define and communicate your uniqueness

Find your brand
You'll find your brand in an eight-step process. I changed the book format slightly for this chapter to help you understand my branding process. I start with a question or questions for you to answer for each step. The sentence stems help you jumpstart your answers, and the examples illustrate one response I have in my own personal and professional branding.

1. Describe your vision of a perfect world.
Question: If everyone on earth learned from you, what would the world look like? What would people experience that they are not experiencing now?
Sentence stem: Imagine a world where…
Example: Imagine a world where everyone says what they mean and means what they say without being mean when they say it.

2. Describe the current reality.
Question: What is the contrasting existing reality? What would a caricature exaggeration of this be? What is the worst situation you ever experienced of people not having the benefit of what you embody? What experiences have you had that make this a powerful subject for you?
Sentence stem: Instead of this perfect world, we have a world where…
Example: Instead, we have a world where people say what they think will get the result they want and/or keep them out of trouble. We have a world where people often speak harshly.

3. What obstacles have you overcome to be who you are and to do what you do?
Question: Why isn't everyone more like you? What excuses do people give you for not excelling in the area that you do?
Sentence stem: I've learned not to let (obstacle) hold me back.
Example: I've learned not to let fear of disapproval hold me back from speaking up when something needs to be said.

4. What unique knowledge do you have?
Question: What do you know that others don't?
Sentence stem: One thing I know that most people don't is…

Example: One thing I know that most people don't is the difference between assertiveness and aggression.

5. What unique beliefs do you have?

Question: What principles guide you? What values do you hold that not everyone does?
Sentence stem: I believe that…
Example: I believe that truth is more important than loyalty.

6. What unique things do you do?

Question: How do you walk your talk?
Sentence stem: I walk my talk by…
Example: I walk my talk by rocking the boat when something needs to be said, even if it risks a relationship.

7. What do people need to stop doing to live in your perfect world?

Question: What do you refrain from doing that others do?
Sentence stem: I walk my talk by refraining from…
Example: I walk my talk by never making excuses for my mistakes or bad behavior.

8. What about your answers is unique to you?

Question: What makes you so special? (If this sounds arrogant, remember – branding is all about what makes you special.)
Sentence stem: I am the only one who…
Example: I am the only one who teaches management skills from the perspective of exactly what to say in hundreds of management situations. *(http://www.speakstrong.com/store/)*

Find your brand, be your brand, communicate your brand

Step 8 is your main expression of your brand. Of course, you'll want to find catchy, pithy ways to word the essence of your brand once you've defined it. Here are some tips to help you do that.

1. Search titles on Amazon and springboard off them.

Use book titles to brainstorm ideas. Since titles can't be copyrighted, you can use other people's titles. This works best if the title is a perfect match and the title you use is obscure. For example, I have a presentation called Brand Aid. *(www.speakstrong.com/hire_meryl/keynotes.html)* That title was inspired by an old, out-of-print book by an unknown author.

2. Twist common phrases and sayings into your own message

Research and study common sayings, clichés, and well-known quotes and phrases. Twist them or springboard off them for unique expressions. For example, "Say what you mean, and mean what you say, without being mean when you say it" is a twist of a common phrase.

3. Use alliteration

The alliteration in "SpeakStrong" adds to its effectiveness.

4. Listen to yourself talk.

SpeakStrong came from listening to myself talk about our tendencies to avoid open dialogue. Listen to yourself talk for the perfect phrases and expressions of your brand.

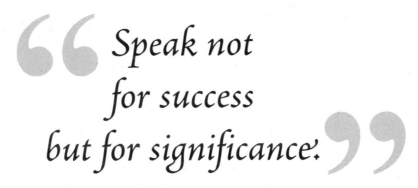

Speak not for success but for significance.

MERYL RUNION

I walk my talk, but do I talk the walk I want?

Skill #49: Talk an inspired walk

Big shoes to fill

The bigger you talk, the harder it is to walk your talk. The bigger you talk, the more likely it is that you'll fall short of living your words. That might lead you to make one of two choices — either to talk about what you really want and give yourself something to live up to, or to tone your words down and cruise. I hope you give yourself something to live up to.

Of course, you also could overpromise and underdeliver. That's not a genuine option.

No ordinary assistant

Here's an example of someone who redefines reality by talking big — but not so big that she doesn't walk her talk. Marcie assists the CEO of a manufacturing company. However, she would never say, "I'm just an assistant." She talks an assistant talk that is worth walking. She refers to herself as an Administrative Professional.

Marcie's original job description included: write memos, set up meetings, deal with customer complaints, sort mail and order supplies. Those aren't the words Marcie uses. Ask Marcie what she does and she'll tell you she composes memos, coordinates events, manages customer relations, prioritizes communication and makes purchasing decisions.

After all, Marcie doesn't just write memos, she takes the time to compose the exact wording to make her point and inspire action. She doesn't just make a few calls to set up a meeting, she truly coordinates events. Marcie knows that every customer counts, and when she deals with an angry customer, she really is managing customer relations.

Marcie determines what letters, emails and memos get to the head of the company. Sure, she's sorting the mail, but it has the effect of setting priorities in the communications at the highest level of the company. And the supplies she orders affect the smooth operation of the organization. She really does make purchasing decisions.

There's nothing wrong with writing a memo. But why call it writing a memo when you're really composing one? Composing a memo is talk that is far more worth walking.

251

More talk worth walking

You don't have to be president or CEO or a celebrity to talk a walk worth walking. You only need to contribute to something you believe in that has value. I think of my friend Jamie who answered the phones for her company. How did she talk her walk? She explained that her job was to make contacting her company a heartwarming, pleasant and inspiring experience for the hundreds of people who called each day.

I am in the process of writing a business communication book. I also could say that I'm in the process of helping my readers take ownership of their lives. That I'm working to elevate the level of dialogue in the world. That I'm helping to create a world where everyone says what they mean and means what they say, without being mean when they say it. Now, that's talking my walk — and it's talking a walk worth walking. My expanded description of what I'm doing here inspires me.

What are you in the process of doing? Read on to find out you can talk an inspiring walk.

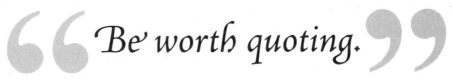

" Be worth quoting."

MERYL RUNION

Dos, Don'ts and Tips, Skill #49
Talk an inspired walk

Amp it up, not tamp it down

I thought about writing a book called *SpeakSmall*, but I decided it wouldn't sell. I'm kidding, of course, but I did record a video interview with the "Acting Director" of the "Center for Lowered Expectations." You'll find it here: *www. speakstrong.com/video/bunnybubbles.html.* It's comedy about how to speak so no one expects anything from you. If that's what you want, go for it—but since you're reading a book called *SpeakStrong*, I trust you're interested in amping up your communication, not tamping it down. Here are your tips.

1. Incorporate words from your branding vision into your daily language

Don't: get so lost in your day-to-day activities that you forget to invoke the bigger vision those activities support.

> **Why not?** Your words will be uninspired and your work will become disconnected.

Do: speak with words that tie ordinary activities into their grand purpose.

> **Why?** To keep the vision alive, and to make each day's activities a part of a bigger whole.

PowerPhrase/What to Say: I'm meeting with a client who wants to elevate the level of her dialogue with her boss so they can be a more positive, powerful team.

Poison Phrase/What NOT to say: I'm meeting with a client who can't say no to her boss.

2. Speak as if every word you use is an invocation

Don't: say anything you wouldn't want to take shape and form.

> **Why not?** On some level, your words do take shape and form.

Do: picture your words as manifesting, and before you speak them, make sure that would be a good thing.

> **Why?** To create a vision that you want to make happen.

PowerPhrase/What to Say: I'd like to run some tests to see what we need to do to bring you back to maximum health. You have so many gifts to give the world; I want to help you be able to give them.

Poison Phrase/What NOT to say: I'd like to run some tests to see how bad it is.

Example: My husband is a natural health consultant who tells it like it is in a way that motivates and creates a vision of optimal health.

3. Use the loftiest words that reality or potential reality support

Don't: misrepresent or lose connection with reality in your attempt to inspire and elevate.

    Why not? You'll lose credibility.

Do: make a list of words that elevate your spirit, and incorporate them into your speech as much as you can without being grandiose.

    Why? Inspiring words keep the eyes on possibilities and positive realities.

    Staying connected to reality keeps you credible.

Example: Some politicians are uninspiring. Others learned empty buzz words that get people excited, but fall flat over time. The leaders who flourish over time are the ones who have a dream, a plan to manifest the dream, the words to draw others into their dream, and the will to walk the talk. They might use the same words as other politicians whose word are empty—but they embed their words with meaning and soul.

4. Talk more about what you want than what you don't want

Don't: over-focus on what's wrong.

    Why not? It drags conversation down.

Do: paint colorful word pictures about what you want to create. Touch on what you want to avoid only as much as the situation seems to require.

    Why? To use the power of attraction, which is more compelling than aversion.

PowerPhrase/What to Say: I'd like to see a front page newspaper article on this.

Poison Phrase/What NOT to say: I'd hate for people not to come because they don't know about this.

Dare to be visionary

Many people refrain from envisioning because they fear setting themselves up for disappointment. They refrain because they've seen too many phonies who promise the world and don't deliver. Or they may refrain because they've been so busy watching their feet that they forget to look up and see the bigger picture. Take a look and see where you want to go. Then talk the walk you want, and walk it. It's a big part of speaking your simple truth.

When you talk the low road I'll still talk the high road...

Skill #50: Elevate conversations

Singular statesmanship sightings

I write this chapter just after a US presidential election ended. I speak for everyone I know when I say — it seemed like the campaigns would never end, and we're so glad they finally did. My friends and associates were in constant states of agitation, triggered by the low-minded political dialogue. The attacks and the counter-attacks, the spin, the accusations, continual speculation and the vicious undermining took its toll. And yet, in this election cycle, there were oasis moments when some politicians and some pundits took a step back and elevated the dialogue. There were moments where Americans got to witness rare displays of statesmanship.

In case you don't know what statesmanship is, it's "wisdom and skill in the management of public affairs." In the election, we saw moments when a candidate turned a low blow around into an opportunity to engage us in an important national dialogue. They were moments when one candidate talked the low road and the other responded by talking the high road. In those moments, we saw glimpses of statesmanship trumping political hackery. We saw examples of how to elevate conversations.

From darkness into light

There's a saying — never wrestle with a pig. You both get all dirty and the pig loves it. Great communicators never consider wrestling with pigs. They elevate conversations so they don't have to get their hands dirty.

When a conversation becomes divisive, they unify. When a conversation gets negative, they guide it into positivity. When a conversation gets confusing, they seek clarity. When a conversation gets mired in problems, they introduce solutions. When a conversation gets manipulative, they get direct. When a conversation gets greedy, they address the common good. When a conversation gets overly intellectual, they get heart-centered. When a conversation gets overly emotional, they introduce logic and reason. And when great communicators find themselves in a hole, they stop digging and seek the opportunity to elevate the dialogue.

When someone tries to pull you down into a hole with them, pull them out of it, or, invite them to join you on level ground.

Misery loves company. People in holes like to drag others into the holes they're in. Great communicators don't take the bait. Instead, they elevate the dialogue. The brilliant ones elevate the conversation without anyone even noticing what they've done.

> *"When they talk the low road, you talk the high road."*
>
> MERYL RUNION

Dos, Don'ts and Tips, Skill #50
Elevate conversations

The skill and the will to elevate conversations will help you Speak Strong like never before. Here are your tips.

1. Create a goal for each conversation and each comment within the conversation

Don't: speak without purpose.

> **Why not?** If you don't know where you want to go, you won't know how to select your words to get you there.

Do: ask what you want your overall conversations to accomplish and what you want comments within conversations to accomplish.

> **Why?** To guide your words to become steps toward a high-road destination.

Example: Heidi met with her employee, Sheila, to address Sheila's errors. Her higher purpose was to reinspire Sheila in her job. When the discussions of errors seemed to drag Sheila down, Heidi switched back to the bigger goal of reinspiring Sheila.

2. Focus on possibilities

Don't: get bogged down by how things are.

> **Why not?** While you need to acknowledge existing reality, the possibility of change is more motivating.

Do: pair each problem with possibilities.

> **Why?** To elevate the conversation.

Example: Carl had to deliver the bad news to Jimmy. He had to tell Jimmy he was cutting him from the basketball team. He spoke to Jimmy about other sports that Carl suspected would be more suited to Jimmy's nature. Jimmy walked out of the conversation completely inspired, even though he had been barred from the sporting activity he thought he wanted. He took up golf, and now, as a professional speaker, Jim tells audiences that the day he was cut from the team was one of the most inspiring days of his life.

3. Emphasize areas of similarity and agreement

Don't: focus on areas of disagreement without referring to the ways you agree.

> **Why not?** Areas of disagreement cause us to see each other as opponents.

Do: point out what you all have in common and where you are like-minded.

Why? It creates a sense of alliance and inspires collaboration.

Example #1: During the US election, politicians would occasionally remind us that, red or blue, we're all Americans.

Example #2: When Jeff and Julie get into arguments about policies in their agency for abused children, Julie reminds Jeff that they're both passionate about the agency mission, they just differ on a few administrative issues.

4. Favor the words "we," "our" and "us" over "I" and "my"

Don't: make yourself and your own interests the main focus of conversation.

Why not? It inspires others to make themselves the focus of conversation.

Do: use the words "we," "our" and "us" as often as reasonable.

Why? To get people thinking in terms of commonalities and collaboration.

Example #1: US President Obama's campaign was "Change WE can believe in" His slogan was "Yes WE can." He spoke more about what WE could do than what HE would do.

An upward spiral

The third law of thermodynamics says that entropy gives matter the tendency to go from a more organized state to a less organized state. Conversation does that as well...unless we make an effort from our side to elevate our talk.

The opposite of entropy is ectropy. Ectropy is a measure of the tendency of a dynamical system to do useful work and grow more organized. That's what we want our conversations to do.

This chapter — in fact, this entire book — is about how to elevate your conversations to their highest order. They are about how to get your words to work for you. I hope it kick starts an upward spiral for your conversations, so it will shape, build and grow the kind of life your heart desires.

When all is said and done, stop talking

Skill #51: Relax into silence

Too many of us are addicted to activity for activity's sake. Too many of us are addicted to talking for talking's sake. Too many of us know how to get things done, but we don't know when or how to stop.

When you find yourself in a hole, stop digging. When what you say stops working, say something else. When all is said and done, stop talking.

Words are wonderful tools. Silence is their sweet reward.

For your PowerPhrase Quote of the Day, visit: *www.speakstrong.com/freestuff/*

Speak
STRONG

APPENDIX

SpeakStrong Article summaries:

You'll find articles at my SpeakStrong.com website with further tips about how to Speak Strong at work and at home. Here are summaries of 25 of my most popular articles. Although I wrote the summaries to give you maximum information, I invite you to read the articles in their entirety. You'll find links to the complete articles at *www.speakstrong.com/articles/*

I also include the specific links after each summary. Enjoy!

Speak Strong

1. *Some Boats Need to Be Rocked*

Article summary: If you live your life trying not to rock the boat, this article explains why some boats do need to be rocked. Like so many people, I learned young to play it safe, put a false front forward and to avoid making waves. I share the story about how I discovered how costly it can be to "play it safe" when a wave I ignored turned out to be an early tsunami warning. Find out more at: *www.speakstrong.com/articles/speak-strong/boats.html*

2. *Beyond Blame: The Dos and Don'ts of Responsibility*

Article summary: Stephen Covey says that to know all is to forgive all — but that doesn't mean you should tolerate inappropriate behavior or neglect to hold people accountable. There's a difference between blame and accountability.

Blame errs on the side of unreasonableness and criticalness.
Accountability forgives the forgivable but does not accept the unacceptable.

Blame examines responsibility to condemn and punish.
Accountability examines responsibility to discover what can be done.

Blame overfocuses on what went wrong.
Accountability focuses on what happened and what needs to be corrected.

Blame is black and white.
Accountability explores complexity.

Find out more at: *www.speakstrong.com/articles/speak-strong/beyondblame. html*

3. *The SpeakStrong Award*

Article summary: It's heroic to Speak Strong, no matter how large or small the situation. Any time someone resists temptation to talk the low road, steps out of their comfort zone or resists their knee-jerk reaction, I say they deserve an award. That's why I give "Pippi SpeakStrong Giraffes" to people who send me their success stories.

My readers love knowing about how others Speak Strong. Learn more here: *www.speakstrong.com/articles/speak-strong/speakstrong-award.html*

4. A *Tale of Pippi and Izzie: How to Elevate Your Word Choice by Elevating Your Thinking*

Article summary: We all experience internal contradictions and competing thoughts, feelings and desires. I illustrate the inner conflict with a metaphor. A giraffe I call Pippi represents rising above the mud of the moment and speaking from an elevated perspective. A lizard I call Izzie represents the reptilian, reactive self that speaks from limited vision. Pippi and Izzie are useful reminders of the competing forces inside us all — forces that influence the way we choose our words.

Do you ever want to be nice and nasty at the same time? Do you ever want to simultaneously affirm and affront someone? Pippi can have one of your ears while Izzie has the other. This article illuminates and integrates the dichotomy. *www.speakstrong.com/articles/speak-strong/tale.html*

5. A *Convenient Truth at Toastmasters: A Tale of Honest Feedback*

Article summary: Honest feedback can be tough to hear, but it's the only kind of feedback that can help you succeed. I learned this lesson when the evaluator for my fourth speech to my Toastmaster's club offered "suggestions for improvement." Although I resisted at first, her evaluations became my favorite, because she gave me useful information I could apply to advance my skills and ultimately my career. People who are willing to "rock your boat" like she rocked mine give you great gifts if you can receive them.

Read the whole article and learn more about honest feedback at: *www.speakstrong.com/articles/speak-strong/Toastmasters.html*

6. A *Sophisticated Vocabulary of Feelings*

Article summary: There's power in naming things, and there's extra power in naming feelings. This posting contains a list of feeling words to help you find the perfect words to communicate what's going on in your heart. You'll also find this list in the back of this book. *www.speakstrong.com/articles/speak-strong/emotions.html*

7. *Beyond the Good Old Boys Club*

Article summary: If you aren't a member of the Good Old Boy's Club, chances are you've encountered it. Here are ten tips to work with or independently from the GOBC:

1. Know the GOBC when you see it
2. Don't assume GOBC dynamics when there are none
3. Be aware of the ways you yourself feed the GOBC
4. Don't let the GOBC define you
5. Create a GOGC — Good Old Girls Club
6. Point out lack of diversity when you see it
7. Acknowledge inclusion
8. Ask for inclusion
9. Don't whine
10. Create your own game

The Good Old Boys' Club doesn't willingly surrender power because it's the right thing to do. The good news is you don't need them to. You can balance the power your own way. Get the full story at: *www.speakstrong.com/articles/ speak-strong/good-old-boys-tips.html*

8. *Constructive Anger: How to Speak Strong when you're seeing red*

Article summary: There's a lot of power in anger. If you suppress your anger, you suppress your power. Anger is like fire. It can cook your food or burn your house down. People who Speak Strong use their anger for constructive purposes. This article offers seven tips to manage your anger constructively. They are:

1. Don't resist your anger
2. Find a way to let off steam
3. Think determination
4. Forget about revenge
5. Don't base your behavior on theirs
6. Set your goals
7. Say what you mean, and mean what you say, without being mean when you say it

Note that revenge and suppression are NOT on the list. Read the complete article at: *www.speakstrong.com/articles/speak-strong/constructive-anger.html*

9. *The SpeakStrong "We Use Recycled Packaging" Sticker*

Article summary: There are many ways to Speak Strong. One is to turn a perceived negative into a positive. A marketer I worked with did that by shipping in recycled boxes and packages marked with a sticker that says "We use recycled packaging." This link is not an article — it's a downloadable image for a Recycled Packaging Avery Sticker Template. *www.speakstrong.com/articles/avery.html*

10. *Take the Time to Say It Right*

Article summary: Gotta-go communication comes in three forms.

1. Dump and run: someone explains their side of an issue, and in the same breath they explain they don't have time to listen to a response.
2. Drive-by delegation: a manager assigns a task with minimal explanation and can't find the time to clarify.
3. Reckless relating: a colleague neglects to reciprocate.

Any conversation worth having is worth having well. If you're the victim of gotta-go communication, Speak Strong. If you're the perpetrator, take the time to say it right. Learn more at: *www.speakstrong.com/articles/speak-strong/gotta-go.html*

11. *Communication Hardball: Reasonableness Is Your Best Revenge*

Article summary: Newton's third law of motion says that for every action, there's a reaction. Too often that plays out conversationally to mean that when someone's words act on you, you react in a way that is determined by their word choice, tone and intent rather than by your own preference. Discover many possible responses by taking moment to respond instead of react.

When someone throws a ball at you, what do you do? Chances are you toss it back. Chances are you toss it back in the same way they threw it to you. If they toss the ball gently, you toss it back gently. If they toss it hard, you toss it back hard. If they toss it so hard you think they're trying to hurt you, you just might throw it back hard enough to hurt them — and a friendly game of catch becomes a vicious game of hardball.

But you could just let the ball go by, duck, throw something different at them, toss the ball back in a surprising way…your choices are endless.

As in catch, you can respond to a verbal hardball in ways of your own choosing. This article explores 14 possible responses to someone who plays communication hardball. They are: placate, apologize, witness, educate, express pain, refute, clarify, appeal, accuse, escalate, terminate, deliberate, mitigate, eviscerate.

Whatever choice you make, choose it because it's the best approach for you. If you must get revenge for someone's harshness, I recommend reasonableness. It's your best revenge. Read the full article at: *www.speakstrong.com/articles/speak-strong/reasonableness.html*

12. *The Secret Power of Tears*

Article summary: Have you had a good cry lately? If the answer is no, you're probably cut off from an important source of power.

The Secret Power of Tears is the most popular article on my SpeakStrong website, with hundreds of hits and forwards. It speaks to the hearts of all of us who have been victims of the war on tears. It invites you to take a look at your attitudes toward tears, and includes a poem by poet and author Jeffrey Armstrong (*www.jeffreyarmstrong.com*) called *The Art of Crying*.

When you don't just allow tears, but actually cultivate them (in appropriate settings), long lost passion for life returns. The secret power of tears is: they unlock your emotions. That adds oomph to your communication. Speaking Strong combines clarity, strength and caring to create a compelling message.

Celebrate life and communicate with a level of passion you thought was reserved for other people.

www.speakstrong.com/articles/speak-strong/secret-power.html

13. *Speak to Create Anticipation: How Foreshadowing Can Hook Your Listeners and Even Get You a Job*

Article summary: Answers are more powerful when people ask the questions first. Foreshadowing gets people wondering and wanting the answer before you provide it. For example, when you tell a joke, you'll get the best laugh if you include just the correct amount of build-up. When you slowly build to an excellent punch-line, you have your listener in stitches. If your build-up is too labored for the punch-line, you'll lose impact. If you reveal the punch-line too quickly, you'll also lose impact. Foreshadow just enough to get your listener wanting to know how it will all turn out — but not so much they want to run screaming from the room. That way you'll hook your listener and maximize impact.

This article includes a tale of a vendor who hooked my interest in his services through foreshadowing. *www.speakstrong.com/articles/persuasion/anticipation. html*

14. *Speak Smart, Speak Sweet, Speak Strong for Communication Clout*

Article summary: True power does not create unnecessary resistance. Sure, you can overwhelm someone with faulty logic, but if you impress them with your reason and good sense, they'll want to know more. You can criticize someone, but if you graciously tell them what you'd rather they did instead, they'll feel better about making the change. You can force an employee to work late, but it might be strategic to incent him to work late, because he's likely to do a better job.

There are three communication power centers:
1. reason/thought
2. emotions/feelings
3. strategy/action

Incorporate all three to give your words maximum power. It's what I call Pippi Power. Pippi Power = IQ + EQ + SQ. That's intelligence quotient + emotional quotient + strategic action quotient. When you display IQ + EQ + SQ, you're using the three available power centers.

Read the article to learn to select the perfect balance of power centers for your audience, and to frame your message in your listener's preferred power center so they will be open to your full message. *www.speakstrong.com/ articles/persuasion/frame.html*

13. *Ten Tips to Speak Strong at a Trade Show*
Poetic article summary:

A trade show is one big production
With planning and display construction.
You'll find nothing selling
If your words aren't compelling
So study this SpeakStrong instruction.

www.speakstrong.com/articles/sales/tradeshowtips.html

14. *Email Mastery: A Speak Strong Approach to Effective E-mails*

Article Summary: There are four keys that keep your emails from getting lost in the depth of your reader's email abyss. They are:

1. Strategic subject lines: Give a clear idea of your message in your subject lines
2. Email overview: for longer emails, open with an overview that helps your reader know what to look for and where
3. Bullets: separate points with bullets
4. Paragraph headers: Create clever headers for paragraphs.

Read more about how to write emails that get results at: *www.speakstrong.com/ articles/email/emailmastery.html*

15. *Dos and Don'ts of Emailing: A Speak Strong Approach to Email Mastery*

Article summary: This article lists essential dos and don'ts to guide you when you compose emails. Here are a few you can apply immediately:

- Don't make your reader search for information.
- Don't write long paragraphs.
- Don't make your reader guess what you want from them.
- Don't make your reader search for your contact info.
- Don't make your reader guess what you are referring to.

- Do use the subject line to indicate contents and desired actions.
- Do place important information where the reader can find it immediately.
- Do write short paragraphs.
- Do determine that every pronoun (he, it etc) has a referent.
- For longer messages, do open with an overview of the contents.
- Do separate different ideas with paragraphs, or send in separate emails.

Read all your dos and don'ts with examples at: *www.speakstrong.com/articles/ email/dosanddon%27tsofe-mailing.html*

16. *How to Write Strong Subject Lines in Your Emails*

Article summary: An email subject line is just a few words, but those few words make the difference between the success and failure of your emails. This article offers eight tips with dos, don'ts and examples. The tips are:

1. Focus on them
2. Include your requested action
3. Present a benefit

4. Think of the subject line as a book title or headline
5. Be as specific as possible
6. Don't cry wolf or hype routine messages
7. Use subject-only headlines for quick messages
8. Use intrigue to entice your reader to open the email.

Get the full explanation and examples at: *www.speakstrong.com/articles/email/ howtowritestrongsubjectlinesinyouremails.html*

17. *How to Give a Performance Review — Dos and Don'ts*
Article summary: Performance reviews are among the most valuable resources in a manager's toolbox, yet many managers don't know how to give a performance review of an employee. Here are 10 dos and don'ts to help you create a positive and productive performance review experience.

1. Avoid surprises by communicating as things arise
2. Prepare all year with great performance management
3. Use preplanned phrases
4. Keep it professional by avoiding personal discussion
5. Maintain balance by including some positives and some areas for improvement in all reviews
6. Show respect
7. Be accurate, avoid making any promises you might not be able to deliver on
8. Review your best employees too, even if you think they're perfect already
9. Document facts, not conclusions

Get the details at: *www.speakstrong.com/articles/performance-management/ performancereviewdosanddonts.html*

18. *'Ask the Right Question' Problem-Solving Worksheet for an Essential Managerial Problem-Solving Exercise*
Article summary: There are eleven steps to ensure that you have given employees every chance to succeed. This worksheet walks you through those steps with questions for each. It will help you manage performance effectively.

Download the worksheet in a word document here: www.speakstrong.com/ documents/problemsolvingworksheet.doc

You'll find my performance flow chart in this book at the end of the article summaries, page 272, and at: *www.speakstrong.com/freestuff/*

19. *How to Stop Passive-Aggressive Behavior in the Workplace*

Article summary: Here are your quick dos and don'ts to deal with passive-aggressive behavior at work.

- Don't react with your own passive-aggressive behavior
- Don't let your doubts silence you
- Don't believe words that contradict action
- Do respond assertively
- Do use Power Phrases to say what you mean and mean what you say without being mean when you say it
- Do let them know how they affect you
- Do ask questions about the true intent of their behavior
- Do hold people accountable for what they do, not for what they say they'll do

Read more at: *www.speakstrong.com/articles/workplace-communication/ howtostoppassiveaggressivebehavior.html*

20. *How to Use Reflective Listening Scripts: The Top Ten Dos, Don'ts, and PowerPhrases to Promote Understanding*

Article summary: Reflective (reflexive) listening is a powerful communication tool because it creates safety for the person speaking, and reassures them they will be heard. However, a few wrong words can undermine your efforts to listen to understand. This article details ten tips to help you listen so others will speak freely. They are:

1. When someone becomes defensive, offer to listen reflectively
2. If you prefer, slip into reflective listening without telling the speaker what you're doing
3. Avoid temptation to switch the focus to you
4. Suspend judgment and keep the focus on understanding
5. Be prepared with neutral phrases to use while they speak
6. Mirror what they say in four areas: the facts, what they think, what they feel and what they want
7. Avoid any need to be right
8. Keep reflecting back until they agree that you hear them correctly
9. Once they feel understood, ask for your turn
10. Follow-up with problem-solving techniques

Read the explanations, the dos, don'ts, and examples for each tip here: *www. speakstrong.com/articles/workplace-communication/reflectivelisteningscripts. html*

21. *How to Handle Interruptions*
Article summary: If interruptions lower your productivity, these ten tips will help you keep those interruptions to a minimum. They are:

1. Anticipate what people might need later to minimize future interruptions
2. Leave detailed messages that elicit a quick complete response
3. Encourage interrupters to find their own answers and help them discover how
4. Respond to interruptions in a way that encourages the behavior you want
5. Determine the urgency of interruptions
6. When it's your boss let him/her know what the interruption is taking you away from
7. Negotiate interruption policies
8. Let people know when you're particularly busy
9. Focus the long-winded
10. Encourage self-sufficiency whenever possible

Read the full explanations, the dos and don't and phrases for each point at: *www.speakstrong.com/articles/workplace-communication/howtohandle interruptions.html*

22. *Trust the process enough to let people question it: Collaborative, credible communication*
Article summary: You're the expert, you know what you're doing, and your approach works with 90% of the people you use it with. So what do you do when someone insists on asking questions before you've laid the groundwork?

Even when you're the expert, credibility requires you to communicate collaboratively. If your listener asks so many questions you feel challenged or if questions interrupt the teaching process, back up and discover how your listener learns best. Then adapt your teaching style to their learning style. You might adapt by using more examples. You might need to explain the "why" behind the "what." You might present an overview of how you impart knowledge so your listener will have a context to understand the details as you convey them.

Learn more about how to collaborate with your students, your employees and anyone else you direct and instruct, so your expertise gets across. *www.managementskilltraining.com/articles/personal.html*

23. *How to Bridge the Four Different Communication Styles: Seven Steps to Communication Style Development*

Article summary: Communication style research uncovers four different communication styles that are determined by two factors — pace and people-orientation.

1. "Visionaries" are fast-paced, people-oriented communicators.
2. "Achievers" are fast-paced, task-oriented communicators.
3. "Reflectives" are slower-paced, task-oriented communicators.
4. "Likeables" are slower-paced, people-oriented communicators.

Each style has its own strengths and weaknesses. And like oil and vinegar, they don't blend perfectly, but they do complement each other.

Here's how you communicate with people who have different styles from your own.

1. Ask the question, what's my communication style? Take a simple communication test to find out. *www.speakstrong.com/inventory.*
2. Invite the important people in your life to take the communication style quiz. Once you understand your own style, enlist the interest of others.
3. Initiate a conversation about conversations with people of other communication styles.
4. When you talk to a "Visionary", make it fun.
5. When you talk to an "Achiever", make it fast.
6. When you talk to a "Reflective", make it logical and accurate.
7. When you talk to a "Likeable", make it personal.

Learn more at: *www.speakstrong.com/articles/communication-styles/stylebridge. html*

24. *Six Steps to Rerail the Derailed Discussion*
How to Talk to Your Communication Nemesis

Article summary: Most people in your life have at least one predictable, irritating, derailing or even damaging communication habit. You can be excused for being powerless in the face of their tactics for a while. But there does come a time when, if you don't figure out how to respond effectively, instead of being a victim of these communication habits, you are a volunteer.

Because people predictably do what they do, you can prepare an effective response. Change the conversation by changing your side of the equation. It's a six-step process.

1. Collect and list things they say that irritate, derail or damage discussion
2. Put your list into categories
3. Note the effect their words have on you
4. Note your habitual response to what they say
5. Create options to respond differently
6. Assess your results and revamp your strategy

Read more at: *www.speakstrong.com/articles/communication-styles/rerail-your-conversation.html*

25. 9/11 and Other Life-Changing Traumas: the Hows and the Whys of Sensitive Conversations.

Article summary: Trauma leaves its mark on everyone it touches. Because our relationships to events are unique, even shared traumas leave different footprints on the individuals they imprint. And because our ways of coping with trauma vary, people who go through traumatic events together often end up conflicting and are unable to support each other.

It is ultimately helpful to talk about traumatic events. If someone in your life is reluctant to talk, don't force, but gently coax them to open up. Here are some tips to do that:

1. Let them talk on their own terms
2. Make it safe for them when they do open up
3. Make sure everything you say is for their needs, not your curiosity. (I had all kinds of questions I would have liked to have asked my friend about but didn't, because it would have been self-serving.)
4. Listen to learn about them

Read the entire article at: *www.speakstrong.com/articles/sensitive-issues/911.html*

26. Educate, Don't Excoriate: SpeakStrong to turn a diversity blunder into a diversity breakthrough

Article summary: The world is full of diversity landmines. No matter how careful you are, it's easy to offend someone with a different background. It's easy for someone with a different background to offend YOU. When they do, educate, don't excoriate.

Explain why a comment was offensive, and offer suggestions for better wording. Consider the blunder as an opportunity to help people understand a culture in new ways.

The entire article is here: *www.speakstrong.com/articles/sensitive-issues/diversity. html*

Meryl's Performance Management Flow Chart

The 'Ask the Right Question' Problem-Solving Worksheet for an Essential Managerial Problem-Solving Exercise provides eleven steps to manage performance issues. This chart illustrates the flow. You can get a color version at: *http://www.speakstrong.com/freestuff/*

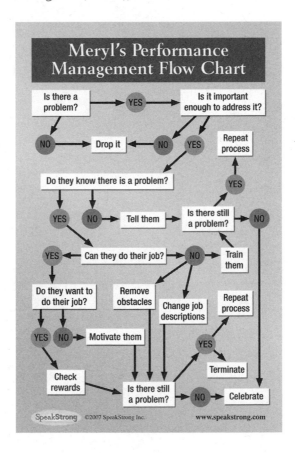

More SpeakStrong articles

All of these articles and more are available at: *www.speakstrong.com/articles/* If the article that interests you isn't in the list, email me at *MerylRunion@ speakstrong.com*. I might write it for you — and I answer almost all communication questions I receive.

More resources from SpeakStrong

Online tools:

These SpeakStrong tools are available at: *www.speakstrong.com/freestuff/ tools_index.html*

Communication Style Inventory

Take the SpeakStrong personality test to determine your communication style and to receive tips on how to communicate with other styles. I regularly hear from readers who are impressed by what they learn. Fill out the questions and we will email you the results.
www.speakstrong.com/inventory/

A World of Truth

A World of Truth is an inspirational flash movie about the world as you always knew it could be. It's my vision for the world. Grab your popcorn — and maybe your Kleenex as well.
www.speakstrong.com/video/worldoftruth.swf

The Legend of Mighty Mouth

The Legend of Mighty Mouth is a SpeakStrong flash movie that tells the tale of corporate transformation through assertive communication. I took my poetic self for a walk to create this one. "It was a small corporation in a desperate town. Problems were up, and profits were down..."
www.speakstrong.com/video/mightymouth.swf

PowerPhrase Tutorial

This is an interactive exercise to create your own Power Phrases to Speak Strong. Let it walk you through the steps and take you to the words you need.
www.speakstrong.com/tutorial/

Bunny Bubbles

In this SpeakStrong Video, I interview Bunny Bubbles, the "Acting Director of The Center for Lowered Expectations." In case you haven't guessed yet, it's humorous, and it's really about how NOT Speaking Strong.
www.speakstrong.com/video/bunnybubbles.html

SpeakStrong Blog

I started the SpeakStrong blog because I was receiving more emails than I could respond to. I also like the input—because sometimes my readers have better ideas than I do. It's great to get people's feedback on my posts, and the discussions can get lively.
www.speakstrong.com/newsletter/

SpeakStrong Newsletter: A PowerPhrase a Week

I've been writing the SpeakStrong Newsletter for seven years now. It's a great reminder to Speak Strong. It includes a section on life in general, the Power-Phrase of the Week, The Poison Phrase of the Week, a question/answer section, and, when I have one, a success story.
www.speakstrong.com/newsletter/newsletbene.html

SpeakStrong Article:
Eight Treacherous Topics: The Things You Think You Can't Say

The touchy three topics we've all been told to avoid are sex, religion and politics. In my perfect world, we would freely exchange ideas on these topics. In my perfect world, no topic would be off limits.

There are more touchy topics than the famous three. I have uncovered eight topics most of us avoid — but should embrace. It can leave you powerless if you need to address these topics but don't.

Let's take a look at what topics you avoid.

The things you dare not say

Take a moment to think about the things you want to say but don't. Consider all aspects of your life — work — home — church — everything.

Got your list?

Each one of your forbidden topics is like a little piece of kryptonite that weakens you, takes away some of your "super powers" and leaves you vulnerable.

When you don't speak up about important issues, it zaps your strength, diminishes your vitality and even erodes your health. There's a saying — "You're as healthy as the things you can talk about." This saying does not just refer to psychological health.

Chances are you don't even know how many things you can't talk about (or think you can't talk about.) Chances are, you censor yourself without even considering saying anything.

The treacherous eight subjects

Most people censor themselves around eight topics. See if this list inspires you to add a few topics to your list.

1) Money

More than 50% of couples keep money secrets from each other and have difficulty discussing financial matters. One of my friends neglected to tell her fiancé before they married that she was $50,000 in debt. I think he had a right to know. He thought so too.

The topic of money is shrouded in embarrassment and pretense. People pretend they have more money than they do. People pretend they have less money than they do. Many work for less than they could command rather than ask for a raise. Most people have someone in their lives that owes them money but are reluctant to ask about it. And people think they're supposed to know how to handle money even if they've never been taught. I know several people who made bad investments because they were unwilling to admit how little they knew about investing.

2) Sex

Mention sex in a group of grown adults and you'll hear titters. You can walk around with a smile on your face, but you had better not tell anyone what put it there. Too bad — they might learn something useful. We are remarkably un-informed about a topic that is so intimate to our lives.

Many discovered sex in the back seat of a car and have never learned how to manage these powerful energies in the most positive ways. We read studies to see what's normal, but we could all learn a lot more just by being honest with each other. If you're one of those people who had a sexual awakening later in life, you might have wondered: "How come no one ever told me about this?"

The topic of sex is shrouded in embarrassment and pretense. People pretend they like sex more than they do or they like sex less than they do. People act like they're more experienced than they are or less experienced than they are. People settle for unsatisfactory sexual relationships rather than ask for what they want.

3) Religion

Religion and spirituality are perhaps even more intimate to our existence than sex, which is why it is both important and difficult to talk about them.

Good luck if you try with anyone who doesn't think just like you do.

A friend who questioned some of the teachings in a bible class found himself "reassured" by the response, "Don't worry. You'll understand it more over time." My friend never did succeed in initiating an intelligent discussion about his concerns. It wouldn't surprise me if there were others in the group who shared his inquiry.

So much of the conversation that does take place about religion and spiritual-ity is dogmatic and proselytizing, which poisons the dialogue for those who seek to relate what they experience or clarify what they question. If more of us felt free to share how spirituality influences us, it would be wonderfully inspir-ing and informative.

4) Politics

The United States is supposed to be a democracy, based upon civilized dialogue and open discussion of issues. Somehow it rarely works that way. Political dialogue is not for the faint of heart these days.

Normally gracious people suddenly decide all bets are off when the topic turns political. Reason and logic give way to tactics, pressure and manipulation. People repeat the talking points of the day with little regard to their validity, and if their arguments don't convince, they get louder rather than smarter.

As a result, illogic dominates the political dialogue.

(Resource: *www.UniteandConcur.com*)

5) Incompetence

When I ask at my presentations how many managers have employees with delusions of competence I get a laugh. Many managers don't address employee weaknesses, so the employees don't know their skills aren't up to par. Often, when an under-performing employee gets a new manager, they resist correction and insist that the new manager is the problem.

The research organization Vital Smarts found that over 50% of medical employees have witnessed incompetence and said nothing. If you don't speak up, you take part in that incompetence and are complicit in harm caused by the incompetence. Sometimes that even means death.

6) Dishonesty

People like to think of themselves as honest and fair — even when they're not. When you identify dishonesty, usually the culprit targets you.

Some types of dishonesty are generally accepted culturally. That doesn't make them honest. Violating copyrights is one widespread example of generally accepted dishonesty.

If you stay silent when faced with dishonesty, you become complicit in rewarding dishonesty. That makes you dishonest yourself.

7) Wants and needs

While some of us are all too willing to talk about what we want, others of us go around as bundles of unmet needs that we never seek to get met — beyond hinting, that is. Often people who never clearly asked for what they wanted feel resentment and seek to punish those who don't guess what they want and don't provide it. Sure, asking for something risks rejection. But not asking ensures it.

8) Joy and pleasure

I once received a comment on an evaluation for a conflict management seminar that stated that because I used so much humor, it was clear that I didn't take the subject seriously. I use humor because I DO take my topics seriously, and humor helps the learning process.

Some people act long-suffering as if it's a claim of nobility. Others are afraid to look like they enjoy their work for fear they aren't earning their pay if they do.

When you let your joy shine, you give others permission to experience joy as well. It's a great message to send.

Expand the scope of your conversations

Your voice is your connection to the world outside you. When you stifle that voice, you stifle that connection.

It does make sense to speak strategically. Check your timing, pick your battles and speak in a ways others are likely to hear. It makes sense at times to play it safe and stay silent. Approach the treacherous topics with care. But don't let cultural norms of silence limit the scope of your conversations.

Say what you mean. Mean what you say.
Don't be mean when you say it.

Now that you've read this article, have you discovered there are a few more off-limit topics than you imagined? Expand the list of topics you can freely discuss and discover what it's like to go through life without "kryptonite" in your pocket. You'll like it.

Risky Conversations Assessment Form

Use this form to decide whether to address an issue or not. You can find a word document version at: *www.speakstrong.com/articles/speak-strong/risky_conversation.html*

1. What do I want to say?

2. What am I saying instead?

3. What is the best that can happen if I speak up?

4. What is the worst that can happen if I speak up?

5. Is the best that can happen worth risking the worst that can happen?

6. Can I live with the worst that can happen if it does?

7. What is the best I can hope for if I don't speak up?

8. What is the worst that can happen if I don't speak up?

9. Is the worst that can happen if I don't speak worth risking the worst that can happen if I do?

10. What is the worst that could happen if I don't speak? What is the likely price of silence?

11. Am I compromising my personal integrity by remaining silent on this issue?

12. Is my silence allowing the perpetuation of an injustice?

13. By remaining silent, am I compromising a long-term value to avoid short-term discomfort?

14. Based on my responses, do I want to speak or remain silent on the subject?

Emotional Map

The Love Letter Technique
According to Relationship Expert John Gray, emotions exist in layers, from more guarded to more vulnerable. Emotions go from:

1. Anger
2. Sorrow
3. Fear
4. Regret
5. Love

If you're ever unsure about what you feel, use this like a map to take you through all possible levels. Gray calls it a love letter technique. That name implies that you only use it in love relationships — but it's useful any time you're not sure what you feel. The process has helped me through many emotional challenges.

Here are some sentence stems to help you work your way through your emotions.

1. Anger and Blame
I don't like it when...
How dare you...
I resent...
I hate it when...
I've had enough of...
I can't stand...

2. Hurt and Sadness
I feel sad that...
I feel hurt because...
It breaks my heart that...
I want to cry because...
I'm disappointed that...
I want...

3. Fear and Insecurity
I feel afraid…
I'm afraid that…
I feel scared because…
I want…
What if…
I'm terrified of…

4. Guilt and Responsibility
I'm sorry that…
I wish I hadn't…
I'm sorry for…
Please forgive me for…
I didn't mean to…
I'm ashamed about…

5. Love, Forgiveness, Understanding and Desire
I love you because…
I love when…
Thank you for…
I understand that…
I forgive you for…
I'm grateful that…

Adapted from *What You Feel You Can Heal* by John Gray.

Start with anger and blame unless another emotion presents itself. Keep working with the sentence stems for anger and blame until you feel some release or you naturally gravitate toward another emotion. Keep moving from sentence stem to sentence stem as you are drawn. You can use emotions from the list of feeling words in the next section and on my website at: *www.speakstrong.com/ articles/speak-strong/emotions.html*

This exercise acts like a powerful emotional map to help you explore and uncover deep emotions. Have a great journey. Your newly established emotional connection will help you SpeakStrong.

Feeling Words

When you embark on an important conversation, do you know how you feel? Most people don't. There's power in the language of feelings. Find the words to describe how you feel, and be effective in making your point.

Emotional Words

abandoned abominable absent-minded absorbed abused accepted accepting accused aching acrimonious admired admiration adored adrift affectionate affected afflicted afraid aggravated aggressive aghast agitated agonized alarmed alert alienated alive alone aloof alluring amazed ambushed amused anguish angry animated annoyed antagonistic anxious apathetic appalled apprehensive apologetic appreciated appreciative apprehensive aroused a sense of loss ashamed astonished attacked attractive attracted audacious avid aware awed awestruck awkward

bad baffled bashful beaten down belittled benevolent berated betrayed bewildered bitter blamed blessed blue bold bored bothered brave bright broken bummed burdened burned-out

calm capable carefree careless caring cautious censored centered certain challenged charmed cheated cheerful cheerless cherished chicken childish clean clear clever close closed clouded clueless clumsy cold comfortable committed compassionate competent competitive complacent complete concerned condemned confident confused considerate contemplative contempt content controlled convicted cornered courageous cowardly cranky crazy cross crushed curious

daring dark dashed dazed dead deceived dedicated defeated defenseless defensive defiant degraded dejected delicate delighted demoralized dependent depressed deprived deserted desired despair desperate despicable destroyed detached determined devastated devious devoted different difficult dirty disappointed disbelieving discarded disconnected disconsolate discontent discouraged disgraced disgusted disheartened dishonest disillusioned dismal dismayed disobedient disorganized disposable distant distracted distressed disturbed divided doubtful downcast downhearted drained drawn dreary dropped dubious dull dumb dynamic eager earnest easy ecstatic edgy effective embarrassed empathetic elated empty enchanted encouraged energetic energized enlightened enraged enriched entertained enthusiastic envious evasive evil exasperated excited excluded exhausted exhilarated expectant exploited exposed exuberant

fainthearted faithful fake fantastic fascinated fatigued fearful fearless feisty festive fidgety fine flat flustered foolish forced forgiven forgiving forgotten fortunate framed frantic free friendly frightened frisky frustrated fulfilled full funny furious

gallant generous gentle giving grieved grieving glorious good grateful great glad gloomy grouchy grumpy guarded guilty gullible

handicapped hapless happy hardy hateful haunted healthy heard heartbroken heavy-hearted helpful helpless heroic hesitant honored hopeful hopeless horrible horrified hostile hospitable hostile humble humiliated hurt hysterical

idealistic idiotic ignorant ignored ill at ease imaginative immune impatient impelled imperfect impertinent important impressed impulsive inadequate inattentive incapable incensed incompetent incomplete incredulous indebted indecisive independent indifferent indignant industrious inept inferior inflamed inflated informed infuriated inhibited injured innocent innovative inquisitive insane insecure insensitive insignificant isolated insulted intense interested interrogated interrupted intimidated intimate intrigued irate insecure insensitive inspired insulting invigorated invisible involved irrational irresponsible irritated irked

jaded jealous jinxed jolly jovial joyful jubilant judged judgmental jumpy just justified joyless joyous jubilant

kidded kind knowledgeable

late lazy leery left out let down liable liberated lifeless light-hearted liked listened to logical lonely loose lost lousy lovable love loved loving low lucky

mad manipulated mean meditative melancholy menaced merry mischievous
miserable misgiving misinterpreted mistreated misunderstood mixed up
mocked modest molested moody motivated moved mournful mystified

naive nasty needed needy negative neglected nervous neutral
neurotic nonchalant nostalgic nosy noticed numb

obeyed obligated obvious odd offended old open oppressed
optimistic ornery out of control outraged overcome overjoyed
overloaded overwhelmed overworked owned

pained pampered panic panicked paralyzed passionate passive patient
peaceful peeved pensive perky perplexed persecuted pessimistic
pestered petrified petty phony pious piteous pitiful playful pleasant
pleased poor possessive positive powerful powerless practical
preoccupied pressured private productive protected protective
proud provocative provoked prudish punished pushy puzzled

questioned quiet quaking

rambunctious reassured realistic rebellious reborn re-enforced receptive
reckless recognized reconciled reflective refreshed regretful rejected
rejuvenated relaxed released relieved reluctant reminiscent remorse
renewed replaced replenished repressed rescued resentful reserved
resistant restless resourceful respected responsible restricted revengeful
revitalized rich ridiculous right rigid robbed romantic rotten rueful rushed

sabotaged sad safe sassy satisfied saved scared scolded scorned secure
seductive self-assured self-centered self-confident self-conscious self-
destructive self-reliant selfish sensitive sentimental serene serious
sexy skillful shaky shamed shaken sheepish shocked shunned shy sick
silenced silly sincere sinful slandered sluggish small smart smothered
skeptical solemn snoopy soothed sorry special spirited spiteful splendid
spunky squashed stifled stimulated stingy strained stretched stressed
strong stubborn stumped stunned stupid stupefied submissive successful
suicidal suffocated sulky sullen sunk sunny super superior supported
sure surly surprised suspicious sympathetic sympathy sympathetic

tacky tactful talented talkative tame tarnished tasteful tearful
teased tenacious tender tense tepid terrible terrific terrified tested
testy thankful thoughtful threatened thrifty thrilled timid tired
tormented torn tortured tough tragic tranquil transformed trapped
treasured trembly tremendous tricked troubled trusted

ugly unaccepted unappreciated unbalanced unbelieving uncertain

unburdened uncanny uncomfortable unconcerned understanding uneven
unfit unhappy unfriendly unique united unjust unknown unneeded
unpleasant upset uneasy unreal unruly unwise uplifted used useless unsure

vacant vague vain valid valued vexed vicious victimized
victorious virulent violated vivid void vulnerable

wacky warlike warm warmhearted warned wary wasted wavering weak
wealthy weary weird whole wild willful wishful witty wonderful worldly
worried worse woeful worthy wounded wrathful wrong wronged

yearning yellow yielding young youthful

zany zealous

About PowerPhrases

PowerPhrases are short, specific, targeted expressions that say what you mean, mean what you say without being mean when you say it.

Short: Keep instructions, feedback and all important communications brief to avoid confusing the issue or diluting your message.

Specific: Chose precise words that provide as much information as possible. For example, specify deadlines. Answer the questions: who, what, when, where and how.

Targeted: Select your words for the results you seek. Have a goal in mind and consider the consequences for every statement you make.

Say what you mean: Communicate what you think, feel and want. Be guided by the truth as you know it rather than the response that is likely to be safe or popular.

Mean what you say: Protect the integrity of your words by following through on what you say. Only speak words you are committed to follow-up on.

Don't be mean when you say it: Be kind in your choice of words. Refrain from using the communication tactics such as:
1) Sarcasm
2) Labeling and name calling
3) Blame
4) Emotional manipulation
5) Absolute language
6) Threats

You can be clear, direct AND kind. Embracing all three standards takes more time than only embracing one or two, but the results are that much better.

The next page has a PowerPhrases poster to remind you to use Power-Phrases. You can find a full color PDF of the poster at: *www.speakstrong.com/freestuff/*

POWERPHRASES!
to get your point across

Be brief: short is sweet

Be specific: paint word pictures

Be targeted: know what you want to accomplish

Be sincere: say what you mean

Be resolute: mean what you say

Be kind: don't be mean when you say it

The SpeakStrong Rules of Responsible Communication

Throughout this book, I refer to setting standards for your own communication, and making agreements with others about how you will speak to each other. I've created my own standards here. I invite you to adapt them to your own needs.

Standards summary:
- Stay Positive
- Be Civil
- Use Candor
- Speak Accurately and Honestly
- Listen Accountably
- Maintain the Three Perspectives

Standards elaboration:

Stay Positive: Emphasize outcome and solutions. Choose your words to elevate and empower others. Examine problems and hold your employees and yourself accountable, not to blame, but to find solutions. Give people the benefit of the doubt as long as there is doubt. Use "possibility thinking."

Be Civil: Be courteous and respectful. Speak the truth without viciousness or attack. Respect others, even if you don't think they earned your respect. Avoid personal attack.

Use Candor: Be straightforward, direct and open. Say what you mean — what you think, feel and want. Practice open communication. Initiate discussions. "Tell the truth but keep the faith."

Speak Accurately and Honestly: Speak with precision, exactness and adherence to facts. A) Be balanced in your use of facts, B) limit yourself to reasonable interpretation of facts in all claims, C) observe contextual correctness, and D) be informative and substantive.

Listen Accountably

Listen more than you speak. Listen as though you will be tested on understanding their words. Clarify your understanding of what you hear. Make it your responsibility that the other person feel heard.

Center for Responsible Communication

Standards of Communication

Stay Positive
- Emphasize solutions
- Elevate and empower
- Be accountable

Use Candor
- Be direct and open
- Reward openness in others

Listen Accountably
- Listen more than you speak
- Listen to understand

Be Civil
- Use courtesy and respect
- Avoid:
  sarcasm
  blame
  labeling
  emotional manipulation
  absolute language
  yelling
  threats

Speak Accurately and Honestly
- Balance your facts
- Interpret facts reasonably
- Be contextually correct
- Be informative and substantive

Maintain the Three Perspectives
Maintain awareness of the following three perspectives:
*yours *theirs, *the one a neutral party would tell.

Maintain the Three Perspectives

Maintain awareness of the following three perspectives: yours, theirs, and the one a neutral party would tell.

Determine:
- What do I think, feel, and want?
- What do they think, feel and want?
- How would a neutral party describe this conversation/situation?

This technique helps you to stay aware of all three perspectives at all times.

Create you own standards

When communication becomes strained, invite a conversation about conversations. Create standards with the people you are close to. Your standards might not look at all like mine. That's fine — as long as they work for you and the people you communicate with.

Speak Strong Quotes for Every Speak Strong Skill

Quotes are like poetry, sound-bytes and the chorus to a song. They capture the essence of ideas and present them in a concise form you can understand.

I've posted quotes for your enjoyment. You can also register for my Speak-Strong quote of the day at: *www.speakstrong.com/freestuff/*

SpeakStrong Step 1: Commit to Code White

Skill #1: Stop saying things you don't mean
- Imagine your life if you could say anything you wanted. Feels good, doesn't it?
- Help a child to find the words to describe their experience and you give them a piece of their soul.
- A well-intended lie is still a lie. A little white lie is still a lie. If you don't mean it, don't say it.

Skill #2: Start noticing what you don't say
- A lie for a lie makes the whole world a mirage.
- A misleading silence is as dishonest as a misleading word.
- Don't play it safe by playing it silent.

Skill #3 Uncover eight lame excuses (and one shameful one)
- Truth doesn't hurt, but letting go of lies comes with a healing sting.
- A wink and a nod may serve the moment, but come with a long range cost.
- Sometimes silence is golden. Other times it's criminal.

Skill #4: Get honest
- Honesty is the safest policy.
- Transparency builds trust.
- Practice honesty with the small things. Then you'll know how with the big things.

Skill #5: Cut to the core
- Some stay in confusion to avoid action. Reality is unimpressed.
- What would you say if you could say anything?
- Truth doesn't care if you believe it or not. Truth doesn't care if you tell it or not. It's still truth.
- As inconvenient as truth might be, ignoring it is even less convenient.
- To err is human. To speak up about errors is divine.

Skill #6: Establish your standard

- There's more to telling the truth than not lying.
- If you distort the truth — even a little — to save a few dollars, you've set the price of your integrity.
- Free speech is not for the faint of heart. Neither is open communication.

Skill #7: Lose your lame excuses

- If they don't want to hear it, they probably need to.
- It's risky to avoid a needed risky conversation.
- Truth holds all the cards — remember that when you play yours.

Skill #8: Talk about how you talk

- Sometimes the most important conversation you can have is about how you have conversation.
- The truth is the truth, even if you're the only one who speaks it.
- Truth is like gravity — it is what it is and it does what it does no matter who champions it and who maligns it.

SpeakStrong Step 2: Say What You Mean

Skill #9: Separate fact from opinion

- Clarity begins at home.
- We all have opinions, but not all of us are opinionated. The distinction is in how rigidly we hold onto our opinions and how skillfully we share them.
- Offer your opinions as useful gifts.

Skill #10: Establish credibility

- If you wait for absolute certainty to speak up, those who require less certainty will control the conversation.
- If in doubt, check it out. Get clear and speak up.
- If you have a horn worth blowing, take a deep breath and let it fly.

Skill #11: Express your opinion (without sounding opinionated)

- Speak simply. People you speak to do not have dictionaries and grammar guides in their laps.
- If you over explain, you'll under convince.
- It's as important to be able to communicate your ideas as it is to have them.

Skill #12: Get over rationality myths
- You don't just interpret facts intellectually. You interpret them emotionally too.
- Get beyond your rationality myths. Feelings matter.
- The greatest thinkers are great feelers too.

Skill #13: Express your emotion
- Speak from your heart and others will respond from theirs.
- Pick words strong enough to pierce the barriers around the heart but gentle enough to protect the heart itself.
- There's a secret power in feelings, and knowing how to use that power is an important part of Speaking Strong.

Skill #14: Expand your emotional vocabulary
- Finding the perfect words is like finding your perfect prince. You might have to kiss a few frogs before you get there.
- The best PowerPhrases are hidden in the last place you might think to look — your mind and your heart.
- When it comes to communicating feelings, most people flunk.

Skill #15: Dare to desire
- When you dare to desire, you risk disappointment. When you don't dare to desire, you risk apathy.
- What do you want? That question is one of my favorite PowerPhrases.
- What you want is important.

Skill #16: Prepare to ask
- If you don't clarify what you want, you probably won't get it.
- Know the difference between wants and needs.
- It's as important to know why you want something as it is to know what you want.
- A conversation worth having is worth planning.

Skill #17: Ask so you receive
- Ask big, ask well and ask often.
- True power does not impose your will on others. True power influences their choices.
- Whining isn't asking.
- The best negotiators can describe what the other person wants better than they can.

Skill #18: Persuade, don't manipulate
- Persuade with words that sizzle without creating smoke.
- Put your best foot forward, but not a false front.
- Use the power of words, but don't abuse it.

Skill #19: Talk to all three brains, (including the one that really makes the decisions)
- It's good to be honest and it's good to be right and it's best to be both.
- It's not enough to be right if you can't convince anyone else.
- Man (and woman) does not decide by intellect alone.

Skill #20: Supercharge your message with persuasion
- Form without substance is empty — but substance without form is unimpressive.
- Lipstick won't disguise a pig, but it might enhance a woman's beauty.

SpeakStrong Step 3: Mean What You Say

Skill #21: Say it so they know you mean it
- A song called "It seems like you sort of light up my life" would never top the charts. Eliminate qualifying words that weaken your messages.
- Avoid weak language that broadcasts weak intent.
- If you don't mean it, don't say it.

Skill #22: Match your talk and your walk
- People don't care about what you're going to TRY to do. They want to know what you ARE going to do.
- High sounding words fall flat without corresponding action
- Commit to walking your talk. It will make you careful about what you say.
- Words speak, actions scream.

Skill #23: Specify and see it through
- Say what you'll do and do what you say
- Dare to be specific. Sure, being specific sets a higher bar — but why should that be a problem?
- Protect the power of your words. Mean what you say.
- No one will take your words seriously unless you do.

Skill #24: Get real but not raw
- If the emperor has no clothes, he might not need any.
- If you're trying to make an impression by putting lipstick on a pig, upgrade your product first.
- Ridicule is as powerful as the target is weak. It does not stand against someone who is well-armed with self-esteem and PowerPhrases.

Skill #25: Don't let weak speak sneak in
- Sometimes Speaking Strong is tough. Sometimes Speaking Strong is tender. But Speaking Strong is never weak
- You can't play big and use weak speak.
- Every word you use that doesn't add to the power of your message weakens it.

Skill #26: Expect to be taken seriously
- People do what you tell them to do…when you expect to be taken seriously.
- If you don't take your own words seriously, how will anyone else?
- Commit to walking your talk. It will make you careful about what you say.
- PowerPhrases are as powerful as your own commitment to them.

Skill #27: Establish boundaries
- Clear boundaries are like good job descriptions. They clarify expectations.
- Freedom comes from good boundaries.
- You teach people how to treat you. Are you teaching them what you want them to learn?

Skill #28: Implement boundaries
- Knowledge isn't power. Action based on knowledge is.
- There's something about good boundaries that challenge people to test them. Meet the challenge.
- You get the relationships you deserve…or at least that you tolerate.
- If Speaking Strong were easy, everyone would do it.

Skill #29: Communicate consequences (not disguised threats)
- Consequences add muscle to your requests, appeals and demands.
- Threats are about punishment and retaliation. Consequences are about outcome.
- Courageous communicators feel fear; they just don't let it stop them.
- Show your power before you use it. It lets people make informed choices.

Skill #30: Meet and greet your communication devil
- React…respond…what's the difference? It's about three seconds.
- It takes courage to turn up the lights and see yourself as you are.
- If people can't follow your instructions, it might have more to do with your instructions than with them.

Skill #31: Stop, drop and purge bad habits
- Speech habits can be addictions. Overcome yours with knowledge and commitment
- The Chinese definition of insanity is doing the same thing and expecting a different result. Are you insane?

Skill #32: Out with the bad habits, in with the good
- Sometimes you only need to introduce a new habit for the old one to drop off.
- People change when the pain gets bad enough, the possibilities get appealing enough, and the steps for change are clear enough.

SpeakStrong Step 4: Don't Be Mean When You Say It

Skill #33: Elevate thinking to elevate speaking
- Don't stoop to their level. Bring them up to yours.
- Possibility-thinking elevates conversations.
- See how things are. See how they can be. Then speak up to bridge any gap between them.

Skill #34: Turn your negatives into positives (that get results)
- If you wish to gossip, do it about the virtue of others.
- Every communication challenge presents a communication opportunity.
- Behind everything you don't want is something you do want.

Skill #35: Express positive realism (not delusional fantasy)
- Pessimists may be right, but optimists live longer. And positive realists live the longest of all.
- Dare to dream and dare to hope and dare to examine reality.
- There is a fine and important distinction between positivity and delusion. So — get real, positive and smart.

Skill #36: Embrace true power
- True power doesn't require an audience or fan club.
- Sometimes you need to stay open at the exact moment every cell in your body wants to shut down.
- True power means being as strong as you need to be and no stronger

Skill #37: Assert yourself (without inviting one of the B labels)
- Don't have a knee-jerk reaction to knee-jerk reactions.
- The only thing worse than confusing passiveness with kindness, is confusing aggression with assertiveness.
- The GOBC doesn't willingly surrender power because it's the right thing to do. The good news is you don't need them to. You have sources of power they haven't dreamed of

Skill #38: Purge passive-aggressive habits
- Passive-aggressive behavior distracts you from your true power.
- A dig hidden in a compliment is still a dig.
- Let your words build bridges, not barriers.

Skill #39: Be a uniter, not a divider
- People you divide might eventually unite…against you.
- Divide and conquer can win you some battles and create some wars you will lose.

Skill #40: Drop the distractions and the deceptions
- Just say it.
- Pay attention to the man behind the curtain.
- Give up the communication games. Strategies are much more fun anyway.

Skill #41: Stop manipulating
- You can manipulate people into giving you what you want, but you can't manipulate them into respecting you.
- Manipulation destroys trust.
- A pit bull is influential, but poodles can work their way into your lap

Skill #42: Get guilt-free in accountability
- Revenge may seem sweet, but sugar rots your teeth.
- The kinder, gentler, softer way is the smarter, wiser, stronger way.

Skill #43: Put sarcasm in its place
- Sarcasm is an ironic remark intended to wound. What's so funny about inflicting pain?
- Witty words entertain, kind words endear.

Skill #44: Identify issues (without using labels)
- "Shock value" is an oxymoron.
- If your conscious mind doesn't set a goal for a conversation, your unconscious mind will.
- The first to speak may take the heat, but leaders lead — they go first.

Skill #45: Hold people accountable (without using blame)
- The harder you push, the harder people push back.
- Any fool can avoid a topic and any fool can attack a topic. It takes skill to speak out gracefully.
- Before you react, remember, people are the least lovable when they need love the most.

SpeakStrong Step 5: Speak Your Simple Truth

Skill #46: Communicate all you are
- The truth has lasting value and you get to keep your soul when you tell it.
- The part you hide just might be a part other people are hungry to know.
- Can you imagine going though life without having a cover to blow? Sweet, very sweet.
- It's hard for a big person to fit into a small box.

Skill #47: Talk your way to self knowledge
- Truth is good for the soul.
- Don't just talk — talk and listen to yourself.
- Falsehood shuns examination. The truth invites it.
- If you don't know yourself, how can you know anything at all?

Skill #48: Define and communicate your uniqueness
- Speak not for success but for significance.
- Your brand may be bigger than you are — or bigger than you knew you were.
- Are you worth quoting?

Skill #49: Talk an inspired walk
- Virtue is its own reward, but virtue shared is an inspiration.
- Be an undercover oracle.
- No one ever inspired anyone by playing small.
- Talk the walk you want.

Skill #50: Elevate conversations
- When great communicators find themselves in a hole, they stop digging and seek the opportunity to elevate the dialogue.
- Take the time to say it right.
- The truth? You CAN handle the truth.

Skill #51: Relax into silence
Say it well and stop talking

SpeakStrong Resources:
Fabulous Formulas to Speak Strong

You already know my favorite SpeakStrong formula. It's: say what you mean and mean what you say without being mean when you say it. I call that *The Ultimate Communication Formula*.

It's ultimate, because it's easy to remember, and it works in all situations.

However, I do have three other formulas that I know you'll enjoy.

Formula #1. The Face Formula to address issues and ask for what you want

The Face Formula has four parts to it — the facts, appreciation, consequence or cost and expectation.

Facts: Begin by describing the facts. This is the observable kind of information your imaginary camera recorded in Skill # 9. Your sentence stems are: I notice, when, the other day, and I see…

Appreciation: Once you explain the facts, use your appreciation statement to create safety. Acknowledge their situation or perspective using sentence stems such as: I understand, I appreciate, I realize and I'd like to understand why…

Cost/Impact: Next is your consequence statement, where you talk about the impact of their actions for you, them and others. Use the sentence stems like, I think, I feel, what happens is…

Expectation: Finally it's time to make your request. That's the expectation. Your sentence stems are: I want, I need, I prefer and please…

Here's an example for you:

Fact: I notice you ordered came in late yesterday and today.

Appreciation: I realize you worked late several nights last week,

Cost: However, what happens is I have to cover for you and behind on my own projects.

Expectation: Please come in on time tomorrow or make arrangements for someone to cover for you.

Just remember to FACE your problems, and you'll be able to Speak Strong.

There's a poster for the FACE Formula on the next page, and you can get a full color free PDF of it at: *www.speakstrong.com/freestuff/*

FACE
Formula to Address Issues and Ask for What You Want

Facts: Situation, behavior.
☞ I notice, when, the other day, I see.

Appreciation: Safety statement.
Acknowledge their perspective.
☞ I understand, I appreciate, I realize, I'd like to understand why.

Consequence/Cost:
How the behavior affects you, them and others.
☞ I think, I feel, what happens is, the risk of it is.

Expectation: What you want.
Requested behavior.
☞ I want, I need, I prefer, please.

Make Your CASE in Conflict

Clarify ..... Their Position
· Help me to understand…
· Let me make sure I understand you clearly…
· Are you aware…? *(I LOVE this one!)*

Assert ..... Your Position
FACE Formula

Seek .... Solutions
· What I want to see happen is for us to negotiate solutions together.
· I suggest that we kick around a few ideas to see what solutions we can come up with.
· If we could come up with a solution that works for us both, would you be interested?
· What would it take to make my request possible?

Evaluate Options, and Build Agreements
· Does this option solve the problem?
· Can you and I both live with this option?
· Is there any way to improve this option?
· Is it realistic?
· Are you and I both willing to commit to it in writing?

Formula #2 The CASE Formula to address conflict

Sometimes, all you have to do is ask, and you receive. Other times, you need to exchange ideas, explore issues and negotiate outcomes. That's when the CASE Formula comes in handy. Here's how this formula works.

Clarify: Begin by exploring their position, attitudes and perspectives. Keep asking questions and exploring until you they have confirmed that you understand them.

Assert: Once you both agree that you understand them, explain your own perspective. Refer back to the FACE formula for this.

Seek solutions: You and the other person sit side-by-side looking at the problem in a mutual effort to find solutions that work for all concerned. A great PowerPhrase to get this process going is:

- If we could come up with a solution that works for both of us, would you be interested?

Evaluate: Review the ideas you came up with and build agreements based on them. Make sure the options you select are realistic and everyone is willing to commit to them.

I include a poster for this formula on the previous page, and you can also get a color PDF of this one at: *www.speakstrong.com/freestuff/*

I also explain the CASE formula in greater detail in my book *PowerPhrases!*

Formula #3. The ACT Formula to say no

You might think saying "no" should be simple, but most everyone I know has a problem with that simple two-letter word. That's why the ACT formula is so helpful.

Acknowledge the request: The first step is to acknowledge the request with a simple phrase like, "I wish I could", or "I can tell this is important to you."

Circumstance: Then briefly explain your circumstance that is the reason why you're declining. Don't go into detail—just say something simple like, "I have other plans."

Tag: Close with a tag phrase that affirms the relationship. Something simple like: "Maybe next time."

That's it! This poster PDF is also available in color at: *www.speakstrong.com/ freestuff/*

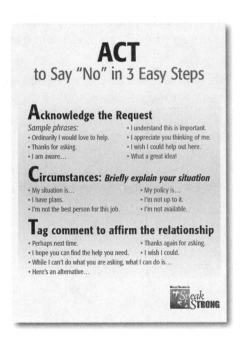

5 C's of Responsible Leadership: Poster.

Get a full color PDF copy of this poster at: *www.speakstrong.com/freestuff/* and listen to the explanation on the Speak Strong at Work CD.

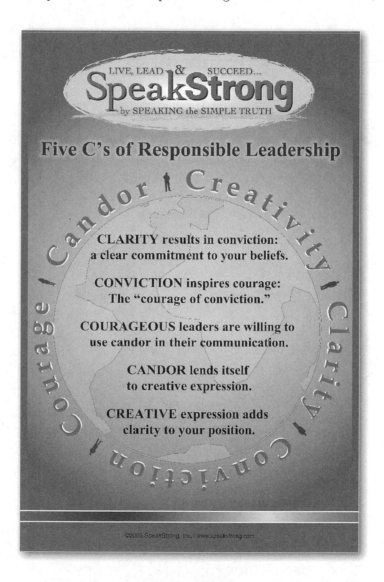

The Totally Integrated Performance System

The Totally Integrated Performance System involves five process, each which involve their own conversations. This chart and the following identifies the

steps. You can get color PDFs of the charts from www.speakstrong.com/ freestuff/ You can also hear about the conversations that need to happen at each step by listening to the accompanying audio CD.

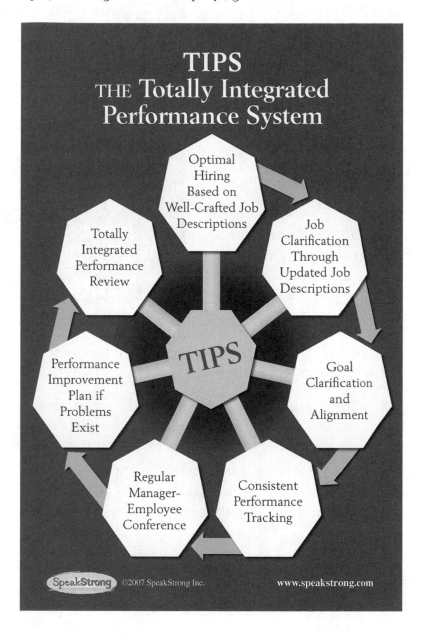

You've got the *PowerPhrases*.
Now get the skills behind them.
It's the logical next step.

I pinpointed over 50 skills that will help you say what you mean and mean what you say without being mean when you say it.

I wrote a story or two illustrating each skill.

Then I provided practical dos and don'ts for each skill.

I provided **PowerPhrases** and **Poison Phrases** to demonstrate what to say and what not to say when you practice each skill.

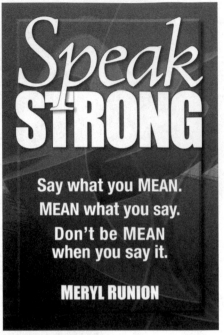

Then I recorded an audio about important conversations for different business situations.

My designer laid it out and made the information *pretty* and *easy to access*.

And I sent it to the printers.

Since then, I've received bulk orders for study groups in organizations and associations, and people tell me it's helping them **SpeakStrong**. They tell me they like it and it's easy to use.

That makes me happy because I really like this book. I hope you do too.

Available at *www.speakstrong.com*